The Widows' Might

The Widows' Might

Widowhood and Gender in Early British America

Vivian Bruce Conger

NEW YORK UNIVERSITY PRESS
New York and London

NEW YORK UNIVERSITY PRESS
New York and London
www.nyupress.org

Library of Congress Cataloging-in-Publication Data
Conger, Vivian Bruce.
The widows' might : widowhood and gender in early British America / Vivian Bruce Conger.
p. cm. Includes bibliographical references and index.
ISBN-13: 978-0-8147-1674-8 (cl : alk. paper)
ISBN-10: 0-8147-1674-1 (cl : alk. paper)
1. Widows—United States—History. 2. Widows—United States—Economic conditions. I. Title.
HQ1058.5.U5C657 2009
306.88'3097309032--DC22 2008044251

New York University Press books are printed on acid-free paper, and their binding materials are chosen for strength and durability. We strive to use environmentally responsible suppliers and materials to the greatest extent possible in publishing our books.

Manufactured in the United States of America

10 9 8 7 6 5 4 3 2 1

For the two most important people in my life,
Elizabeth Ann Russell Bruce and Darius John Conger

Contents

Acknowledgments

The list of those to whom I am indebted in helping me complete this work is, indeed, long. I could not have accomplished this task without the financial and emotional support of a great many people and places, and that help is very gratefully acknowledged. My only regret is that the people I recognize here will never understand the extent to which their assistance, patience, and understanding eased my way through every step of a process that was both a wonderfully joyful and enlightening exploration and a long, arduous, and sometimes painful undertaking.

The faith various institutions have demonstrated in me by their generous financial support is deeply appreciated. First, I extend my thanks to Cornell University: to the History Department for providing not only the opportunity to study with and learn from some of the best scholars in the country but also financial support through the Martha Barrett Scholarship and the Gertrude A. Gillmore Fellowship, and twice through a Daughters of the American Revolution Fellowship; to the Sage Graduate School for awarding me the Three-Year Teaching Fellowship; and to the Women's Studies Program for providing me with a research grant from the Beatrice Brown Award Fund. I thank St. Michael's College for a Faculty Development Grant. I thank Ithaca College for generously supporting me throughout the years with two Provost's Office Small Grants, a Provost's Office Grant for Faculty Summer Research, and a School of Humanities and Sciences Emerson Collaborative Grant. Finally, I thank the American Historical Association for awarding me a Littleton-Griswold Research Grant and the American Antiquarian Society for awarding me a Frances Hiatt Fellowship. These awards provided me not only with time away from teaching responsibilities but also money for travel to archives and historical societies.

I would be remiss if I did not begin my thanks to various libraries and archives with the single most important institution responsible for the completion of this work. I thank very much the librarians at the Mormon

Family History Center in Ithaca, New York, for all their help. For two years, whenever the Family History Center was open, I was there coding wills. The volunteer librarians placed countless microfilm orders, helped me manage uncooperative microfilm readers, provided additional space for me, and found rooms in which I could eat lunch. Over the years, they were unfailingly friendly and cooperative; in fact, they gave me access to my sources when they were otherwise scheduled to be closed or on vacation. We became very good friends, and their interest in my research gave me an additional source of inspiration. I owe a special debt of gratitude to them.

I also want to thank the librarians at Forbes Library, in Northampton, Massachusetts; the Essex Institute, in Salem, Massachusetts; Plimoth Plantation, in Plymouth, Massachusetts; the Massachusetts Historical Society, in Boston, Massachusetts; the Maryland Historical Society, in Baltimore, and the Maryland Hall of Records, in Annapolis, Maryland; and the Library of Congress in Washington, D.C., for their generous and gracious assistance in my quest for unpublished letters, sermons, account books, and legal records.

I want to thank my fellow graduate students at Cornell University for their loyal support during my years in residence at Cornell. I also want to thank the members of the history graduate student research forum for allowing me to present parts of my work to them for their insightful comments. I especially want to thank my very good friend Michael Wilson. Throughout our years together at Cornell, he was a friendly but critical reader of several of my chapters, he was a constant source of moral support and social interaction, and, most important of all, a warm and loving friend who shared the good as well as the bad times with me. Professors I. V. Hull and Rachel Weil of Cornell University read my work closely and made intelligent and thought-provoking comments on it.

I want to thank my colleagues in the Kenyon College History Department, Joan Cadden, Pam Scully, and Ellen Furlough. They generously gave me their scholarly advice and friendly support as I struggled to finish my book while teaching full time. Most important, however, I want to thank William Scott for reading and critiquing my work at every phase of the long process of bringing this book to fruition. He has been an invaluable colleague and a wonderful friend. His comments, sometimes brutally honest but always insightful and helpful, have made this work what it is. I can never repay what he has done for me. I only hope he knows how grateful I am and that there is a special place in my heart for him.

I want to thank my colleagues in the Ithaca College Department of History, especially Joanne Izbicki and my very good friends Leslie Horowitz and Karin Breuer. They read various chapters of this work at bi-weekly meetings during which we critiqued, agonized, gossiped, laughed, and cried over beer and sandwiches. They offered valuable comments and even more valuable emotional support. Where would I be without them?

The anonymous readers of the manuscript pushed me hard to make this a better book. Their suggestions were sometimes painful but always helpful. Ultimately, of course, I bear complete responsibility for the final product, but I appreciated their input and I hopefully I lived up to their expectations.

When I first went to Cornell to work with Mary Beth Norton, I was shy and insecure about my ability to complete a Ph.D. She must have seen the potential in me, for throughout the past ten years she has willingly and even enthusiastically turned me into a professional historian with a great deal of confidence. While I was still doing coursework, she provided invaluable comments on my written work, gave me the opportunity to be a teaching assistant for her courses, and passed along important advice about getting through graduate school and about being a professional historian. Her copious, in-depth comments on this book have made it a much more precise, clear, and analytically rigorous work. I thank her for that. However, she has come to be more than an adviser; she has come to be an invaluable friend and colleague. For all that Mary Beth Norton has generously given to me, I am truly thankful.

Although my mother, Elizabeth Ann Russell Bruce, did not live to see me return to college as an adult, while she was alive, she always supported my desire to do so, and I am certain that she was guiding me throughout the process, pushing me when I got discouraged, and providing me with the spunk and the determination I needed to see it through. I am what I am today because of my mother, and for that I will be eternally grateful.

My husband, best friend, and most avid supporter, Darius John Conger, has seen me through the joys and the traumas of my academic career. He gave me guidance when I sought it and let me struggle on my own when I needed to. Throughout the years, he cooked and cleaned for me, listened eagerly as I talked about my work, waited patiently as I went off on research trips, provided invaluable computer assistance, encouraged me, and, most important of all, loved me. I could not have accomplished my goals without him by my side.

Introduction

"Lay in a Stock of Graces Against the Evil Day of Widowhood"

On August 30, 1673, in Boston, Massachusetts, Dorothy Upshall, widow of Nicholas, wrote a will in which she divided her earthly goods among two daughters, a grandson, three granddaughters, one brother, and two sisters. Thirty-five years later and about 402 miles south of Boston, in Charles County, Maryland, Elizabeth Diggs, widow of William, left her estate to six sons and three daughters, demanding that daughter Mary receive her share immediately while her other children wait until all her debts were paid. Eighteen years later and 440 miles further south, in Charleston, South Carolina, Catherine LaNoble, widow of Henry, bequeathed her estate—the landed portion of which, she specifically noted, her mother had given her—to two daughters, a son-in-law, a grandson, and a granddaughter.[1] Nearly one thousand widows over a 120-year time span across Massachusetts, Maryland, and South Carolina repeated this seemingly mundane ritual of devising their estates, whether personal property, landed property, or both.

Far from being mundane, will making signaled a significant private and public event in a woman's life, in her family's life, and in her community's life. At the most personal level, leaving a will meant that a woman was facing her own mortality. It must have been a highly emotional time, a fearful time fraught with internal and external conflict. But it also must have been a powerful time. A woman who created a will believed she had something of value to leave, and she wanted to determine who would receive it. Even if she and her husband had talked over the family's future, it was an act over which she had the ultimate say. At a more formal level, widows' wills reflect the place widows occupied in early British America. Widows were no longer wives and mothers with clearly defined gender roles within the household but rather fell within several contested sites of socially constructed gender roles. Cultural, legal, communal, and economic ideals ensured that widows would not be allowed to wield absolute power and control generally reserved for men. However, as heads of households, they were expected to oversee the family and to represent its interests as their husbands had once done. A widow who left a will understood her responsibilities to her family and to her community, and she must have felt a great deal of satisfaction at being able to contribute to another's economic well-being. But just as they did not necessarily bequeath their estates as men did, neither did all widows across colonies and time bequeath their estates in the same manner. As widows' wills reveal, many widows successfully contested or appropriated their rights and responsibilities for their own reasons, reasons based on age, economic status, tradition, family relations, personal experience, and individual quirks.

The title of this book, "The Widows' Might," expands upon the biblical parables found in the gospels of Mark and Luke. In Mark 12:41–44 and in Luke 21:1–4, we learn about a poor widow who put "two mites" into the collection box along with the rich who "cast in much" as they proceeded through the Women's Court in the Temple at Jerusalem. A mite was a small bronze or copper coin worth about an eighth of a cent and was the smallest denomination made at the time. Whatever the monetary value of the mite, the real message was clear. Although the amount the widow gave seemed insignificant in comparison to what the rich contributed, what made her gift extraordinary was that she gave "all she had, even all her living," while the rich gave their "superfluity," their surplus. Her contribution was greater because her sacrifice was greater and thus more meaningful. The widow's mite symbolizes women's strength, courage, and sacrifice in the face of abject poverty and their abiding faith that God will provide for them. Some of the widows in this study were, indeed, poor when they bequeathed what little estates they had left. Most, however, were women of some means. In both instances, early American widows did have the mite and the might, the economic and social power, to publicly proclaim in their wills their concept of the early American family. This is not meant to diminish the religious significance of their actions. Widows read the Bible and understood the story of the widow's mite; like her, they had faith in God. Widows also read advice books and heard sermons addressing their complex and complicated gender roles in early American communities.

As a result, they gained faith in their own strength, courage, and "might" to provide for their families and friends in the meantime.

Modern researchers recognize that widowhood is a critical stage in women's lives and that the disruption caused by a husband's death and a widow's need to remarry depends not only on the extent to which her husband was a part of his wife's life but also on the status of "widow" in the community, a social role strictly prescribed by custom.[2] Contemporary observations apply equally well to seventeenth- and eighteenth-century Anglo-American widowhood. Until recently, historians of colonial women or communities have downplayed, even dismissed altogether, widows as unimportant, irrelevant, or—as in the case of witchcraft—socially and economically anomalous (if not highly problematic). Because they assumed that marriage and rapid remarriage were the prevailing experience of seventeenth- and eighteenth-century women, widows usually occupy an obligatory paragraph, section, or chapter in histories of Anglo-American women.[3] Those earlier historians generally assumed that knowledge of widows contributed little to the study of early American womanhood and to the study of early American society. When they did study widows, they did so largely to shed further light on the lives of married women. Widows offered a contrast to married womanhood. As in any study of "the other," understanding what married women were not helped to clarify what they were. Yet widows were not simply an "other." They were not generally conceived of as being outside the norm. In fact, other women and many men took the presence of widows in their midst as a matter of course. They were constituent members of society, and, like all social groups, they were both troublesome in some ways and useful in others. They were more visible and had potentially greater influence within their communities and on gender roles in general than has previously been understood. What ultimately makes widows an important group to examine is that they were among the completing definers and constructors of their society.

In 1692, Cotton Mather claimed that the "vast Numbers of Poor widows in Every neighborhood" in Boston proved that many women "may at some time or other, tast the Sad, Sowre, Tear-ful cup of Widowhood." He believed that women who never expected to face widowhood would "soon find the Days of Mourning brought upon them." According to Mather, all women would be well advised to "lay in a stock of Graces against the Evil Day of Widowhood." In 1718, Mather explained that his congregation contained at least eighty widows, about 20 percent of the membership. He attributed the high proportion to the fact that Boston's population consisted of "so much of Sea-faring People."[4]

While there are few reliable, concrete colony-wide statistics, historians provide more accurate figures about the incidence of colonial American widowhood than Mather's. As the following numbers reveal, widowhood varied by colony and across time, and the proportion of widows in the population differed. In late seventeenth-century Essex County, for example, widows made up less than 9 percent of the adult female population and made up approximately 20 percent of those over age thirty. In 1687, widows made up 10 percent of all Boston ratepayers. Widows were 11 percent of the New Haven, Connecticut, proprietors and 5 percent of the heads of households in the towns of Hartford, Wethersfield, and Windsor. The best figures for seventeenth-century Maryland suggest that women outlived their husbands twice as often as the reverse and that, in a society where men died early, "almost invariably" every woman in the Chesapeake experienced widowhood.[5]

In eighteenth-century Beverly, Massachusetts, widows outnumbered widowers by seven to one. Sixty percent of all marriages in Woburn ended with the death of the husband, and at any one time, 10 percent of adult women experienced widowhood. As the timing of Mather's sermon to the widows of Boston made clear, both King William's War (which ended in 1697) and Queen Anne's War (which ended in 1713) took a heavy toll on Boston marriages. A 1742 census revealed that, by the middle of the century, widows made up nearly 30 percent (1,200) of all adult Boston women. More specifically, widows constituted approximately 8 percent of Boston's total population and 10 percent of all ratepayers in 1742. In Marblehead, Massachusetts, widows also made up 10 percent of the ratepayers. In Prince George's County, Maryland, by 1775, nearly one-fourth of the women over age fifty-eight were widows. And, finally, in one parish in colonial South Carolina, widows made up 51 percent of the adult female population and 27 percent of the entire adult population.[6]

Clearly, widowhood was a common experience for women in colonial America. The statistics indicate, however, that the rates of widowhood varied sharply, depending on war, disease, and maritime employment. They also suggest that over time, rates of widowhood increased, and widows rarely accounted for less than 10 percent of the adult female population. The widowed population, in fact, was probably much larger than 10 percent, since many widows lacked the wealth to qualify as ratepayers, a key measure for demographers.[7] Remarriage rates and differences in who actually remarried help explain the statistical consequences of a husband's death for Anglo-American colonial women, but they do not explain what it meant to be an individual widow or what it meant to be a member of a group of widowed women.

Historians of early American women initially presented us with opposing images of widows. On the one hand, colonial widows possessed a great deal of power in their communities because they were wealthy. Inheritance could provide widows freedom and independence. Most men who had land to bequeath did so to their wives, even if they denied them the right to sell or dispose of it. Young women with children were more likely to control large portions of their dead husbands' estate than were older widows with grown sons. Moreover, widows' ability to control when and whom they remarried granted them power.[8] Because of this, a "characteristic glamour . . . hung round every widow." She could provide her second husband with an inheritance that would enable him to pay his debts, and she was, therefore, a widely sought-after commodity.[9] Control of wealth gave widows an edge over "competitors in the marriage market." This, in turn, encouraged an "imperiousness or even downright tyranny" in widows and created a "widowarchy."[10] However, many widows "of affairs" chose not to remarry, and they led independent and financially secure lives.[11]

On the other hand, widows did not always remarry quickly, many widows did not have minor children at their husbands' death, and thus most widows were not rich. Most inherited neither large amounts of land nor personal goods. Even though some men bequeathed their widows their entire estates, those estates often consisted of one-room houses, livestock, household goods, little cash, and few slaves. The widows suffered from continual harassment by creditors and insecure land holdings. Colonial widows frequently depended on their adult sons and exerted little influence over family matters and children's behavior. Although eighteenth-century widows made up an increasingly large proportion of the total population, they played no major role in local commerce. Widows were not rich and powerful businesswomen. Because "economic productivity . . . depended on the cohesion of family units headed by men," widowhood was an "interlude" during which a woman carried out her husband's wishes for maintaining a well-ordered family. Few widows took advantage of their situation because they internalized the lessons taught to them in the advice books about their proper economic and social roles.[12] This was no "widowarchy." Two diametrically opposed words seemed to construct early American widowhood: "relict," a mere remnant, a deserted or discarded person, and "she-merchant," the affluent trader and head of household who was a powerful and independent member of society.

Recent research helps us bridge the two concepts by reconceptualizing gender in early America, thereby allowing us to reject the starkly drawn images in favor of a more nuanced understanding of widowhood. In her path-breaking book, *Good Wives*, Laurel Thatcher Ulrich argues that women's lives were far from static and submissive and that, while women were subservient to men, they could assert themselves to a certain degree within the social framework of life. Mary Beth Norton, in *Founding Mothers and Fathers*, argues that Filmerian political theory, resting on the Fifth Commandment that one honor one's mother and father, created a situation in which the state had a major stake in preserving well-ordered families and parental authority. This enabled seventeenth-century elite women, and, in particular, widowed mothers, to wield political and economic power in their families and within their communities. More recently, Ulrich analyzed John Winthrop's inclusion of numerous women in his history of the Massachusetts Bay Colony. According to Ulrich, Winthrop (the iconic Puritan patriarch), as well as ordinary men and women, recognized that "women . . . mattered in the cosmic scheme of things." Ultimately, she claims that high-status women and older women (many of whom were widows) were essential to the colony. Both historians suggest that this was "a world considerably less 'patriarchal'" than we've been led to believe.[13]

The historians Karin Wulf, Cynthia Kierner, Terri Snyder, Linda Sturtz, and Cara Anzilotti[14] suggest that this is true to a large extent for the early eighteenth century, as well. In exciting and innovative theoretical models, they explore how women used marital status, wealth, and a gendered cultural ideology to gain autonomy and agency within a society that attempted to define them as marginal. They convincingly argue that the domestic world of women and the public world of men were not constituted as exclusively separate physical and psychological spaces—and thus complicate the previously starkly drawn images of widows. Household and public were realms of activity in which both men and women participated (sometimes successfully, sometimes not), even though women, unlike most men, did so through a complex process of negotiation within hierarchical categories of race, class, and gender. Kierner, Wulf, and Anzilotti argue, however, that women's public roles remained sex-specific and served the needs of elite white men and the patriarchal structure and thus limited the degree of autonomy and agency women possessed.[15] Yet, ultimately, all see a decline in women's status (albeit to different degrees and occurring at slightly different times) and a concomitant growing dependence on men as American society became increasingly masculine and women's access to the public arena of court and politics declined.[16] My analysis of widows who never remarried complicates, even challenges, this declension model.

I focus on widows who did not remarry because they (unlike widows who remarried and reassumed the role of wife) were in a unique position to define or redefine their norms and construct or reconstruct their worlds in response to both the prescriptive literature directed toward them and the actual circumstances in which they found themselves. Widowhood (for women as well as for society as a whole) was normative, not marginal; widows were not necessarily always problematic. While American culture appeared to be predominantly masculine by 1750, my focus on widows suggests that we need to rethink our understanding of prerevolutionary society. I do not want to engage in a discourse of masculine oppression and female resistance, but I do want to make clear the tensions inherent in competing gendered definitions of "widow." Through widows we can better understand the structure of the colonial family, community, legal system, and economic structure. They rippled through each of these realms, being affected by and affecting them in anticipated and unanticipated ways. Colonial American history comes not only from the masculine voice of magistrates, ministers, didacts, selectmen, sons, and brothers. It comes also from the feminine voices of widowed petitioners, churchgoers, authors, shopkeepers, and, most important, testators. Listening to those voices reveals the complexity of behaviors, family life, encounters between people, and economic roles.

Because seventeenth- and eighteenth-century law stipulated that only single women and widows could leave wills, and because it was believed that the few who remained widowed bequeathed only personal property, those historians inclined to study widowhood were disinclined to examine it through widows' wills. As a result, women's public sentiments for the most part remain silenced by the numerical dominance of men's wills and by the assumptions of the historians who used those sources. Men with little or no real property to bequeath usually did not leave wills, signifying that they understood the supposed insignificance of personalty (that is, nonlanded property) in the patriarchal system. Yet, widows with only personal goods to dispose of—just like those with real property—left wills, indicating that they, despite society's emphasis on the signifying power of realty, wanted to give meaning to their possessions, as well as to exercise whatever control they could over their own lives and over the lives of their friends and families. Indeed, historians have pointed out the financial importance of personalty for widows, especially as the American economic system changed from family capitalism to corporate capitalism. Even though women may have typically "only"bequeathed personalty, such bequests were their way of shaping familial, kin, and community structures, as they understood them.[17]

Moreover, for women, will making was not just a culminating act; often, it was also their first and only public expression of their usually private thoughts and beliefs. There are frustratingly few extant letters and diaries written by colonial women before 1750. According to Mary Beth Norton, writing required not only a reason to write but also "access to paper, a high degree of literacy, and some leisure time, all of which most American women did not achieve" until the late eighteenth century. Literacy rates for women lagged well behind those for men; no woman kept a diary in the seventeenth century, and very few women did so well into the eighteenth century—about the same time that boys' access to writing instruction was extended to girls.[18] Therefore, an analysis of the thoughts and intentions women expressed in their wills—not just in the specific bequests, but in the explanations of or the justifications for those bequests—provides a necessary foundation on which to build our understanding of colonial widows and widowhood. Widows' wills were obviously legal instruments, but they were much more than that, as a close and careful reading of the documents reveals.

I examined the wills of widows in Massachusetts, Maryland, and South Carolina. My data derive first and foremost from probate records for all widows and for an equal number of men in Charles, Prince George's, and Kent counties in Maryland; Suffolk, Essex, and Hampshire counties in Massachusetts; and *all* wills in South Carolina from the first widow's will through 1750. More specifically, my data set includes 1,885 wills and 1,122 inventories: 962 widows' wills (51 percent) and 923 men's wills (49 percent) and 608 widows' inventories and 514 men's inventories.[19] Of these, 1,282 wills (68 percent) are from Massachusetts (653 women, 629 men), 317 (16.8 percent) are from Maryland (165 women, 152 men), and 219 (11.6 percent) are from South Carolina (110 women, 109 men). From these wills, I gathered data on the age of the testator, the total number of male and female heirs, the type of realty (that is, landed property), household goods, clothing, personal goods, servants or slaves, stock, crops, and intangibles the testator bequeathed or the intestate had in her or his estate. For each category of goods bequeathed, I recorded the first four recipients, as well as the conditions and type of conditions placed on the bequests. I also noted the identification of executors and administrators. For each inventory, I determined the value of the estate by adding in debts due to the estate and subtracting the debts owed to others from the estate.

Massachusetts and South Carolina were the two most influential colonies of their respective regions (New England and the Deep South), which means that regional traits in these colonies were likely to be the most prominent and easily examined. That provides insight not just into colonial widows but also into emerging regional distinctions caused by differences in economic and cultural systems. Maryland is important because it is a second southern sample that adds more data from a longer time frame and because it offsets concerns that Charleston distorts the South Carolina sample. The use of data from South Carolina enabled me to include information from a city comparable to Boston, which in turn helped me sort out the northern/southern factors from the urban/rural factors. I ensured geographic, economic, and social diversity within the colonies by examining widows from large towns and small villages, from urban and rural areas, from inland and seaboard communities.

Working with a large data set involves some tradeoffs. For example, it was impossible to research the lives of individual widows or even a group of widows, as Lisa Wilson did for widows in Pennsylvania,[20] but it enabled me to begin to explore if widows in one part of the country thought and acted the way that widows in another part of the country did—as well as how and why (or why not, of course). It made it possible for me to provide a collective picture of widows in early America, which in turn allowed me to analyze patterns, relationships, and created identities that might not otherwise be visible. Ultimately, it also enabled me to understand widowhood as a transatlantic construction, as a way of thinking about gender that transcended artificial regional and temporal boundaries.

I also explored the gender dynamics suggested by my research into the probate records. A vast array of prescriptive literature, such as the Bible, sermons, especially New England funeral sermons,[21] advice books, and plays (Charleston, South Carolina, residents regularly attended concerts, balls, plays, and other such amusements), was published in England and then widely circulated in the colonies throughout the seventeenth and eighteenth centuries. Within those texts, ministers and others variously labeled widows as sober, grave, temperate, just, honest, faithful, charitable, peaceable, modest, chaste, kind, virtuous, and pious but also as deceptive, wanton, angry, scheming, haughty, sorrowful, pitiful, discontented, odious, and sinful. Although extensive, this catalogue of prescribed behavior presents only a partial picture. This same literature reveals a more practical image of colonial widows as models for "the Excitation of Heads of Families bereaved of their Husbands."[22]

While elite women read books, the ideas contained in them reached the lower orders when ministers preached, when excerpts or serialized versions appeared in newspapers, when disputes reached the courthouse, or when neighbors talked. Ostensibly, the words all advice book authors used to describe widows depicted their true character. In fact, the words more accurately signify how writers and ministers wanted widows to be remembered and imitated—or disdained.[23] To say this is not to deny that widows conformed to at least some ideals. Indeed, many appear to have done so, especially if we take the sermons at face value and believe the tribute paid to colonial widows. However, examining the collective body of ideal images provides a more nuanced, and perhaps more realistic, understanding of the boundaries within which most colonial widows maneuvered. Widows understood the social expectations that they would conform to cultural standards. Not only were widows different from one another, but the advice offered was inconsistent and ambiguous. This ambiguity arose primarily from the nature of widowhood itself.

Court records reveal the place widows held in colonial society, intergenerational disputes, and community networks, not only through the laws imposed to regulate widows' lives but also through the direct challenges widows made to the laws. While church records, poor relief rolls, lawsuits, and petitions disclose widows' tenuous social and economic positions, those same lawsuits and petitions, as well as the numerous newspaper advertisements widows placed, suggest that widows played a strong and vibrant role in the economy. Widows operated within a cultural structure, a family structure, a community structure, a legal structure, and an economic structure. While widows "spoke" less frequently and less vocally than men, we hear their voices loud and clear in their wills, petitions, court appearances, newspaper advertisements, poetry, advice books, and rare letters. In these multiple ways, their words bring widows clearly into the world around them and reveal whether their private sentiments coincided with their public declarations. Widows acted out their lives and constructed their identities, identities that have gone unexamined, in multiple contexts. As Rhys Isaac argues, "It has become a truism . . . that full personhood requires having a validating story of one's own, just as collective identity requires that one's gender or ethnic group have a duly acknowledged place in the master narratives that are taken for the society's history."[24] I explore, therefore, the stories women told about themselves in relation to stories that were told about them to place them more concretely in the master narrative that is colonial American history.

Like many historians, I came to this project assuming that the practices associated with widowhood would vary greatly among the three colonies. However, ideas crossed the Atlantic Ocean and spread along the eastern seaboard. While the ways in which widows created a place in their communities varied slightly in their specific regional contexts, transatlantic print culture, laws, and economic systems created an understanding of widowhood that was consistent over time and across colonies and countries.[25] Therefore, as will become obvious as we move through different aspect of widows' lives in the coming pages, those lives and the identities they created appear remarkably similar whether they occurred in Massachusetts, Maryland, or South Carolina, and this is especially so for Boston and Charleston.

Before I leave this discussion, it is important to address what some may call my "Massachusetts-centric focus" in this research. It is true that numerically widows from Massachusetts dominated because, during the period from 1630 to 1750, there were simply more widows who left wills in Massachusetts than there were in either Maryland or South Carolina. In fact, the population of each colony in 1750 suggests this was not an aberration. The populations of Massachusetts, Maryland, and South Carolina in 1750 were 188,000, 141,000, and 64,000, respectively.[26] Moreover, while I spent a long time in the archives and historical societies in both Maryland and South Carolina, ultimately there was more additional primary evidence to be found for Massachusetts. But ignoring the other colonies would have produced an account different from that which I wanted to relate.

I begin each chapter with an opening anecdote that relates a story from one widow's life. These vignettes are important because they not only put an intimate, personal face on select widows but also, and more important, illustrate the key concepts on which the chapter focuses. Each chapter explores in depth the different roles widowhood entailed.

Chapter 1 explores the ideology and the reality of remarriage. Because the rate of widowhood was high in both England and America, large numbers of widows, writers, ministers, playwrights, and members of the community believed they had to deal with those widows. On the one hand, the prescriptive literature projected what the authors hoped would be an ideal way of thinking about remarriage. In projecting their ideals, the various writers were neither clear nor consistent about their solutions to the so-called problem they established. On the other hand, prescriptive literature did not reflect reality or create a reality for widows. But the confused or ambiguous discourse of the advice literature did give widows a new vocabulary to use to describe themselves. They could create an identity through public opinion. By reading books, listening to sermons, and watching plays, widows could pick and choose, to a certain extent, how they wanted to be viewed and how they wanted to live their lives. It would be unrealistic to argue that such materials created a stable self-concept for all widows; instead, individual widows constructed their own identity out of a sometimes disordered world. Together, those collective identities help us understand early American widowhood more fully.

Chapter 2 examines the ways in which widows appropriated social and cultural norms embodied in the law and legal processes. Laws regarding dower, inheritance, and intestate estates conveyed male-defined cultural ideals and social norms that instructed all community members, especially widows, about gender roles. The laws imposed a male hegemony and codified masculinity. The law, however, was also a discourse and an arena of conflict among the various groups that accessed that law. Although widows did not always have full access to legal resources, they had specific ideas about how conflicts should be resolved, especially when they attempted to alter the restraints on their gender.

Chapter 3 explores how widows exploited the fact that they were as much "fathers" as mothers to their children and stepchildren and that they were members of families and households. Such a role expanded the widow's rights and responsibilities. It also placed her in an anomalous position with respect to her own household and to the wider community. Part of the responsibilities embedded in the masculine roles assumed by widows was raising and protecting the children. Colonial funeral sermons preached for male community members asserted that a man's responsibility was "in his ship as in his house," to maintain, even command "good order, wise government, and religious worship" within his family. Wives became masters of their ships and of their houses at their husbands' deaths. Acting as a father meant that a widow had to put aside her emotional attachment to her children, order her family strictly, teach her children to read, and look after their fortunes—functions normally undertaken by the husband.

Because the necessity for widows to conduct worldly business went beyond tending to their own households, chapter 4 explores their roles as recipients of charity, as providers of charitable assistance, as friends, and as neighbors. It also examines their roles as citizens in the polity, who assumed both rights and obligations of citizenship, providing for the common good even if mostly within the domestic realm.

Chapter 5 explores what it meant socially, culturally, and spatially when widows handled money, acted as creditors, or sought credit. I investigate how this participation shaped the organization of the shop/marketplace or transformed customarily noneconomic sites into a locus of financial transactions, how women's reputations were enhanced or harmed by their involvement with money and credit, and how the world of money and commerce that is the "circulation of goods" influenced their "personal lives."

But it is to some extent an artificial construct. What this structure reveals is not only how widows bequeathed their estates but also their complexly interconnected and intertwining lives; in fact, at times it seemed almost impossible to distinguish one aspect of their lives from another. Widows assumed responsibilities that took them into the legal system, created new relationships within the household, highlighted their significance to the neighborhood, and pushed them into the commercial realm. Wills, letters, and newspapers reveal not only widows' role in consumer society but also complicated female networks where women were both divided and connected by their status, assumptions about gender, and widows' self-identity. The roles and responsibilities widows undertook at various times overlapped much as a mathematician's Venn diagram.

The foundational research for this book is based on quantitative data and statistical analysis. However, I've chosen to keep that numerical analysis to a minimum, opting instead to focus more on widows' words and deeds. Throughout I have paid particular attention to different aspects of widows' worlds as they moved beyond their roles as wives and mothers and into ever increasingly masculine public roles. I am mapping out colonial American widowhood by triangulating individual widows' lives, the ideology pertaining to widows, and recent theories of early American gender. I am looking at not just women whose husbands have died, but, more important, the meanings and consequences of that state of being, the conceptual significance of those women's ways of believing and behaving.

In general, sermons and advice books described two broad economic categories of widows: poor and wealthy. Most authors sympathized with the plight of poor widows, but they wrote very little about their proper behavior. Poverty implied both a passive acceptance of paternalistic support systems and a withdrawal from familial and communal responsibilities. Colonial writings on widowhood focused on those wealthier widows who possessed the means as well as the motivation to fulfill the prescribed qualities. The writers prescribed two realms, household and community—the first normally female, the second almost always a male space. Neither clergymen nor advice book writers, however, established clearly defined boundaries for these spaces. Such categories oversimplified the complexities of colonial widowhood that allowed the women to violate the conventional gender norms of their communities.

Only widows who followed the rules in the prescriptive literature were worthy of "remembrance and praise."[27] No widow could have adhered to all the rules—they were simply too complex, too ambiguous, and too contradictory. If a widow excessively mourned her husband, she neglected her children and community. She also questioned God's wisdom. If she did not, she found herself accused of sexual licentiousness and arrogance. To best serve her children, she entered the public realm but, in doing so, risked being accused of unwomanly assertiveness. If she failed to assume her public responsibilities or married a greedy man as her second husband, she was accused of neglecting her children. Widows, as women who acted as men, exemplified the resourcefulness of all colonial women in the face of the severe limits placed on them by a society that could imagine them only as frail and imperfect copies of men. Perhaps Cotton Mather best expressed this ambiguity: "Some Women have the Names of Men, a little altered, as Jaquet (from Jacoba) Joanna, Joan, Jane, Jennet (all from John), Thomasin, Philippa, Frances, Henrietta, Antenia, Julian, Dionysis, and the like; *But all our Widows are put upon thus doing the works of Men may their God help them!*" [emphasis added].[28]

However, the authors of the prescriptive literature could not control the lessons widows took from the advice or how widows used it in their daily lives. Clearly, some women hoped their widowhood would be temporary, while others enthusiastically embraced financial independence, but for many women widowhood was not a choice, and they did not have the option to withdraw from or could not afford to be pushed out of the so-called masculine world. Therefore, in the profusion and confusion of advice, widows learned to negotiate the often conservative and limited boundaries prescribed for them. Widows did not just respond to the advice literature; they created their own identities from it. I am not analyzing masculine oppression and female resistance (although sometimes that was the case), but I am arguing that the category "widow" allowed individual women to negotiate their space in society; it enabled them to be strong, resourceful, and competent—or weak, deferential, or incompetent when it served their and their families' interests. They used the contradictions and inconsistencies to their advantage in forging their identities as widows.

Ultimately, I see early American widows neither as feminists nor as serving the needs of the patriarchy. Widows were distinct from married and single women and from husbands and fathers. They used prescriptive literature; household, communal, and economic rights and responsibilities; and the legal system to fashion a fluid and flexible identity that redefined traditional gender boundaries. Our contemporary interest in examples of female independence should not obscure the very real struggle for subsistence that many colonial widows confronted. Widowhood could be a constraint on women's lives. It could also be an avenue for women to expand their roles. Widows were no longer wives and mothers with clearly defined roles within the household. Although domesticity influenced their public activities, widows entered this realm as women assuming maternal *and* paternal responsibilities. This ambiguity allowed widows to be among those defining and constructing their society. It also enabled them to be visible and vocal heads of households and members of their communities as they engaged with the courts and the economic world.

A fitting place to move more deeply into this exploration of widowhood is with Rebecca Holmes Amory. Like the vignettes with which I begin each chapter, her life puts a human face on widowhood. However, Amory's extensive family letters and account book and the advertisements she placed in newspapers enable me to dig deeper and more consistently into her life and into those issues. As I move from chapter to chapter, I reveal the rich details of her life as she faced the tragedy of widowhood, as she assumed family responsibilities, as she created a new identity for herself, as she stepped out into the neighborhood, and as she undertook a wide variety of economic roles. Here I start where her life started and leave off right before her widowhood. Her parents, Rebecca Wharfe and Francis Holmes Sr. were born in Massachusetts and were married in Boston in 1693. They had six children, all of whom were born in Boston. Francis

Holmes Sr. was a merchant with a warehouse at Long Wharf and owned the Bunch of Grapes tavern in Boston. He also owned land in Charleston, to which he began traveling for business in 1702, just nine years after he and Rebecca were married. When he moved to Charleston permanently, in 1721, he took two of his four sons with him. They became merchants and shippers in Charleston.

Rebecca Holmes, her two other sons, and her two daughters (Rebecca and Ann) stayed in Boston, making Rebecca at this point a surrogate widow, the female head of the northern half of the family. Unfortunately, records do not indicate who made the decision or why the decision was made to separate the family. We do know that she ran the tavern while Francis was living in Charleston. To complicate this family structure even further, one of her grandchildren—Francis Holmes III, son of Francis Jr. and Elizabeth Holmes—lived with her in Boston while his parents remained in Charleston. Francis Holmes Sr. died (when Rebecca Holmes was aged fifty-six and they had been married thirty-three years) while still living in Charleston. He bequeathed to his wife some clothing and household goods, a slave, and £1,666—all in lieu of her dower rights in his estate. He divided his South Carolina land among his four sons, he left his daughter Rebecca £500, and he ordered that his remaining property in Boston be sold. Rebecca not only continued to run the tavern[29] but also purchased outright her husband's brick house on King Street, as well as his warehouse on Long Wharf. Like other older colonial widows, Rebecca Holmes did not remarry. Older widows usually did not have dependent children to support and thus were more economically secure. In addition, the work they did find was adequate for their personal needs, and frequently their husbands left enough wealth to support them. If not, in Massachusetts, a widow's dower rights entitled her to a minimum of one-third of all her husband's real property for her lifetime, as well as one-third of his personal estate forever.[30] However, when a widow remarried, as a *feme covert*, she would lose control of the real property (although it would legally remain hers) and she would lose outright the personal property she brought to that marriage. Consequently, older widows more often chose to remain widowed; indeed, Rebecca Holmes lived for another five years as a Boston widow. She makes an interesting "role model" for her daughter—living altogether for ten years as a powerful and independent woman—first as a surrogate widow and then as an actual widow.

In 1721, the younger Rebecca Holmes married Thomas Amory in Boston. His parents, Rebecca Houston and Jonathan Amory, were born in

England but then migrated to Charleston around 1685 (by way of Dublin and the West Indies).[31] Thomas Amory and his sister were born in Ireland. His father became a wealthy merchant in Charleston, importing large quantities of English goods and then disposing of them from his warehouses to traders, planters, and shopkeepers. He also served as Charleston representative for several Boston merchants.[32] His mother (who was a widow with property when Jonathan married her) died shortly after they arrived in South Carolina; his father married again. From that marriage, Thomas Amory acquired three stepbrothers and stepsisters. They all lived in Charleston. Like his father, he was a merchant; he lived for thirteen years in the Azores (on the island of Terceira, where he settled in Angra, the main city on the island and a key trading point). Rebecca Holmes and Thomas Amory lived together as man and wife for eight years. As we will learn in the following chapters, when Thomas Amory died, Rebecca's life changed, sometimes dramatically and sometimes more routinely. In that she was not alone; she did, however, give voice to her experiences through letters, something that most early American women did not leave behind.

1

"Though She Were Yong, Yet She Did Not Affect a Second Marriage"

The Cultural Community and Widow Remarriage

In a revealing courtship ritual between two powerful widowed Bostonians, we see Madam Katherine Winthrop testing the boundaries of her power, independence, and self-identity as a wealthy woman, we see the extent to which she internalized as well as challenged the messages of prevailing advice literature, and we see how she—like other women—reconstructed ideas of widowhood through the contingencies of their lives and the choices they made. Throughout the give-and-take of this courtship, it became clear that the inducements for her to remarry would have to be great—ultimately greater than her suitor Samuel Sewall was willing to provide.[1] Between October 1, 1720, and November 11, 1720, Samuel Sewall, one of Boston's richest merchants and Chief Justice of the Massachusetts Superior Court, recorded in his diary the details of his brief and ill-fated courtship of the widow of Waitstill Winthrop.[2] At the time of the courtship, Katherine Winthrop was fifty-six years of age, with two married daughters and a seventeen-year-old son. Sewall, sixty-nine, had five daughters and two sons.

A careful reading of Sewall's description of this courtship reveals that colonial Americans' convictions about remarriage involved much more than economics.[3] Family, friends, neighbors, custom, age, and social expectation shaped the choice widows made between widowhood and remarriage.

Sewall began his courtship cleverly. He visited Madam Winthrop, seeking both her sympathy for the recent loss of his wife and her advice about courtship of a new wife. Although "She propounded one and another for me," he insisted "none would do."[4] Several visits later, Sewall expressed his hope that his visits would not be "disagreeable" to her daughter Noyes and his concern that her son, the "Chaplain of the Castle," lived with her. Sewall finally admitted that he wished she would "be the person assign'd for" him. She turned down his proposal, explaining that she could not leave her children. He asked her to think about it and continued the courtship.

Sewall gave her books, sermons, and cakes as enticements to marriage. Winthrop kept "harp[ing] upon the same string," adamantly maintaining that she must take care of her children and her business and "could not leave that House and Neighbourhood where she had dwelt so long." He countered that "she might doe her children as much or more good by bestowing what she laid out in Hous-keeping, upon them." Sewall next suggested that because her son would soon come of age and marry, "it might be inconvenient for her to dwell with her Daughter-in-law, who must be Mistress of the House." He assumed that Winthrop would be subsumed into her son's household and that a widowed mother, dependent not only on her son but on her daughter-in-law, would create problems. The implication was that as his wife and sole mistress of the house, Winthrop would exercise more power than as a widow. When that did not sway Winthrop, he switched tactics and suggested that her wealth "might do som Good to help and suport" him.[5] Not surprisingly, her answer did not change.

When Sewall visited Winthrop on October 17, she greeted him "Courteously, but not in Clean Linen as somtimes." Yet Winthrop did allow Sewall to take some liberties; he not only held her bare hand (he had to remove her glove to do so) but also kissed her (he declared those kisses "better than the best Canary [wine]"). Usually, however, Winthrop avoided being alone with him and placed obstacles between them when they were together. Winthrop explicitly addressed her beliefs about sexual matters several visits later when she claimed that the "Apostle Paul affirm[ed] that a single Life was better than a Married" and that "she had not pleasure in things of that nature as formerly." For Sewall, that made her "the fitter to make me a Wife." Winthrop remained unmoved, and Sewall remained undaunted; he turned next to friends and family for assistance.

Sewall twice visited Winthrop's sister, Madam Mary Mico (who possessed "a parcel" of books—perhaps including some advice books aimed at widows[6]), to enlist her aid in persuading the widow to marry him. Mico initially rejected Sewall's pleas for help, arguing that she was "in the same condition" (by this time, she had been widowed for two years and remained so until her death in 1733). He understood the power of female networks, but not well enough. Perhaps Madam Mico was jealous of the attention her sister was getting, or perhaps she did not want to lose a close female companion who shared life experiences with her. Whatever her reason for initially rebuffing Sewall, she later conceded that if "her Sister were for it, she should not hinder it." But she never agreed to actively help his cause.

When he next visited Madam Winthrop, she "took occasion to speak pretty earnestly about my keeping a Coach," which her friends advised "must be set on Wheels, and not by [be] Rusting."[7] Sewall declared that he could not afford to keep a coach and that his estate to her would be himself; he hoped her estate to him would be the same. The following notation in Sewell's diary suggests his discussion of the affair also went beyond family:

> As were drinking at the Governour's, he said: In England the Ladies minded little more than that they might have Money, and Coaches to ride in. I said, And New-England brooks its Name. At which Mr. Dudley smiled. Govr said they were not quite so bad here.

When Sewall presumptively asked Winthrop how soon he could make their negotiations public, she tartly replied that they were "like to be no more public than they were already," suggesting her disapproval of the prominent men of the town gossiping about her.

On November 2, having apparently taken his friends' counsel, Sewall offered Madam Winthrop £100 a year upon his death as a marriage settlement and asked what she would give him if she died first. She indicated that she knew that he had given all of his estate to his children by a deed of gift and could not live up to his end of the bargain. He denied the charge, claiming he owned land in the colonies as well as in England.[8] On November 7, Sewall again pressed his marriage proposal, saying that he loved her (she would only admit to respecting him). He also disingenuously complained that while he offered his proposals without any advice from friends or family, she "had so many to advise with, that twas a hindrance."

At last, convinced of Winthrop's rejection, Sewall told her he would not bother her any more. As he walked out the door, he reminded her that she had "enter'd the 4th year of her Widowhood." On November 11, he noted, "Went not to Mm. Winthrop's. This is the 2d Withdraw." Thereafter, Sewall mentioned Madam Winthrop only in passing and never again wrote of their courtship. On March 29, 1722, he married the widow Mary Gibbs.[9] Three years later, Katherine Winthrop died a widow at the age of sixty. In her will, she named one son, two daughters, her daughter-in-law, four grandsons, three granddaughters, her sister, and numerous nieces and nephews as heirs.[10]

When Sewall suggested that Winthrop could better provide for her children by giving them their full portion of her estate through a deed of gift than by trying to raise them through her management of the estate, he addressed widows' economic power and familial responsibilities. When he assumed that Winthrop would be controlled by her son, he suggested the constraints on widows' independence within the family. When he discussed Katherine Winthrop's lack of attention to her physical appearance and her evident determination to avoid physical contact, Sewall alluded to both Winthrop's and the community's fear of sexual misconduct implicit in widowhood. Finally, when he mentioned the community and the social networks formed by her "friendly neighbors," he identified the ambivalent role the community played in a widow's decision.[11]

In the same city, eight years after this courtship, Thomas Amory died suddenly on the morning of June 19. Unlike Katherine Winthrop, Rebecca Amory was a young widow; she was twenty-seven—a full thirty years younger than Winthrop, and she and Thomas had been married only six years. Also unlike Winthrop, Rebecca Amory had five children under the age of six to care for. Amory's brother Isaac, living in Charleston, South Carolina, wrote her, "I here make you all the offers of Service in my Power tho at so great a distance and wish I could be with you to help you tho I hope you'l find many Other freinds[.]"[12] He understood the importance of a support network, even if it could not be family. As did Madam Winthrop, Rebecca Amory was to rely on friends for advice.

When Thomas died, Rebecca was granted administration on his estate, which was valued at slightly more than £2,600 and included a wide variety of furniture, household goods, clothing, books, slaves, livestock, a house, land, wharfage, and stills.[13] This large estate reflects the success of his various business undertakings, which enabled him to leave his widow well situated materially and financially. Yet, even under these circumstances, it seemed likely that Rebecca Amory would remarry for two reasons: first, her youth and wealth made her a prime candidate in the Bostonian marriage market; and second, she needed a husband to manage the large estate and to be a father to her orphaned children. But Rebecca Amory remained widowed until her death, in 1753. Perhaps she and Katharine Winthrop took to heart prescriptive literature against remarriage, or perhaps demographics dictated their status. More likely, they exercised the newfound autonomy widowhood engendered and simply chose not to remarry. In the process, they embraced new identities for themselves.

As wealthy, high-status, independent women, Winthrop and Amory do not represent all widows in colonial America or even all widows in New England. They do, however, exemplify the individual and communal struggles around widowhood and remarriage. There is no concrete evidence that either woman read the large body of prescriptive literature about widowhood. But that all the parties involved, however tangentially, could not agree whether Madam Winthrop should marry Samuel Sewall reflects the ideology prevalent in early America. As this ritual suggests, it was not easy to draw clear boundaries around those who did and who did not support widow remarriage and why they believed as they did. It was a complicated and sometimes confusing matter, but one in which widows exerted their power over their own lives and their own identities—that is, over their concept of widowhood and traditional gender boundaries.

The ideals promoted in sermons and conduct books were neither aimed at an elite few nor limited in geographic and temporal scope; in fact, they represented a transatlantic and intercolonial ideology of remarriage. For example, in England, the most popular conduct book, *The Whole Duty of Man, Laid Down in a Plain and Familiar Way for the Use All, But Especially the Meanest Reader* [emphasis added], went through sixty-four editions between 1659 and 1842; *The Ladies Calling* went through at least twelve editions up to 1787; and *New Whole Duty of Man: Containing the Faith as well as Practice of a Christian* went through thirty-seven editions between 1741 and 1853. Total sales of advice books neared one thousand copies. All this suggests that they indeed reached a large and socially diverse audience.[14] Likewise, colonists—whether they emigrated from England or were born on this side of the ocean—read, reread, and memorized the contents of these books.

Almost every early American woman owned a Bible, a prayer book, and *The Whole Duty of Man*.[15] Probate records indicate that these books frequently appeared in women's estates. In Massachusetts, nearly half of all widows' estates contained books and other reading material. In Maryland and South Carolina, respectively, about 40 and 45 percent did so.[16] The will of William Norris of Prince George's County, Maryland, suggests one way some women came into possession of these books. Norris bequeathed his daughter two of Richard Allestree's most popular tracts: *The Whole Duty of Man*, which included private devotions and rules for the proper conduct of each household member, and *The Government of the Tongue* (1674), a manual about ethical speech.[17] Widows in all three colonies also bequeathed such reading material. However, because widows in Massachusetts and South Carolina tended to live in urban areas and possessed greater wealth—and thus had the leisure time to read—they were more likely than Maryland widows to bequeath books. The range of prescriptive literature went beyond the Bible and a handful of titles. Inventories listed more than a hundred separate titles; in addition to history books, dictionaries, and legal treatises, there were the more ubiquitous psalm books, an extensive variety of religious treatises, numerous sermon books, as well as *The Ladies Library*, *The Compleat Housewife* (first published in England in 1727, this book appears to be the first cookbook published in America), *Ruth's Recompense* (written in 1628 by an English Puritan minister, this is a commentary on the biblical book of the widow Ruth), and Garland's *Of Vertuous Dames*.[18] *The Ladies Calling*, which appeared most often in southern colonial homes, was used as a guide to proper female conduct. Other writers of conduct books paraphrased or copied verbatim whole passages from it. Also popular in the southern colonies was *The Ladies Library*, a compilation of passages taken from works such as *The Ladies Calling* and Mary Astell's *Serious Proposal to the Ladies* and *Some Reflections upon Marriage*.[19]

The continuing popularity of Cotton Mather's *Ornaments for the Daughters of Zion*, printed originally in 1692, is supported by two pieces of evidence. First, the English evangelist George Whitefield, who discovered *Ornaments* on a trip through New England in 1741, recommended it to all the women of Boston and sent it to Benjamin Franklin to reprint for the women of Philadelphia.[20] Second, and more important, the inside front cover of a copy of a third edition, dated 1741, bears the following inscription: "Dorothy Griggs Her Book ad 1743" and "Dorothy Griggs and her Daughters Book." That Dorothy Griggs took the time to inscribe the book in both her own name and in her daughter's name is highly significant. According to Laurel Thatcher Ulrich, such acts "set a person apart" and became "crucial props in unobserved intimate ritual." With this advice book and through this simple act, Griggs created a female identity and "a world of meaning" across two generations and in the process transmitted her cultural ideals to those who followed.[21]

Mather understood the importance of his message beyond his neighborhood and parish. On March 17, 1718, he wrote to Samuel Sewall that "You have [done] so much . . . for the widow, that I cannot but believe my poor *Marah* [*Marah Spoken To: A Brief Essay to do Good Unto the Widow*] will be welcome to you." Sewall noted in his diary that when Mrs. Denison visited him, he gave "her a Widow's Book Bound, having writ her Name in it."[22] Mather also sent "a little number of" copies of his *A Visit to the Widow* (identified as a paraphrased title for his *Marah Spoken To*) to ministers in neighboring towns where there were a large number of widows. He hoped that the ministers would then disperse the copies among the widows.[23] In addition, local governments in New England frequently handed out free books and printed sermons. In those communities that did not give away books, officials often gave public readings of them.[24]

Those who did not or could not read also heard the ideals preached at midweek and Sabbath services. Because some New England churches seated as many as hundred people, the number of people exposed to sermons was quite large.[25] Spoken and printed sermons were also disseminated and discussed in frequent private meetings in homes throughout New England. In his funeral sermon for the widow Bridget Usher, Thomas Foxcroft pointed to both Usher (her husband, Hezekiah, preceded her in death by twenty-six years) and the widow Martha Dassett (who died the same year as Usher and whose husband John preceded her in death by twenty-three years) as "Patterns of Constancy to the Publick Worship . . . and they practiced (even to the last) the good old Way of writing after the Minister. They were swift to hear; and by this laudable . . . Method, took care to hear for the time to come, as the Prophet speaks."[26] Women as well as men spread the messages contained in this advice literature. Although it would be interesting to know the extent to which they adhered to or subverted ministerial teachings in their weekly gatherings, unfortunately no evidence remains of the notes they took or the discussions they held.

Equally popular were Renaissance and Restoration English plays.[27] Although English plays were rarely read or performed in Puritan Massachusetts, they were very popular in Maryland and South Carolina. At a time when most people were illiterate, plays both entertained and instructed, reaching many who avoided ministers and churches. In the South, people from a variety of classes and levels of education attended frequently and discussed knowledgably the content of the productions. Most of the repertoire and actors came directly from England, bringing to the southern colonies secondhand versions of the contemporary London stage—complete with discussions of sexuality, debates over morality, and merry and tragic widows.[28]

Widows presented a conceptual dilemma for seventeenth-century authors. Prescriptive literature attempted to precisely define the roles, rights, and responsibilities of maidens, wives, and widows. However, widows were neither maiden nor wife, neither yoked nor independent, neither mother nor father. Or, rather, it was not that they were none of these things but that they were all of these things. They did not fit comfortably into a well-ordered hierarchical society or into any well-defined niche; therefore, they could not be easily constrained by the boundaries that framed the lives of other Anglo-American women.

Discussion of remarriage in the prescriptive literature revolved around a key issue: which posed more danger to a well-ordered society, widows who remarried, or widows who did not? Three factors determined remarriage patterns: the "rules" that the elite prescribed, the practices the popular culture chose to follow, and the wishes of individual widows. These inextricably linked forces created confusion about widow remarriage. In light of the high marriage rates and constrained lives of single women, the authors of British and colonial prescriptive literature, whether sermonic or theatrical, confronted independent women primarily at widowhood. Independent women were an unsettling phenomenon in communities built on the hierarchical and patriarchal nuclear family. The reactions to the condition were neither clear nor consistent. Men of power felt compelled to eliminate as much ambiguity as they could. As they instructed the community, they interpreted widowhood to their best advantage. Ordinary folk, who accepted ambiguity more readily than the elite, challenged and reinterpreted the teachings of clergy and magistrate.[29] Widows used this tug-of-war between elite and popular prescriptions surrounding widowhood to their advantage.

The female *exempla* from ancient history, the Bible, and religious treatises had long been used to educate women about their proper behavior. Beginning in the sixteenth century, books written in English for a general middle-class female audience expanded the scope of these writings. The ascent of Henry VIII to the throne, in 1509; his marriage to Catherine of Aragon; his many succeeding marital problems; and the successive ascents of Mary and Elizabeth Tudor to the throne focused the English population on the nature of marriage and on women's public presence, both at court and in society. At a time when a rigid hierarchical nuclear patriarchal family structure symbolized social, cultural, and economic order, royal difficulties and controversies raised the specter of disorder created by marriage, death, and the rule of women.[30] The unruly woman had become the new reality, and writers subjected family life to intense scrutiny."[31] Within an unstable milieu, scholars, clergymen, and playwrights debated the nature of women, discussing their faults, as well as their virtues. In contrast to the unruly women they saw all around them, they identified and promoted an ideal gender role that described the supposed natural differences between men and women and between different categories of women.

Conduct books aimed specifically at widows appeared in the late sixteenth century.[32] Renaissance writers directed books, plays, and sermons at "the principal and most distinct scenes, in which a woman can be supos'd regularly to be an actor": maiden or virgin, wife, and widow. Although a great many of the works presented exaggerated, ambiguous, and even convoluted images, authors drew out the inherent contradictions to enable their readers to make the right choice. Each phase of a woman's life shared similar qualities, such as piety, meekness, and modesty. Yet, each phase entailed quite different rights and responsibilities—and widows could easily understand their options, especially since they had likely encountered this same material when they were single and married.[33] A poem by the English dramatist Thomas Middleton ostensibly allowed his readers to choose between good and bad, virtue and sin, and the maiden, married, or widowed state.

> In a maiden-time profest,
> Then we say that life is best;
> Tasting once the married life,
> Then we only praise the wife;
> There's but one state more to try,
> which makes women laugh or cry—
> Widow, widow.[34]

Although he recognized the ambiguous nature of widowhood as a time of loneliness or a time of happiness, he suggested it as a viable alternative to being single or married. Similarly, in *Tis Merrie When Gossips Meet*, three women debated the relative merits of the three phases of a woman's life. The widow argued that she had the most freedom because she had no husband waiting for her at home who would smell liquor on her breath and question what she was doing. In addition, her "red-hair'd" husband "would let me grone, and grone, the veriest Clowne." Ultimately, however, apprehensive that some women might make the wrong choice, both Middleton and Rowlands clearly settled the issue. The former proclaimed, "of these three, the middle's [wife] the best, and that give me"; the latter admitted that she "would not linger out my youthfull prime" if she found the right man and even urged the maid, who had a wealthy but homely suitor avidly pursuing her, to marry him because he would maintain her well.[35] In fiction and in reality—as with Madam Winthrop—women gathered to discuss and debate the difficulties of living with men and the efficacy of remarriage at a time when male power was pervasive. Such gossip created "solidarity among women, providing a forum for them to share their experiences and work out their ideas."[36]

Anglo-American prescriptive literature maintained that a widow, with the death of her husband, lost not only half of her life but the "defender of [her] own Chastitie, saver and keeper of [her] bodie, father and tutour of [her] children, wealth of [her] house, housholde, and goods," as well as her "governour and Lord."[37] These multiple losses spelled disaster for a widow and for the community. They implied that a widow's second husband should step in to restore order. Still, it was rarely that simple, especially when women like Katherine Winthrop and Rebecca Amory chose not to remarry.

Several very different seventeenth-century advice books highlight this ambivalence toward remarriage. In 1632, T.E., the author of *The Lawes Resolutions of Womens Rights*, the first book in English on the legal status of women, initially stated that "the widdow married again to her owne great liking," indicating that widows willingly remarried. He then noted that this widow remarried "not with applause of most friends and acquaintances." T.E. justified the widow's decision to remarry on the grounds that "young, rich, [and] gracious" widows had no other choice. Such widows were relentlessly pursued, even harassed, by all the town's "bachelours and widowers. . . . This kinde of life the widdow liked not," and to "set mens harts and her owne at rest shee [was forced to] chuse amongst them."[38]

By contrast, the English dramatist Thomas Heywood's *Gunaikeion*, written in 1624, argued that widows seemingly had a choice. He claimed that the friends and kin of a young noble widow "continualle layd open the sollitude of widdowhood, the comfort of societie, and all things that might persuade her to a second marriage." She steadfastly refused the community's pressure to remarry, arguing that "should I happen upon a good man, such as my first husband was, I would not live in that perpetuall feare I should bee in, lest I should loose him; but if otherwise, why should I hazard my selfe upon one so badde." While Heywood praised widows who committed suicide upon their husbands' death, he more realistically urged widows "to imitate the Turtles, who if one be taken away by death, the other will never chuse an other mate."[39] In the end, like Middleton and T.E., he offered widows no choice at all: ideal widows did not remarry.

On the other hand, Hannah Allen's autobiography explored the depression of widowhood and the redemptive powers of remarriage. Hannah was married in 1656. After her husband died, eight years later, she "began to fall into a deep melancholy." She became so depressed that she attempted suicide, trying perhaps to live up to the ideal presented by *Gunaikeion*. Three years later, however, shortly after her remarriage to a widower with whom she "lived comfortably," the melancholy disappeared as quickly as it had appeared.[40] Again, the choice was clear.

Colonial ministers drew from the most authoritative Anglo-American prescriptive writing, the King James version of the Bible, which described widows as sad, lonely, and suffering the "greatest losse and dammage, that can bechance her in the worlde."[41] In 1718, the Puritan minister Increase Mather observed that with the loss of a "desirable Husband," a woman suffered a "sore Affliction" much greater than the death of a child, and his son Cotton Mather noted that a "Widow is at first encountred and affrighted and amazed with a dismal prospect of Difficulties which appear insuperable." Widows themselves testified to fact that widowhood was a time of great mourning and readjustment. As Rebecca Amory wrote, "I dout not you have heard the malloncholy news of . . . my Dear husbands death . . . this surpriseing event of providence has left me in a very aflicted condishon[.]"[42] Because of the seemingly insurmountable barriers that widows faced, the younger Mather devoted an entire sermon to explaining the distressing and pitiful state in which widows lived and urging the community's benevolence and patience toward poor widows. Significantly, neither Mather urged widows to remarry to alleviate their distress. They adhered to the belief expressed that a "good woman" not only refrained from seeking a second mate but refused all unsolicited offers of marriage, remarrying only when forced to do so.[43]

Authors of the prescriptive literature were unclear about precisely when a widow needed to free the turtle dove and yoke herself to another. Seventeenth-century writers urged widows to remain unmarried, but, recognizing that that was not always a possibility, they also urged widows to remarry when circumstances forced them in that direction; finally, they urged widows to imitate Hannah Allen only if they found they could not adjust to the sad and lonely state of widowhood. Part of the lack of certainty over remarriage stemmed from the recognition that widowhood could be a time of more than being "desart and desolate" and, indeed, that widowhood could provide women with a degree of autonomy.

Through the numerous references in the Old Testament to the rights of honor and privileges of protection due to widows and fatherless children ("orphans"), society not only accepted widowhood but also recognized that it could free widows from male guardianship. According to Numbers 30:3-9, although vows made by unmarried women could be voided by their fathers and vows made by married women could be voided by their husbands, "any vow of a widow . . ., any thing by which she has bound herself shall stand against her." But such a vow could also stand for her; a widow was responsible for her own life and the decisions that she made. In preindustrial societies dependent on verbal contracts, such a privilege accorded widows significant power. *The Lawes Resolutions of Womens Rights* confirmed that the vow of a widow "no man had power to disallow of, for her estate was free from controlment."[44] The theme of powerful widows free from constraint runs throughout the prescriptive literature from Sir Thomas Elyot's *Defence of Good Women* (1540) through *The Whole Duty of Woman* (1753).

Elyot portrayed widows in a positive light, stressing their independence, intelligence, and strength.[45] He argued that some women possessed masculine virtues that made them capable of undertaking public life. His exemplar was the Syrian Queen Zenobia. As a married woman, she walked an ambivalent path between never questioning her obedience to her husband and recognizing the boundaries of her husband's power over her. As a widow, Zenobia, freed from such constraints, pursued her talents and power. Widowhood enabled her to exercise the civic virtues that Elyot believed women possessed. Only as a reigning queen did Zenobia act like a man in a man's world. To wield the power all widows had, she suppressed the feminine.

Echoing these men, Mistress Littlegood, author of the *Juniper* lectures, parodied advice books that told women it was best for them remarry. To the gathering of friends at her house where those present lamented the "great pains we poor women take," she pledged that she would never remarry because she had "not been troubled these thirty-two years with so grievous a burden as a Husband."[46] Her vow subtly suggested that older women should not remarry, but she primarily asserted that, as a widow, she had lived nearly half her life free from the constraints of marriage, and she refused to eschew that freedom for any reason. The most ardent espousal of the liberty of widowhood came in *The Ladies Calling*. Allestree argued that being married once was enough for any woman and that, having done it once, women were unlikely to do it again because they who "have commonly fortitude enough to encounter and baffle" the many problems in their lives can find little gain in remarriage.[47]

In 1743, the widow Elizabeth Timothy, printer of the *South Carolina Gazette*, published "verses written by a young Lady, on women born to be controul'd." The anonymous author did not explicitly address the issue of widowhood, but clearly the constraints of marriage—first or second—were on her mind.

> How wretched is a Woman's Fate,
> No happy Change her Fortune knows,
> Subject to Man in every State.
> How can she then be free from Woes?
>
> In Youth a Father's stern Command,
> And jealous Eyes controul her Will;
> A lordly Brother watchful stands,
> To keep her closer Captive still.
>
> The tyrant Husband next appears
> With awful and contracted Brow;
> No more a Lover's Form he wears,
> Her Slave's become her Sov'reign now.[48]

However, most authors refused to grant widows the liberty of widowhood espoused by Mistress Littlegood. More prevalent was the fear of women alone, without male constraint. One author argued that because a widow had lost her husband, that is, her governor, she was "tost at all adventures, as a shippe, lacking a master, and is carried without discretion and consideration, as a childe when his overseer is out of the way."[49] He believed that most women did not have enough sense to care for themselves and should be handled like children. The most virulent and misogynist attack on remarrying widows appeared in Joseph Swetnam's 1615 *The Arraignment of Lewde, Idle, Froward and Unconstant Women*. In advising men who might be anticipating marrying a widow, Swetnam expressed a profound hatred of widows. He wrote, "woe be unto that unfortunate man that matcht himselfe unto a widowe for a widowe will be the cause of a thousand woes." Widows will "looke to governe" and "commonly [they] are so waspish, and so stubborne, that thou canst not wrest them from their wills.[50] Once a widow learned to live without the constraining hand of a husband, she tried to turn the gender order upside down by becoming the governor of the family.

To solve the problem of ungoverned women, advice books and sermons urged widows to revere their dead husbands and to give themselves wholly [and holy] over to Jesus Christ.[51] A widow was to take Christ as her second husband, living her life in frequent and intense prayer and forgoing the "trimming and araying of her bodye,"[52] much as the widow Winthrop did. Thomas Pritchard, in *The schoole of honest and vertuous life*, advised widows that if they took the liberty of remarrying, they should certainly "wey well this restraint of your liberty." He then urged widows to "cast your hope upon God, depend upon his providence, comit the matter wholy to his hands."[53] One of the few female voices on the subject was the eighteenth-century English author Eliza Haywood, who, in *The Female Spectator,* praised widows

> who have past with Honour your two first Stages of Life, and support the third with a becoming Fortitude and Patience, . . . in whose faithful Hearts our Husband still survives . . . [and] who continue wedded to the Memory of your first Love, and fly all second Offers, though accompanied with Titles, Wealth, and every gilded Prospect, so enchanting to the less constant of your Sex.[54]

For ministers like Cotton Mather, Benjamin Colman, and Thomas Foxcroft, and diarists such as John Saffin, the biblical Anna (Luke 2:36) offered an ideal model. Anna was widowed after living with her husband for seven years. She remained a widow until her death at age eighty-four.[55] For an example closer to the Boston community, Mather turned to Elizabeth Cotton, at whose funeral he claimed, "When she first became a Disconsolate Widow [at age twenty-one], she . . . settled her Espousal to her Saviour."[56] Beyond the concerns of a hierarchy turned upside down, opinions on widow remarriage focused primarily on two areas of concern: sexuality and economic status, but again in a complex and ambiguous manner.

On the one hand, according to St. Paul the community must fear younger widows for the sexual turmoil they could create. The widow

Winthrop's declaration that she no longer took pleasure in sex and Mather's statement that widows should forgo "trimming and araying" their bodies addressed a serious concern that independent, unchaperoned widows would not be chaste. Take, for example, the New Testament, which Winthrop quoted. In his Epistle to the Corinthians (7:8-9), Paul advised unmarried and widowed women that "it is good for them if they abide even as I. But if they cannot contain, let them marry: for it is better to marry than to burn." Paul refined his advice in 1 Timothy 5:3-15. He counseled widows age sixty or more to remain single and young widows to remarry. According to Paul, older women had fulfilled their role as wives and mothers. Young widows, however, threatened a well-ordered society because they "had begun to wax wanton," wandered "from house to house" as tattlers and busybodies, and, more important, had not borne children. Those who steadfastly refused to remarry and bear children had "already turned aside after Satan."

The Anglican clergyman Thomas Becon advised remarriage as the only way for young widows to remain chaste. Experience demonstrated "how light, vain, trifling, unhonest, unhousewifelike, young widows have been in all ages and are also at this present day."[57] The Puritan minister Cotton Mather, unlike other advice book authors, voiced similar concerns about the chastity of widowers. He asserted that widowers frequently succumbed to temptation, dishonoring God with their unchaste behavior. To avoid temptation, as well as to uphold their reputations, Mather also urged widowers to remarry.[58] Nonetheless, moralists in both early modern Europe and the colonies viewed sexually uncontrolled widows as much greater threats to the social order than widowers.

On the other hand, many seventeenth- and eighteenth-century commentators viewed poor widows as objects of God's and men's pity. In 2 Kings 4:1-7, the prophet Elisha aids a poor widow who fears losing her two children because her dead husband has left her deep in debt. Magically, Elisha turns a single jar of oil into many jars of oil for her to sell to pay off her debts and to keep her children without having to remarry. Some, fearing widows' economic independence, argued that God intended women to be subject to men; independent widows, therefore, violated God's natural order.[59] The issue went beyond a gendered natural order, however. Widows often controlled significant property, providing ambitious and enterprising males effortless access to property and status. Thomas Pritchard urged women to remain widowed and to avoid men who have spent their own wealth and "peradventure will attempte" them—that is, entice or seduce them.[60] At least implicitly, Pritchard made a connection between widows' sexual and economic liberty. Similarly, Cotton Mather argued that, although the Bible gave women liberty to remarry, to ensure that a second husband "may [not] Count Hers more than Her," he cautioned an older widow to not marry a much younger man.[61] In 1725, the widow Spratt from Maryland wrote her niece about the widow Lloyd, who, she noted, had been left "3 h[und]r[ed] pounds a year jongter [jointure] and 800 more if she lives a widow and half the plate and goods . . . so she will make [a] pritty matche for some body."[62] The widow Spratt failed to note, however, that the widow Lloyd would have more money if she remained unmarried than if she remarried. Control over large estates and the passage of such estates to future generations generated considerable discussion.

At the most basic level, widows who failed to pay enough attention to their children's future increased the likelihood that the community would be responsible for those children. The issue was more ideologically complex, however. In making the connection between sexual and economic freedom more explicit, many advice book authors reminded widows that their desire for sexual gratification often jeopardized their children's financial future by giving control of their children's estate to an avaricious second husband.[63] John Dunton feared that a remarrying widow would use her husband's fortunes "to make her a better prize to a second husband: she goes into another family, as if she were a Colony sent out by her son, he must pay for the planting her there."[64] Similarly, Eliza Haywood, a rare forceful female voice, asserted that widows with children should never remarry. Yet, she turns Dunton's argument on its head in her admonition about independent and powerful men:

> it is a great Misfortune to lose either of our Parents while young, and unable to take Care of ourselves, yet is the Danger much greater when the Place of a Father is fill'd up by a Stranger, than it can be under a Mother in-law: —The Reason is obvious; —the one can do of himself, what the other can only accomplish by the Influence she has over the Husband.

Unfortunately, widows "are made to believe, that in quitting their State of Widowhood they shall do a greater Service to their Children than they could do by continuing in it.[65] Given that Haywood wrote these words more than twenty years after Katherine Winthrop rejected Samuel Sewell on the grounds that she needed to protect her children's fortunes, it is likely that Haywood did not influence Winthrop but rather may have been reflecting positions of power and control that widows were already protecting.

As this survey of the prescriptive literature suggests, widows confronted a dizzying array of options. Because a widow ruled over her family as her husband had and represented her family's interests in the wider community, her behavior greatly concerned that community. Still, widows were given some leeway to decide how they would fit into their communities' patriarchal structure. Each author offered what she or he believed was the ideal prescription. If a widow, however, read several advice books or heard several sermons, she understood that she enjoyed great discretion—much more so than other women—but it was a discretion that could prove at best ambiguous and at worst confusing. This uncertainty was accentuated in the options offered them by British playwrights, novelists, and poets beginning with the Restoration.

When women became a regular part of the audience for early English plays, for many observers, they "were as much part of the spectacle to be commented on as women on the stage."[66] The concern about the spectacle of women both in the audience and on the stage had two effects. First, audiences demanded plays that could be judged as "matter for serious discussion." Second, playwrights clearly articulated fears about the "problematic relationship between power and sex," in which female liberty threatened the social order. Plays about women reflected political and economic disorder of post-Cromwellian Britain. The British stage dwelled on discontinuity and rupture, rather than communal consensus and conformity. As such, it offered an arena of passionate exchange rather than concrete resolution.[67]

Most British dramatists introduced the widow problem with the widow's refusal to remarry. Plays provided alternate ways of understanding widow remarriage by exploring issues that failed to conform to abstract ideas. Individual dramatists offered pointed advice, but the broader repertoire presented a variety of opinion, as is evident in these key dramas explicitly about widowhood: *The Puritan: or, the Widow of Watling Street*, *The Widdowes Teares*, *The Widdow*, *The City Heiress*, and *The Widow Ranter*.[68]

In most of these plays, the widows ideally remain passively loyal to their dead husbands, to their vows of chastity, and to their Christian duties. In one sense, the widows conform to society's hierarchy and to the counsel of advice book authors. It is, however, more complex than that.

The playwrights portrayed young widows as disloyal, scheming harlots, signaling chaos, the need for masculine control, and the importance of patriarchal order. If such widows did not remarry, their independence and untamed sexual liberty threatened to disrupt society. However, older wealthy widows offered men sexual experience, social mobility, and sustained gender order. The plays also offer a woman's perspective that women in the audience would have understood. Although the widows in Aphra Behn's plays eventually remarry, they all express ambivalence toward remarriage. They remarry on their terms, not on society's terms. Several dramas portray widows who, in defiance of convention, choose to never remarry. These plays accord widows freedom to demonstrate their virtue and independence, as well to disdain male-dominated institutions.

Reflecting the era's prescriptive literature, several sources portray the most traditional response to widow remarriage. In *The Widow of Watling Street*, the widow Lady Plus proclaims to her relatives her determination to never remarry. Beyond asserting that she could never find another man as good as her husband, she reveals the precariousness of her position by proclaiming that she would be "the common talk at table in the mouth of every groom and waiter, if e'er more I entertain the carnal suit of man."[69] When the widow Eudora in *The Widdowes Teares* contemplates remarriage, her friend answers that "I am asham'd and abhorred to thinke so great and vow'd a patterne of our sex, should take into her thoughts . . . a second love. Wives should be stil yong in their husbands loves[.]"[70]

Several playwrights suggested that widows could neither be trusted to remain loyal to their husbands nor to make sound, rational judgments about their lives. In Susanna Centlivre's *The Gamester*, the Widow Wealthy's sister reflects such fears when she decries, "What in that Mourning Weed resolv'd on Matrimony, and is your Lord forgot already . . . does your dead Husband's Picture that dangles at your Watch there, serve only to put you in mind of another?"[71]

Despite the widow Lady Plus's initial refusal to remarry, she decides to wed her suitor after being tricked into believing that she must remarry to save her deceased husband from purgatory. According to the irate nobleman who reveals the scheme to Lady Plus (a man as full of animosity toward widows as Joseph Swetnam):

> Upon whom can I justly cast this blot, but upon your own forehead, that know not ink from milk? such is the blind besotting in the state of an unheaded woman that's a widow [emphasis added]. For it is the property

> of all you that are widows (a handful excepted) to hate those that honestly and carefully love you to undo you. Who regard you least, are best regarded; who hate you most are best beloved. And if there be but one many amongst ten thousand millions of men, that is accurst, disastrous and evilly planeted; whom Fortune beats most, whom God hates most, and all societies esteem least, that man is sure to be a husband. Such is the peevish moon that rules your bloods. An impudent fellow best woos you, a flattering lip best wins you; or in a mirth, who talks roughliest, is most sweetest; nor can you distinguish truth from forgeries, mists from simplicity: witness those two deceitful monsters, that you have entertain'd for bridegrooms.[72]

Similarly, the widow Eudora eventually agreed to marry her suitor, who then immediately revealed his anxieties about her decision by asking her:

> doe not you wives nod your heads, and smile upon another when yee meete abroade? . . . Do you not brag amongst yourselves how grossly you abuse their honest credulities? . . . How you vow Widdow-hood in [your husband's] life time, and they believe you, when even in the sight of their breathless corpse, ere they be fully cold, you joine embraces with his Groome or his Phistion or perhaps his poisoner; or at least . . . solemnly plight new Hymineall bonds with a wild confident, untamed Ruffine?[73]

The seemingly easy conquest of the widow Eudora, the discussions of widows' weakness and the likelihood that widows will violate the vows to their husbands lead another male character in the same play to test his wife's loyalty by faking his death. After his "demise," his wife follows his body into his tomb where she mourns and fasts as a proper widow. But then, tempted to end her vigil by a young, virile soldier, the widow succumbs to the scheme. Ultimately, widows appeared wild, sexually untamed, and ready to defile the honor of their widows' beds. Even if the cause appeared honorable, widows could easily upset a well-ordered society constructed along specific gender roles. "Unheaded" widows foolishly turned the world upside down. Men had to step in to protect widows from themselves and to protect the community from the havoc wrought by widows who could not distinguish truthfulness from deception.

But that deception ran two ways, for, in these plays, the widows viewed men as interested in them only for their money. Some rebelled against their situation, and others used it to their advantage, especially those widows who highly valued their liberty and independence. For example, Lady Plus understood the constraints suffered by most married women and initially asserted that she had no intention of giving up her freedom. The widow Valeria also resisted remarriage: "Its a dangerous age," she proclaims, in which "poor simple dealing women had need look about em." While men pursue her for her money, she declares that she will not remarry until she finds "one that loves me for my self Sir, Not for my wealth."[74] Similarly, in Behn's *The City Heiress*, the widow Galliard repeatedly turns down proposals for marriage. She refuses to give in to either social or sexual pressure to marry someone who does not love her; she also refuses to marry someone she does not love.

In *The Widdow*, when his friend Francis asks Ricardo why he wants to marry the widow Valeria, Ricardo answers that he has no estate left and claims rather incredulously: "Why, do'st think if I had kept my land still, I should ever have look'd after a rich Widow? Alas, I should have married some poor young Maid, got five and twenty children, and undone myself." These sentiments echo Joseph Swetnam when he declares that a man seldom "marrieth with a widowe for her beauty nor for her personage, but only for her wealth and riches."[75] The widow Valeria, however, turns the tables on Ricardo. She announces that she has deeded away all of her estate. She then offers herself in marriage to her various suitors. Two of them abandon her when she reveals that she possesses no estate. Only Ricardo steadfastly maintains his love, winning Valeria's promise to marry. Ricardo, who from the beginning of the play appeared only interested in Valeria's estate, ultimately follows his heart without regard to the economic consequences. Love triumphs over greed. But does it? In the end, Ricardo gains access to Valeria as well as to her large estate.

In *The Widow Ranter*, Aphra Behn looks at remarriage from the widow's economic perspective. The widow Ranter is no fool. She acknowledges that she knows the young men love her only for her money, claiming, "if it were not for that, I might sit still and sigh, and cry out, a Miracle! a Miracle! at sight of a Man within my doors." However, she also recognizes that her wealth gives her power. She exclaims, "We rich Widdows are the best Commodity this Country affords." She does not shy away from openly using her wealth to find a good husband. Along the same vein, but in a much more forceful female voice, the widow Roxana explains her decision not to remarry her long-time lover: "as I had money enough, and needed not fear being what they call a cast-off Mistress, so I had no need to give him twenty Thousand Pound to marry me."[76]

Unlike the religiously based prescriptive writers, playwrights rarely explored the tension between a widow's remarriage wealth and her children's future. In fact, none of the widows in these plays had children. The struggle over who controlled her wealth focused only on a widow and her suitor(s). This likely reflects the young age of the widows in the plays. This also likely reflects the fact that these plays responded to audience interest—and, apparently, most playgoers preferred stories about young, nubile women, rather than haggard matrons. More than anything else, playwrights dwelled on a widow's licentiousness. The widow Lady Plus's brother asks, "for what should we do with all our knights, I pray, but to marry rich widows, wealthy citizens' widows, lusty fair-brow'd ladies?[77] To him, young, rich widows provide the best alternative for men who need economic security—and, because of young widows' wantonness, they will be anxious to marry such men.

However, in controlling those who sought her, through her control over access to her money and her body, the widow gained power. Therefore, dramatists sought to wrestle control from widows by impugning their reputations.[78] In trying to persuade a suitor to quit his pursuit of her, the widow Lady Plus asks him to "put off all [his] suits." Behind her back, her manservant uses her words against her: "Put off all their suits, quotha-a? ay, that's the best wooing of a widow indeed, when a man's non-suited; that is, when he's a-bed with her." Later, when the widow's servants discuss her refusal to remarry, her maidservant claims that her mistress refused all suitors "like an honest, chaste and virtuous woman; for widows ought not to wallow in the puddle of iniquity." Her manservant disagrees, however: "Many widows will do't, whatso comes on't."[79] Her maid servant grudgingly agrees, saying "their filthy flesh desires a conjunction copulative." Whether or not the servants believe that their mistress is licentious, the specter of sexual misconduct remains. The disagreement between maid and menservants suggests differing gender perspective. Women believed that widows were honest and did not give into sexual iniquity because they understood the consequences of such actions and may have realized that they would find themselves in the same situation one day. Men believed that most widows found it impossible to be virtuous and gave into their natural licentiousness. The maidservant's reluctant acceptance of the manservant's claim reflects the ambiguity of widows' reputations.

In *The City Heiress*, the widow Galliard's main suitor, Tom Wilding, alleges that, although her relatives—especially her mother—might require her suitors to be "sober discreet person[s]" and although she has to pretend to be a deeply religious woman, she is in reality made of "no such sanctifi'd Materials." He believes that religion merely provides a mask under which the sexually experienced widow hides her true desires. Despite her independence, disdain, and haughtiness, he seeks the "soft, witty, [and] wanton" pleasure she provides "when she loves." But Wilding has a rival, Charles, whose uncle urges him to assert his power over Galliard with manly roughness because "women love importunity" and "willing Rape is all the fashion." Accordingly, Charles accuses Galliard of using her feminine wiles to trick him into marrying her. He justifies his actions on two accounts: first, he claims he is treating her so roughly only for "charity, care of your Reputation" and to ensure that no other, more dangerous man (Wilding) will lie with her; second, he asserts that "a widow of your Youth and Complexion can be praying for nothing so late, but a good Husband" and that, by raping her, he is ensuring her of one.[80] Wildly passionate upon remarriage, widows were to have their sexuality and independence contained and controlled even if it required rough handling and fashionable rape.

Even though it appeared that widows could easily be controlled sexually, that was not necessarily the case. Two other female voices present yet another vision of widowhood that makes clear the inextricably linked issues of sexuality and independence. In Susannah Centlivre's *The Basset-Table*, the Lady Reveller engages in this revealing conversation with a friend:[81]

> Lady Reveller: Is it a Crime to have a Number of Lovers? If it be, 'tis the pleasantest Crime in the World. A Crime that falls not every Day to every woman's Lot.
>
> Lady Lucy. I dare be positive every Woman does not wish it.
>
> Lady Reveller: What Pleasure is there in one Lover? 'tis like being seen always in one Suit of Cloaths; a Woman, with one Admirer, will ne'er be a reigning Toast.
>
> Lady Lucy: I am sure those that encourage more, will never have the Character of a reigning Virtue.
>
> Lady Reveller: I slight the malicious Censure of the Town, yet defy it to apease my Virtue; Nature has given me a Face, a Shape, a Mein, an Air for Dress, and Wit and Humour to subdue: And shall I lose my Conquest for a Name?

Again, the wildly independent Roxana shrewdly expounds on current gender roles and rails against the gendered ambiguity she (and by implication, all widows) face:

> While a Woman was single, she was a Masculine in her politick Capacity; that she had then the full Command of what she had, and the full Direction of what she did; that she was a Man in her separated Capacity, to all Intents and Purposes that a Man cou'd be so to himself; that she was controul'd by none, because accountable to none, and was In Subjection to none. I added, that whoever the Woman was, that had an Estate, and would give it up to be the Slave of a Great Man, that Woman was a Fool, and must be fit for nothing but a Beggar; that it was my Opinion, a Woman was as fit to govern and enjoy her own Estate, without a Man, as a Man was, without a Woman; and that, if she had a-mind to gratifie herself as to Sexes, she might entertain a Man, as a Man does a Mistress; that while she was thus single, she was her own, and if she gave away that Power, she merited to be as miserable as it was possible that any Creature cou'd be.[82]

Despite the novel voices of the Lady Reveller and Roxana, however, all five plays end by restoring order to the family and the community. In *The Widow of Watling Street*, ultimately Lady Plus chooses to remarry, and, in the closing lines of the play, both honorable men and heaven applaud that decision.[83] Acknowledging the tension inherent in widowhood, the playwright guided the widow Lady Plus and other widows in the audience towards remarriage. Ricardo, a "decayed young gentleman" and suitor to the widow Valeria, argues that such a marriage was as natural as:

> your College for your old standing Scholer,
> your Hopsitall for your lame creeping Souldier,
> your baud for your mangled Rorer,
> your open house for your Beggar,
> and your Widow for your Gentlemen.[84]

All the people or places on the left of the phrase "for your" were expected to provide aid or comfort for the people on the right of the phrase. To Ricardo, his natural right to the widow Valeria, and presumably to her wealth and her body, is as unquestioned as a beggar's right to charity or a sick person's right to treatment in a hospital. Old scholars, disturbers of the peace, and gentlemen force others to provide for them, denying colleges, hospitals, charity houses, prostitutes, and widows' discretionary power. These feminine agencies serve masculine agents. Their clients justify their existence.[85]

In *The Widdowes Teares,* the widow Eudora seemsd to be caught between two competing beliefs. One advises widows not to remarry and to remain loyal to their dead husbands. Following St. Paul, they are asked to become celibate. Others acknowledge widows' carnal passions and advise them to control their sexuality. For most males, remarriage, not celibacy, was preferable. Young males desired not only lusty wives but also their dead husband's estate, and the only alternative from this perspective seemed the radical and unacceptable action of having "all young widows spaded for marrying again. For the old and withered, they shall be confiscate [forfeited property] to unthrifty gallants and decayed knights."[86] The age of a widow determined consequences. Playwrights negated the power of young widows by depriving them of their sexuality and negated the power of old widows by depriving them of their wealth.

In *The City Heiress,* Aphra Behn gave a different twist to the notion of men governing widows. That Wilding never gives up pursuit of the widow Lady Galliard exposed a key issue for widows and for society. In response to Galliard's questions about his true motives for courting her, he replies, "unless being sensible you have not discretion enough to manage your own affairs your self, you resolve, like other Widows, with all you're worth to buy a Governour, commonly called a Husband. I took ye to be wiser."[87] Wilding tries to convince the widow that, although society dictates that a woman needs a man to control her life, he believes that she is smart enough to reject that notion in favor of her freedom and independence, and particularly her sexual freedom and independence. Behn suggested that allowing women flexibility and discretion did not lead to social disorder. Ultimately, however, even she retreated to the conventions of the seventeenth century by having the widow Galliard remarry.[88]

This body of Anglo-British prescriptive literature reflected and constructed the inherent confusion faced by the widow Priscilla Fones. On November 17, 1629, she wrote the following letter to John Winthrop, asking his advice about remarriage:

> I intrated your help [with that] . . . which hath bred me much grife and troubel of mind my selfe being uvery fearfull to chang my condicion[.] all

> my frinds perswade me it will be best for me to chang but my selfe hath no hart to it[.] in the man I see that which I chefly ame at in a husban which is grace and godlynes with gifts sutabel to his calling though in outward estate he coms short of any that hath bin yet moued to me these things with his importunity and paines in coming so fare hath bred such destraction in my mind as truly I know not what to doe but mine eis are towards the lord for derection in this waity busines god brother help with your prayers and best aduise for I haue now cast my selfe uppon you and my father and mr. Whit[.] I haue only giuen him this answer that I will doe nothing without the aduise of my frinds.[89]

Although most widows seemed more comfortable with their choice, Priscilla Fones's "griefe and troubel of mind," her fear of "chang[ing]" her "condicion," and her plea that she "had not hart" to remarry arose from the conflicting messages given her by the prescriptive literature, her understanding of widows' lives in her community, her friends who told her it would be best for her to remarry, and her own goal to find a wealthy second husband, which her current suitor fell "short of." Fones turned to an older man, a "governor," to guide her decisions. Although she had come from England, the issues her letter raised were relevant in New England. About a year later, Winthrop arrived in Boston, bringing with him a transatlantic ideology about widow remarriage. Fones, like many other widows, especially Katherine Winthrop, with whom this chapter opened, would not remarry without a great deal of struggle, despite—or, indeed because of—the fact that the rate of widowhood was high in both England and American in the seventeenth and eighteenth centuries.

If the question for the didactic authors was which posed more danger to a well-ordered society, widows who remarried or widows who remained widows, then the answer remained uncertain. However, if we change the question to how often widows did remarry, the answer becomes clearer. Remarriage was not unusual for either men or women. Widowers, however, remarried twice as often as widows.[90] A significant percentage of widows failed to remarry. Research for France and England indicates that only about 20 percent of French widows and 25 percent of English widows remarried. Age was a likely factor. Widows under age thirty usually remarried, while those over age fifty remained widows until their death. In premodern England and Europe, permanent widowhood was quite common, especially for older women.[91] Colonial American remarriage rates conform to the English and French pattern. On average, two-thirds of all widows in seventeenth- and eighteenth-century America remarried. As colonies became more settled, the remarriage rate for widows declined. The proportion of women who remarried in all colonies decreased by half, from 11 percent in the seventeenth century to 5.5 percent in the eighteenth century. Remarriage was more common in rural areas than in cities.[92] Depending on the widows' ages and where they lived, from the time of the initial European settlement, permanent widowhood characterized about one in three colonial widows. The variations caused by place and time—and how widows thereby negotiated gender boundaries—are also instructive.

New England widows in both the seventeenth and the eighteenth centuries rarely remarried. In Plymouth Colony, 75 percent of all women married just once. Like their English and European ancestors, when Plymouth widows remarried, they did so at half the rate of widowers.[93] There are, however, discernible chronological variations. In the seventeenth century, wealth, age, and location affected remarriage rates. In urban areas such as Boston and Salem, older and wealthy widows infrequently remarried. In Windsor, Connecticut, the remarriage rate for widows who had been married less than ten years was nearly three times higher than for widows who had been married at least twenty years. In Wethersfield, Connecticut, only 30 percent of all widows remarried, and almost all of those were under age fifty.[94]

The pattern changed slightly in the eighteenth century. Only 37 percent of Wethersfield women over the age of seventy were still married. In Woburn, Massachusetts, only 18 percent of widows remarried. Although younger widows continued to remarry at a much higher rate than older widows, it was common for younger widows in settled or well-established communities, where they could find economic support outside marriage, to remain unmarried.[95]

As the advice book literature suggested, young widows likely remarried more often than older widows for several reasons. First, at least some in the community expected them to remarry. Second, they were more likely to have young children to support. And, because they were young, they were unlikely to have accumulated significant wealth. Remarrying helped ensure their own and their children's well-being. Third, young women were more desirable to men because they were more attractive and more sexually active than were older widows—and they were capable of bearing heirs for their new husbands. Their existing children could also provide additional labor for the newly reconstituted household. Additionally, young widows usually controlled their children's portions of their former husbands' estates. This wealth could provide significant assets to the new household. Widows were also experienced household managers. Older widows, in contrast, probably did not have dependent children to support and were more economically secure. The work they found was adequate for their personal needs, and frequently their husbands left enough wealth to support them. Others relied on adult children and friends to support them. Consequently, older widows more often chose to remain widowed—and we must not lose sight of female agency; demographics alone did not determine a widow's remarriage prospects.[96]

The remarriage pattern in the Chesapeake and in the southern colonies was at once different and simpler than that in New England. Nearly all seventeenth-century widows in these colonies remarried quickly. Chesapeake women married several times. Recent histories of Maryland suggest that two-thirds of the colony's widows remarried quickly—after less than a year of widowhood—and that they remarried four times as often as widowers. The patterns for Virginia are similar. Throughout the seventeenth century, between 60 and 70 percent of widows remarried, with young widows more likely to remarry than older widows.[97] Widows in the southern colonies faced pressures similar to those faced by young widows in New England, but the demographic instability of the region greatly exacerbated those pressures, and there were more young widows than older widows. The rates of remarriage were much higher in the South, where the plantation economy offered few alternate means of support and less family support. Remarriage provided widows with a more secure future than they could provide for themselves alone. Widowhood in the South and in the Chesapeake was more likely to be a temporary phase in a woman's life than it was for widows in New England.

Although eighteenth-century widows in the Chesapeake region and in South Carolina did not remain unmarried at the high rates of New England widows, after 1700, however, widows in those regions remarried less frequently than they had before that date.[98] Remarriage patterns among widows in eighteenth-century Virginia replicated those observed in New England. Only 9 percent of all testators' widows remarried, and those who did remarry were young. The percentage of widows who remarried declined from 60 percent in 1700 to just over 43 percent by 1749. Only 46 percent of the widows in eighteenth-century St. Andrew's Parish, South Carolina, remarried. Southern colonies widows gradually, over time, remarried, albeit at lower rates. In eighteenth-century America, there were increasingly more evenly balanced sex ratios in the Chesapeake and in South Carolina and fewer potential marriage partners for widows in New England as the population moved farther west. As the numbers of the permanently widowed increased between the seventeenth and the eighteenth centuries, ministers, magistrates, and members of the community increasingly discussed the social, legal, and economic issues widows faced in male-dominated, hierarchical societies.

Whether a widow should remarry or not centered on three inextricably linked factors: her age, her wealth, and her sexual freedom. But precisely because these were not three distinct or discrete issues, the transatlantic discourse about remarriage presented conflicting opinions that were not resolved by 1750. Because the rate of widowhood was high in both England and America, large numbers of widows, writers, ministers, playwrights, and members of the community believed they had to deal with those widows.[99] On the one hand, the prescriptive literature projected what the authors hoped would be an ideal way of thinking about remarriage but also reflected, to a certain extent, a reality that could not be avoided. In projecting their ideals, the various writers were neither clear nor consistent about their solutions to the so-called problem widows represented. Youth, money, and sexuality could wreak havoc on a society ruled by men according to male virtues. Yet, youth, wealth, and sexuality enhanced a woman's ability to attract men and to find a husband, women's primary role in society. Men sought out such women, who, using these assets, gained a measure of control over their lives. On the other hand, what made them most attractive to men also increased their personal power to control their lives and to influence the community. Their assets made wealthy, fecund, and winsome widows potentially powerful and dangerous. Prescriptive literature did not reflect reality or create a reality for widows. But the confused or ambiguous discourse of the advice literature did give widows a new vocabulary to describe themselves. They could create an identity through public opinion. By reading books, listening to sermons, and watching plays, widows could pick and choose—to a certain extent—how they wanted to be viewed and how they wanted to live their lives. They created their own order out of a seemingly disordered world.

The Bostonian widow Rebecca Amory revealed her thoughts of widowhood in correspondence with her brother Isaac in Charleston, South Carolina. Her brother William had just died, and she took the opportunity to chide Isaac for putting his wife and children in jeopardy by neglecting his own health: "I wish you could be persuaded that you cannot serve yr fammily soe much any way as by taking care of your own life." It was the firm widowed voice of experience. She continued to press the issue, writing several months later that "I believe it would be much advantage to your health to summer here & hope you wont neglect it." In case he did not get the point, she said, "I hope my sistar will urge you to it for fear of being a widow."[100] But her anxious words belie her experience. Rebecca Amory had learned the power of female independence. Indeed, she asked Isaac to "let me know what circumstances he [William] has left his children in." Then she flexed her economic muscle by claiming that "I should be willing to doe aney thing in my power for them yt they needed," adding cryptically, "you know my circumstances."

As indicated by the many heated debates widows engaged in over the strengths and weaknesses of maiden, wife, and widow, they understood their society's expectations of them, but they also understood how best to negotiate the sometimes rough waters of widowhood that redefined their lives. At her husband's death, according to Cotton Mather (who among all advice book authors most realistically portrayed widowhood), a widow faced "new Anxieties and Encumbrances." There were "Debts to be paid, and Mouths to be fed, and abundance of Cares arising, which till now she was a Stranger to!"[101] The statistical evidence suggests and the lives of Katherine Winthrop, Mary Mico, and Rebecca Amory confirm that many widows knew how to handle those responsibilities without remarrying. They, rather than passively let circumstances define them, actively redefined their identity.

Upon learning of a legacy left her husband by a relative in England, Rebecca Amory wrote a long letter in response. Throughout it, her grief over losing her husband was palpable.[102] Like other widows, she did not want to appear unseemly; therefore, she highlighted three key points: first, as a widow, she suffered a "very aflicted condishon" (which she mentioned twice); second, she was the administrator of her husband's estate, but, as it was "as yet unsettled," she was financially vulnerable; and, finally, she asked the relative to pursue this matter only for the good of her children, "of whom he was ye tenderest father & thear lose unspeakable" (which she claimed four times). However, her concluding entreaty that "I must pray . . . that you would send copey of the will" indicates that she knew her legal rights and responsibilities. As the next chapter shows, Rebecca Amory was but one among many widows who understood the law and knew how to use it to their advantage as they crossed ambiguous gender boundaries to carve out new identities for themselves.

2

"Prosperity & Peace May Alwais Him Attend That to the Widdow Prove Himselfe a Friend"

Widows and the Law

On December 28, 1704, Benjamin Schenckingh Jr., William Smith for his wife Elizabeth, William Elliott for his wife Catherine, and John Emperor for his wife Amarintia, submitted a petition to the South Carolina Court of Chancery justifying their suit against Elizabeth Schenckingh's estate.[1] At Bernard Schenckingh Sr.'s death, his children included the petitioners, a daughter, Hannah Grange, "all which he had by a former Venter [wife]," and a son, Bernard, "whome he had by Elizabeth Schencking his late Wife." Bernard Sr. died intestate. The court named his second wife, Elizabeth, administratrix. After taking the dower share of her husband's estate, Elizabeth duly gave the four plaintiffs their shares of the estate and "reserved" one-sixth for Hannah and one-sixth for the younger Bernard. Her actions conformed to South Carolina law regarding the division of an intestate estate.

Shortly thereafter, Elizabeth Bernard Jr. died an intestate minor, having never received his share of his father's because Elizabeth "Kept the possession and Management" of this estate and "therewith Acted and did as she thought Fitt." The plaintiffs argued that, as Bernard's next of kin, they were entitled to his share. They "severall times demanded to be paid by the said Elizabeth their respective shares," yet "she could not be prevaled upon to Comply with their reasonable and Just and fair request." They threatened her with "recourse to the Law to recover their right." Bernard Schenckingh's estate totaled £2,115; Elizabeth's dower amounted to £705; each child received £235. Bernard Jr.'s £235 divided four ways would have totaled approximately £58. In South Carolina at this time, the mean value of estates was £1,718 and only a third of the population left an estate worth less than £500. Money does not seem the primary issue in the suit. Elizabeth Schenckingh's stepchildren seemingly resented her economic freedom and her independence from family or community.

Elizabeth Schenckingh, with "butt a Little time to Live," reached an accommodation with her stepchildren. For not giving her "any [further] Trouble as Long as she lived," she promised to bequeath them not only the £235 but also "some thing . . . for their Civillity and forbearance." However, when she died, she bequeathed what the petitioners termed a "Triviall Legacy" of £100. Seemingly duped by her, the plaintiffs asked the court to grant them Bernard Jr.'s estate according to English intestacy law. Her executors answered the petition on two points of law. First, they claimed that the children were not Bernard's next of kin, only half-brothers and -sisters, and thus not legally entitled to his estate. Second, they claimed that in South Carolina "no such distribution as is Demanded by the said Complainants is Compellable to be made by the said statute . . . or by any other Law Statute or Custom." Because South Carolina did not formally adopt English common law until 1712, Elizabeth Schenckingh's literal and figurative will prevailed.

Unlike Schenckingh and the many others widows who left wills, Rebecca Holmes Amory died intestate. She may have died before she had the opportunity to write a will, or, as court records suggest, it may have been intentional. A petition by Ann Coffin, Amory's sister, argued that her mother, Rebecca Holmes, died intestate possessed of "considerable Real and Personal Estate which has never been Divided among her Heirs as the Law Directs." She asked the magistrates to force Amory, who was the administrator, to divide the estate according to law. The case remained unresolved for another eight years. At that point, Amory argued that she could not divide the property among all the Holmes children without destroying it. Although the court ultimately granted Rebecca Holmes's house and land to Amory and required her to pay to the other heirs their share of the estate, she had had control over this vast estate for twenty-three years. Intestacy presented widows both the greatest vulnerability and the most flexibility and power. It was as ambiguous as widowhood itself. Perhaps Rebecca Amory learned from other widows in the community (especially her mother) that it was better not to be encumbered by specific bequests, bequests that frequently had restrictions attached to them.[2]

The cases of Elizabeth Schenckingh and Rebecca Amory highlight the variety of legal options available to colonial widows in South Carolina,

Maryland, and Massachusetts. They reveal the specter of women of wealth uncontrolled and uncontrollable. While colonial law[3] sought to order relationships as well as to facilitate change, including relationships and change between men and women,[4] these cases reveal the ways in which widows appropriated social and cultural norms embodied in the law as well as legal processes to further their interests and how they pushed the boundaries of colonial law to ensure their independence and autonomy. Historians argue that widows' relationship to the law deteriorated significantly during the eighteenth century.[5] While it is true that some widows may have suffered a decline over time, other widows well understood their society's expectations of them as guardians of children and their own legal rights. Those widows successfully negotiated the sometimes rough waters of widowhood, often by imposing their wills on the courts but more often by skillfully manipulating the law to their advantage.

Most widows ventured into court to prove their husbands' will, present accounts of the estate, and recover or pay outstanding debts; gender played an ambiguous but important role when they did.[6] Although only two sixteenth- and seventeenth-century advice books explicitly discussed the "rules" by which widows were to "behave Themselves" in public, such authors implicitly understood that widows "must go abroad to solicite her businesses in person, what she cannot do by the proxie of her friends." Prudent widows guarded their "own interests" and "boldly" defended their rights without "becoming agitated to the point of immoderate language."[7] In stepping in that public space, a widow was advised to turn to a learned, yet aged man who would covet neither her body nor her money—and who was not a "pleader in the law." A widow represented by a lawyer eschewed her femininity and took "on the heart of a man." She became a troublemaker and would make men "loathe her and hinder her of the succour" that widows naturally deserve. Men were expected to be persistent, strong, and shrewd, but widows were expected to maintain their female demeanor.[8] Hiring an attorney indicated that a widow was determined to win her case on the basis of the merits of the case rather than by relying on the goodness and sympathy of the court. Widows who took such a step rejected their deferential and supplicatory status.[9] Believing that "prosperity & peace may alwais him attend, that to the widdow prove himselfe a friend,"[10] they entrusted their estates to men of good reputation or high status without fear.

In the various colonies and over time, the law reflected a paternal authority with competing and contradictory goals, but always determined to preserve its rights and privileges.[11] Colonial widows operated within as well as rebelled against these boundaries. Laws regarding dower, inheritance, and intestate estates revealed a male consensus-building system and conveyed male-defined cultural ideals and social norms that instructed all community members, especially widows, about gender roles. The laws imposed male hegemony and codified masculinity. The law, however, was also a discourse and an arena of conflict among the various groups that accessed that law.[12] Colonial law was a dialogue between the men who wrote the laws and the widows who sought to use it for their own ends. Widows used lawmakers' normative values to manipulate it for their own benefit. Despite the law's bias against female power, widows frequently used it to suspend the normative sanctions against female liberty and power.

Although widows did not always have full access to legal resources, they had specific ideas about how conflicts should be resolved, especially when they attempted to alter the restraints on their gender. When the widow Ann Marcomb prayed that the Maryland Provincial Court prove itself a friend to widows by ensuring that her title to her deceased husband's estate would be confirmed to "Commisserate her Meane Estate," she was acknowledging that she understood the power of the magistrates who enforced the law, as well as her rights under that law.[13] She projected an image of a poor, pitiful widow left alone without male protection and provision to convince the justices that she deserved their support.

English custom and law dictated the legal boundaries of women's lives by defining them as dependent on and ruled by their husbands or fathers. A seventeenth-century legal scholar declared that a woman is "understood either married or to bee married and their desires or [are] subject to their husband, I know no remedy though some women can shift it well enough. The common Law here shaketh hands with Divinitie."[14] The author referred to Genesis 3:16, in which God explains to Eve her relationship to Adam: "thy desire shall be to thy husband, and he shall rule over thee." The eighteenth-century legal scholar William Blackstone expanded on the biblical injunction by explaining how women lost their legal identities upon marriage:

> By marriage, the husband and wife are one person in law; that is the very being or legal existence of the woman is suspended during the marriage, or at least is incorporated and consolidated into that of the husband; under whose wing, protection, and cover she performs every thing.[15]

Yet, English laws provided widows several ways to avoid remarriage. As a *feme sole*, a widow regained her legal identity. She could do things that she could not do as a married woman. Moreover, a widow could assume responsibilities as her children's legal guardian or as executor (or administrator) of her husband's estate.[16] Such responsibilities provided her with power. One seventeenth-century legal treatise argued that a widow should not administer her husband's estate "because the office is troublesome," and, indeed, many passed the responsibility to their sons or co-administrators.[17] However, after accomplishing the administrator's duties, widows could retain the residue of the estate. The provision often made being an administrator beneficial, rather than troublesome.[18] Beyond giving widows a legal identity and the right to oversee their husbands' estates, English law established dower to ensure the economic survival of widows.

Only a man's direct descendants were his legal heirs, and, prior to the creation of dower law, a widow had no claim on her husband's estate. She remained simply a protector of his real property until his children reached the age of majority. First by custom and then by law, dower created a widow's right during her lifetime to one-third of all real property that her husband owned during their marriage whether he died testate or intestate. Theoretically, dower compensated a widow for the contribution she had made to the marriage, provided her with sufficient economic means to maintain herself and her children, kept her off relief rolls, and preserved the rest of the estate for his heirs.[19]

English law tried to ensure that an unscrupulous husband did not deny his widow her dower. A husband could bequeath his widow more than her third rights, but he could never give her money or goods in lieu of her dower. If a wife believed that her husband left her less than her rightful third, she could renounce his will and claim her dower rights in his estate. The law limited, however, a widow's access to her husband's estate. If a woman accepted more than her third, her husband's debts, which could not be paid out of her dower, could be paid from her legacy. A woman could not claim both her dower rights and a bequest of real property in lieu of dower because it would cause "serious [economic] disadvantages for the legal heir," her children.[20]

Common-law dower rights did not initially include the widow's right to her husband's personal estate, but over time custom, ecclesiastical law, and manorial law greatly expanded a widow's right to dower. Practices varied widely across communities and legal jurisdictions,[21] but they all provided the widow with some economic support after her husband died. Yet, dower guaranteed a widow only limited claims to her husband's estates because expanding a widow's dower rights, while protecting the community from liability for a destitute widow and her family, infringed on the heirs' right to their father's estate and infringed on the husband's power to control his family even after his death. Eventually, new local laws granted complete testamentary freedom to the husband and eliminated widows' right to dower in personal property.[22]

The 1670 Statute of Distributions standardized the distribution of an intestate's estate and a widow's interest. It granted her, in addition to her dower rights in her husband's real property, one-third of her husband's personal goods forever (the remaining two-thirds were to be divided among his children). This right provided valuable economic support for widows whose husbands' estates included household goods, tools, and livestock. However, the legislators gave priority to creditors' rights over widows' rights in this instance. Because administrators sold personal property to pay off a decedent's outstanding debts before they distributed the estate, the benefits of intestacy law for widows could be negated by a heavily indebted estate.[23]

Men who inherited their estates prior to marriage could protect this property from dower law through both a "use" (an agreement that transferred his land to feofees but that ensured that he remained its legal owner) and a jointure (the property or rent designated for a widow in a prenuptial contract if her husband predeceased her).[24] Such husbands could forever bar their wives from dower by passing their land through a legal fiction beyond the wives' reach, and they could simultaneously substitute less valuable jointure for dower.

Colonial lawmakers demonstrated familiarity with the English common law, as well as with English local customs, but they bent those laws to suit their own purposes.[25] So, too, did colonial widows. In 1675, through her attorney, the widow Dame Margaret Yeamans, widow of Sir John Yeamans, Baronet and former governor of South Carolina, petitioned for her dower rights in fourteen slaves that had belonged to her husband.[26] These slaves were about to be shipped out of the colony and sent to Lady Willoughby Yeamans, guardian to John Yeamans. In response to Margaret Yeamans's petition, the Council ordered that the slaves that were "now remaining at Wappoh shall be and remain there security to answer and make good what Dower may be recovered by the said Margarett Yeamans." Yeamans was determined she would not be denied her rightful third of her husband's property under English law. In concurring with Yeamans's demand, the court recognized slaves as real property. Under dower law, Yeamans would have had no legal right to the slaves if the court had recognized them as personal property. Although the slaves passed to her only for her lifetime, winning her case ensured Margaret Yeamans economic security, if not unlimited control over the slaves.[27] In 1690, South Carolina legislators clarified the classification of slaves by declaring that they "shall be deemed and taken as all other goods and chattels . . . and all negroes shall be accounted as freehold in all other cases whatsoever, and descend accordingly." This meant that slaves passed to widows as dower whether their husbands wished them to or not.

From the colony's founding, in 1670, settlers in South Carolina tried—almost desperately at times—to ensure that the colony would recreate a civilized, well-ordered English society within its boundaries. Pamphlet writers and settlers alike promoted South Carolina as a place for individuals to advance socially and economically with a government "as nigh as convenient can be to that of *England*." The administration of the law was highly centralized. Charleston was the seat of all judicial proceedings; although the legislature did not publish any body of laws for another seventeen years, on December 12, 1712, the colony formally adopted English common law.[28] This wholesale adoption of English law entailed the embracing dower and intestacy law and their inherent assumption of paternal control of family wealth both before and after the death of the male head of household. But because husbands in South Carolina often died young, leaving widows with young children to care for and no elder sons to rely on, South Carolina lawmakers and judges took a more ambiguous stance toward widows' rights and power than did Englishmen or northerners, especially in response to demands made by widows.[29]

Two actions opened up the possibility of greater wealth and power for widows. In 1696, the legislators reversed their position by defining slaves as personal property.[30] Five years later, they explicitly adopted the Parliamentary Act for the Better Settling of Intestates Estates, which stipulated that, when a man died intestate, his wife would receive one-third of his personal estate unconditionally. In addition to their lifetime interest in their husbands' landed estates, widows gained complete control their share of their husbands' personal estates. Widows benefited more from the intestacy law than they did from dower law from this point forward. In a highly commercialized economy like South Carolina's, personalty could be more valuable than realty because it provided widows with the liquidity and capital they would need to participate in the market. That was one way to ensure that widows could provide for their own and their children's economic futures. The reclassification of slaves would have even greater consequences for both men and women as the colony turned increasingly to slave labor and slaves became a primary source of capital.

In 1743, Sophia Hume's husband left a will in which he bequeathed her £1,000 "in full Recompence and Satisfaction of any Dower Thirds," giving the rest of his estate to his brother to pay off his debts. But he died owing £4,000 to his brother. Sophia Hume could have renounced the bequest and taken her dower portion, which would have been safe from creditors until she died. Instead, she chose to relinquish both the bequest and her dower rights to her brother-in-law in exchange for "the interest from the investing of 1/3 of the proceeds of any sale of this land for her lifetime." They agreed that until they sold the lands, she would receive one-third of the rents and profits from the land. The magistrates did not question the arrangement that she had made because they understood the necessity for widows to safeguard their own and, more important, their children's economic interests. Hume's strategy could have backfired if her brother-in-law had proved a poor or dishonest business manager, but for her the risk was apparently worth the security of a steady income and freedom from managing a debt-ridden estate.[31] She found a safer arrangement outside a dower law that imposed more constraints on her than she was willing to bear. The arrangement also demonstrates that dower did not always work well in an expanding commercial economy such as South Carolina's.

Such arrangements did not always work out. On November 12, 1725, the court heard arguments in a case in which John and Mary Stanyarn sued Joseph Seabrook, executor of Robert Seabrook's will. Mary Stanyarn was Robert Seabrook's widow; the Stanyarns brought suit to recover Mary's share of the estate given to her in a "deed poll" rather than the bequest left her by Seabrook. Robert and Mary had signed a postnuptial agreement in which he gave her an unspecified amount of household goods, money, plate, jewelry, bedding, pewter, tools, land, and slaves forever. On September 22, 1720, Robert made a will in which he bequeathed Mary slaves and a plantation containing 372 acres, along with half of his cattle, horses, mares, sheep, and hogs. That the Stanyarns wanted the terms of the deed to stand while Seabrook wanted the terms of the will to stand suggests two perspectives: either the deed was worth more than the bequest and Seabrook, as executor, was trying to retain as much of the estate for himself as he could, or Mary Stanyarn wanted the household goods, but especially the plate, jewelry, and money, to better engage in commerce and embrace the growing consumer culture.

Joseph Seabrook argued that the deed of gift was void because, by law, a husband could not directly give his wife—legally himself—any property or goods. He believed that widows should have only the minimum protection guaranteed by a law, a law by which women remained dependent on husbands or sons. He also believed that a widow who sought more than her guaranteed minimum rights put an undue burden on the family and on the community. To him, Mary Stanyarn had recklessly stepped outside the legal and ideological boundaries constructed for widows. Several marriage settlements and deeds of gift in South Carolina suggest that her actions were not unusual and that widows sometimes gambled that the terms of such agreements would ultimately provide them with more than their dower rights. Although the gamble did not pay off for Stanyarn, widows understood their legal and economic position, and they worked the situation to their best advantage if they could.

Thomas Baker of Berkeley County also died intestate on June 13, 1717, with "Considerable Personnal Estate . . . of a very Considrable Value Sufficient to pay all his just Debts with a Sufficient Overplus." The court named Johannah Baker administratrix, and she took possession of the estate. Magistrates expected widows to follow the prescriptive literature and to put their children's financial future ahead of their own immediate concerns for economic survival. If so, Johannah Baker disappointed them. Because their six children were minors, she legally maintained possession of the estate until each child reached the age of majority or married. Johannah Baker refused to give her daughter, Mary Baker Flood, her share of the estate on her marriage. After Mary and her husband repeatedly asked Johannah Baker for Mary Baker's portion, Johannah Baker gave "out in Speeches that she will sell at Public Vendue every thing that belongs to the said Estate and will Convert the money from thence arising to her own use and that She will neither render any Account or lett" Mary Baker and her husband have any part of it.[32] Mary Baker, as head of her household, decided that she would pass on Mary's portion when she wanted and that she would not be controlled by her dead husband or her son-in-law.

The power that Johannah Baker wielded proved elusive for other widows. Anne Rowsham's husband, William Jr., died intestate. As administratrix, she was responsible for collecting £500 owed to her husband. In creating an identity as a well-behaved dependent widow, Anne Rowsham claimed that her father-in-law, William Rowsham Sr., "Designing and Intending and well knowing your Oratrixes weakness and unexperience in the affaires of the World," made a deal with her. If she agreed to give him the £500 in debts, he promised to bequeath her one-third of his real and personal estate for her widowhood and £200 outright. She agreed. When William Rowsham Sr. died, Anne Rowsham discovered that he had left her only one-third of the profit of his stock of cattle and slaves and one-third of his personal estate. The only real estate that she received was one room in the house "wherein she now Lives to Lodge in During her Widowhood." By dower law, of course, he was not responsible for leaving her anything because she was not his wife. She had gambled away her share of her husband's estate, but she believed that widows should rely on men for support and protection, "not in the Least Suspecting or Mistrusting [his] Fraudulent and Evill Design to deceive her." Rowsham's executor refused to give Anne even her diminished legacy. In creating another identity for herself as an assertive, independent widow, she exerted her power by going to court seeking redress against these injustices. She declined to sit passively by.[33] William Rowsham Sr. believed that he had protected his daughter-in-law's minimal rights; he refused to live up to a bargain that gave her more than that. However, Anne Rowsham was also not willing to give up what she understood to be rightfully hers under the system.

In 1672, women composed 17 percent of the white South Carolina population; in 1708, they composed only one-third of the white population; and by 1728, their share had increased only to 44 percent. In 1730, each South Carolina household contained, on average, fewer than three children.[34] As a result, because many men died without a wife or children, the magistrates faced no pressure to alter dower and inheritance laws.

Unlike South Carolina's, Maryland's charter did not stipulate that English laws and customs extend to the colony, although Maryland legislators believed that some or all of English law "might be received as the colonists saw fit." There was no printed body of laws until 1700, but Thomas Bacon's and William Kilty's compilations of the various acts and resolutions of Maryland indicate that between 1637 and 1700, legislators passed numerous temporary laws concerning the probate of wills and succession to an intestate's estate.[35] The Acts of Assembly, common law, local custom, and Acts of Parliaments influenced Maryland law and guided the courts. Like English and South Carolina property law, lawmakers in Maryland created laws by and for the benefit of male heads of household and magistrates.

Probate laws reflected a belief that men by right controlled their estates and their families before and after their deaths. Widows, who clearly understand their customary and legal rights, influenced those laws as legislators repeatedly repealed and revived them over the years. Four cases suggest that influence.

The first two cases demonstrate how widows pushed the magistrates to recognize their traditional rights. In 1659, Rose Scotcher requested that "according to the Custome of the Province shee have allowed her necessary furniture for her Chamber before the Estate be devided." She knew that widows were usually given, if not a full dower third, then at least a small piece of their husbands' estate before the heirs divided the remaining portion—and she wanted legal possession of her share. Two years later, when Ruth Knowles informed the court that her husband's estate owed more debts than it could pay, she sought "such maintainance as is usually allowed to other widdows for thaire relefe." Knowles understood and demanded that the magistrates adhere to the local practice of granting a widow her bed, bedclothes, a few household goods, her wearing apparel, and some provisions when an estate could neither pay the deceased's debts nor provide his widow with her dower.[36] Although the lawmakers and magistrates may have seen these pleas as requests for charity, widows saw them as customary rights.

The following cases demonstrate how widows pushed for their legal rights. When Edward Commins's widow attempted to sell part of the land he had bequeathed her, the buyer refused to "perform the bargain" unless the Lord Proprietor gave him permission. At question was whether the widow "could Sell the Said Land from her Children." The key phrase here is "from her children." As in England, widows were not their husbands' legal heirs, and the widow Commins's sale of land worried the buyers. They sought confirmation that the land they bought from her would be secure when the children came of age and demanded their property rights in their fathers' estate. Because Edward Commins had bequeathed the land to his wife without condition, the court ruled that she could "make Sale thereof Lawfully." In this case, although her interests potentially conflicted with her children's interests, the magistrates adhered to Edward Commins's will and gave her the power to sell the land in question. Just before she was to remarry, Mary Mulliken gave her three children land, livestock, and household goods. She declared that her personal estate would be divided among her children at her death and, more important, that "the Seat of land . . . with all howses Edifices buildings Orchards and

Gardens" she currently lived on would be first for her own "proper use" and that she then would be free to give it "to . . . whosoever I shall like of or think fitt."[37] Mary understood two key points about the property she brought into the marriage: her new husband could take legal possession of the personal property and could bar her children from their share of their father's estate by ruining or selling it, but he could not sell it or bequeath the real property. Her deed of gift protected her rights and her children's rights to the property. She reaffirmed her legal control over the estate that she brought to the marriage; in the end, she alone would judge the character of the recipients, and she alone would be responsible for her children's future.

Perhaps wishing to eliminate the flexibility of probate law that the widows Scotcher, Commins, Knowles, and Mulliken used to their advantage, the legislators stepped in. The 1671 "Act for the Preservation of Orphans Estates" declared that previous laws were "very defective & noe waies sufficient" for maintaining the economic well-being of children whose fathers had died. In addition to stating that all wills "shall be firme and Inviolable," the act itself specified two important provisions: in the event of intestacy, the widow became administrator of her deceased husband's estate, and, after debts were paid, the widow received one-third of the estate, and the "Rest is to be divided amongst the Children." This law, while ostensibly expanding widows' rights, also could be meaningless for a widow whose husband died heavily in debt. Although Maryland counted slaves as personalty and thus they could be sold to pay debts according to common law, the legislators declared that slaves could not be used to pay the deceased's debts "if there are sufficient other goods." Maryland lawmakers tried to prevent the ravage of a widow's estate by prohibiting the sale or rental of slaves unless necessary. Moreover, granting widows a full third share of all slaves absolutely meant that widows possessed and could bequeath a significant source of wealth and power.[38] Yet, the law gave priority to creditors' needs over widows' needs and aimed at preserving the estate of the children and not at safeguarding the economic well-being of the widow. It marked an important step toward the creation of a better-defined boundary for widows. Or did it?

That widows' control over estates continued to plague the colony—or at least the leaders of the colony—is suggested by the 1681 "Act for the Better Administration of Justice in Probate of Wills, Granting Administrations, Recovery of Legacies, and Securing Filial Portions."[39] The lawmakers reiterated their belief that "itt is most necessary that there bee a setled succession from the dead to the Liveing." Using the gendered language of family, they claimed that "Certainety is the Mother of Repose." Like the earlier act, the law provided that, after the deceased's debts and funeral expenses were paid, the widow was to receive "one full Third parte thereof" and the rest was to be equally divided among the children. Again, slaves were not to be used to pay debts. This act was continued in 1682, 1684, 1686, 1688, and 1692—a repetition that in itself suggests how difficult it was maintain to a clear legal boundary around widows' lives.[40]

An amendment to the "Act for the Better Administration of Justice" passed in 1695 and again in 1699 stipulated that widows who were bequeathed portions of their husbands' estate had to either take that portion in full satisfaction of their dower rights or refuse their legacies and accept their third of their husbands' real and personal estate "as Widdows whose husbands dye Intestate." This amendment was ostensibly passed to save the children from "utter Ruine."[41] According to lawmakers in colonial Maryland, all of these acts failed to prevent the waste, sale, or destruction of orphans' real estate. They believed that even though such orphans were the children of "p[er]sons of greate estates whilst liveing," the estate that accrued to them on reaching age was generally of much less value than when initially probated. The lawmakers established clear guidelines under which guardians could clear and plant only a portion of the total estate large enough to raise, keep, and maintain the children until they reached the age at which they could rightfully take possession of the estate themselves.[42]

In 1705, the assembly amended the act yet again. This time they changed English dower law, providing that husbands could not negate their widows' dower in real estate by bequeathing them part of their personal estate. The justification for the changes demonstrates concerns of Maryland lawmakers:

> many men have bequeathed and devised or hereafter may bequeath or devise to their wives by their Last Wills a Considerable part of their personall Estate intending no doubt but not expressing that such bequest or devise should be in full of such wives part portion or third part of the Testators Estate and yet such wives widows and relicts have not only claim'd such bequest and devise as legacys but have farther claim'd their part of the remaining Estate of their deceased husbands[.][43]

Following a long-standing pattern, the legislators pitted widows' needs against their children's needs, deciding in favor of the children. Legislators apparently feared that widows, by claiming both dower and bequest, would deplete the portion available for the children. The law argued that if a testator bequeathed "a considerable part" of his personal estate to his wife, she could not then claim her dower share in his real estate. If a testator bequeathed "any part" of his real estate to his wife, she, likewise, could not then claim her dower share of his real estate. Unless the testator explicitly indicated otherwise, all bequeathed real estate was for the widow's lifetime only. In either case, she had forty days to choose between her bequest and her dower rights.

The Maryland courts did not want the widow to have both a legacy and dower. But what happened if the widow failed to make a timely choice? In 1715, the General Assembly ruled that if a widow did not choose between devised and dowered personal estate within the allotted time, she would be given a third of the clear personal estate "besides her dower of [her deceased husband's] reall Estate in full of all such devises or Legacys." If she did not choose between devised and dowered real estate, she would be given only what was devised to her and "thereby barred of her dower . . . Unless it shall appear to be the designe of the devisor that such widow shall have both devise and Dower."[44] In 1727, widows' options were even more narrowly proscribed. After that date, the widow who failed to choose between devised and dowered personal estate was given only what was devised to her "and shall not have or claim any more of his Personal Estate, than shall be so bequeathed."[45]

By the early decades of the eighteenth century, men in Maryland were more likely to die at older ages than in earlier decades, leaving widows and adult children with competing interests in their estates. As the magistrates recognized, it was neither necessary nor desirable to give control of the husband's estate to his widow as guardian of older children. Legislators reclaimed children's rightful shares in their father's estates. Lawmakers more narrowly defined dower provisions as they increasingly viewed dower as a means of charity, rather than as clearly established rights for widows. Widows defined dower differently.

When their husbands' estates were presented in probate court, Sarah Moore, Mary Neale, and Rebecca Howard renounced their husbands' wills and thereby fell back on intestacy law. None of these widows explained why they "refuse[d] to accept the bequest left [them]" or why each was "determined to have her thirds." However, a closer examination of their husbands' wills and inventories and the changing legal structure suggests some possible explanations.[46] Both Henry Neale and John Howard died leaving large personal estates, £1,163 and £1,015, respectively. Both men possessed more than twenty slaves and more than twenty head of livestock. Although they put no conditions on their wives' bequests, Neale and Howard divided their personal estates equally among their spouse and children. Mary Neale shared her portion with eight children and would have received £129. Rebecca Howard shared her portion with five children and would have received £169. In both cases, by renouncing their husbands' wills, the widows received a much larger portion of their husbands' estates than was bequeathed to them. Mary Neale tripled her share, and Rebecca Howard doubled hers.[47] Henry Moore had died leaving a personal estate of only £174; he left half to his son and half to Sarah for her widowhood only. By renouncing his will, Sarah received a smaller share of the personal estate (one-third), but she received this share forever. She had the freedom to bequeath an estate to whom she pleased. These widows hardly suggest they were "Mother[s] of Repose," and they certainly did not see their dower as paternal protection.

In a similar case decades later, Thomas Ringgold Sr. willed his wife, Anna Marie, in lieu of dower, the use and occupation of his "plantation with all appurtenances, slaves, horses, cattle and sheep, plantation utensils, and crops growing thereon for her lifetime." He also gave her use of all the tenement houses and land, as well as all plate and household goods, for her lifetime. He appointed his son, Thomas Ringgold Jr., his executor. According to testimony given years later, Anna Marie Ringgold renounced this will and accepted her dower rights. She and her son, Thomas Jr., then made an agreement in which she gave him control of the entire estate and he promised to pay his mother an annual sum as well as interest on the £3,000 devised to her by his father.

In 1776, Thomas Ringgold, Jr., died in possession of his father's estate. In his will he left his mother, in lieu of what his father devised her, a life interest in the house she lived in, some land, household goods, slaves, and an annual annuity of £600. From this estate she was to set aside £3000 for heirs he specified.[48] As for his wife, it appears he left her seemingly secure but clearly in a passive relationship to his mother: Anna Marie was to pass along her £600 annuity to Mary. Like her mother in law, Mary Ringgold renounced her husbandís will and instead elected her thirds of the estate. By doing so, she deprived her mother-in-law of the bequests given her by Thomas Ringgold, Jr. Anna Marie Ringgold had, after all, renounced her own husband's will and then traded away her dower rights for what she obviously perceived as a guaranteed lifetime settlement from her son, a settlement that was now in danger.

Throughout the correspondence between family members, both widows' brothers acted for them: John Galloway for Mary Ringgold and James Tilghman for Anna Marie Ringgold. Although their brothers negotiated the dispute, the letters contain occasional glimpses of Mary and Anna Marie Ringgold. John reported, for example, that Mary's grief "seems to increase on her daily. That amazing Resolution which she has hitherto been blessed with begins to fail. She tells me her situation appears more terrible to her the more she thinks of it and I believe it is never off of her mind. She wishes for some female friend . . . be prevailed on to spend this winter with her."[49] James Tilghman, expressing no such sympathy, charged Mary with trying to deny her mother-in-law a rightful share of the estate. Despite Anna Marie's willingness to pay Mary £1,000 for not renouncing the younger Thomas's will, on January 14, 1777, the latter "renounced the several bequests and devises made her by her Husband." A letter written by her brother John explains why.

> Every opening has been given to Mrs. Ringgold and her friends to put my Sister on Some certain footing and not altogether dependant on the £600 a year for a Support which was allowed on all sides to be not sufficient . . . but they would not enter into any kind of Conversation tending that way. . . . My sister plainly sees that if she missed the present opportunity of putting herself in easy Circumstances that she should not have any more than the £600 to depend on which would leave her in indigent Circumstances the remaining part of her life . . . and was justifiable in renouncing the will.

He reported that, instead of being greatly disturbed by her decision, she said that "her mind is more at ease then it has been for a long time and she has no one to look up to be depended in for a Sufficiency to live on and she is convinced her Husband always wished that should be the Case." Mary Ringgold intended to take her share of the slaves, livestock, carriage, and household goods and the house rent-free and "throw the overplus of the Thirds into the Estate." John blamed Anna Marie Ringgold for refusing to remove "the vast number of difficultys" and for forcing Mary to renounce the will and "fly to her thirds for maintanance." He even suggested that she jeopardized her grandchildren's future by refusing to negotiate. "I cannot help saying my Sister has been exceedingly communicative to her Mother in this matter . . . but not one Syllable could she ever extort from her." In closing, he remarked that "I doubt whether the women belong together."[50]

The case entailed the competing needs and the competing recourse to legal protection of two widows in the same family; it also points up several issues relevant to all widows in seventeenth- and eighteenth-century Maryland. Widows faced risks when forced to rely on their sons or husbands—or both—to look after their economic future. Thomas Ringgold Jr. put neither his mother's nor his wife's fortunes in jeopardy intentionally. Yet his actions did just that. Although both widows held dower rights in their husbands' estates, the law failed to disentangle whose rights took precedence, demonstrating the inability of dower law to safeguard widows' minimum stake in their husbands' estate. The actions of each woman revolved ultimately around meeting their minimum financial needs in order to safeguard the estate for their children. Both women understood their just share of the estates, their definition of a "Genteel maintenance," and their strong sense of economic independence. Ultimately, both women fought for what they believed was rightfully, if not legally, theirs. Lawmakers in early Maryland accorded widows a degree of freedom and protection under the colony's initial dower and intestacy laws. Once the colony became economically and demographically stable, beginning around 1700, however, Maryland widows' needs came increasingly into conflict with their children's needs and with the view of the community that as widows they were trying overstep the legal boundaries established to protect those children. Magistrates tried to halt what they saw as widows' grasp for power and control under those laws. Widows increasingly rebelled against the new laws, trying to retain the rights and freedoms they had gained in Maryland's unstable, early years. Stability meant the reimposition of traditional limits on widows.

Massachusetts's dower and intestacy laws ensured that husbands and fathers had more control over their wives, children, and family structure than did husbands and fathers in either South Carolina or Maryland. Puritans established probate laws that ensured the survival of a "hierarchy of relationships among all members of society." Built into the New England's legally constructed hierarchy was the assumption that the legislators did not need to protect a widow's economic interest because, if a widow found her inheritance or intestacy rights inadequate to provide for herself, then her children, particularly her sons, would care for her "out of feeling of love and duty."[51] From the start, living in a more settled and stable community than either Maryland or South Carolina, Massachusetts widows never gained the freedom enjoyed by southern widows prior to 1700. But the situation was more complex.

New England widows played an active role in shaping the law to suit their own needs even if that meant overstepping ideological bounds and incurring the wrath of family, friends, and magistrates. In 1641, the Massachusetts Bay Colony adopted its first legal code; the *Body of Liberties* simply stated "if any man at his death shall not leave his wife a competent portion of his estaite, upon just complaint made to the Generall court she shall be relieved."[52]

The law, which seemed to satisfy the intent if not the letter of English dower laws, placed the interpretation of "a competent portion" in the hands of individual judges. Although the elders of the community took the place of the husband in maintaining a well-ordered family in a well-ordered social structure, the law buttressing New England males' authority ensured that widows no longer had a legally guaranteed minimum estate with which to maintain themselves and their families. The legislators placed widows in a supplicant position by making them seek relief from the court. Lawmakers refined this statute in 1648, but they had already set in motion a tradition of widows actively seeking their legal rights, as was evident from the large number of petitions presented and court cases initiated by widows throughout the late seventeenth and early eighteenth centuries. Ironically, facing a more traditional situation than southern widows, Massachusetts widows were encouraged to be more legally assertive.

The Book of the General Laws and Libertyes Concerning the Inhabitants of the Massachusetts, recognizing that "no provision hath yet been made for any certein maintainance for Wives after the death of their Husbands," clarified the terms of dower rights. Of the property her husband "was seized of," a widow was entitled to one-third of all the real property for her lifetime and one-third of all the personal estate forever.[53] Two points about this law are important. A widow's right to her husband's real property was not a right of succession but a right of dower; and, as in England, she was not entitled to dower if she and her husband had made a prenuptial agreement guaranteeing her a jointure. Land that a husband sold with his wife's consent was not dower land. Ultimately, the act ensured male control of property in the community.

The new dower law constricted the benefits a widow received from her husband's estate by making her choose between her jointure and her dower rights. Forcing widows to choose protected the estate from a double claim and safeguarded the economic rights of children. Although the law recognized widows' capabilities by conceding that they had enough knowledge of their husbands' estates to make the best decision, it constrained their economic control over the estate. The ramifications of the law can be seen in the following brief notation entered into the legal records when the widow Button's inventory was probated: "Court declared that the widow Button, having land made over to her as a dowry from Mathias Button, had no right to her proportion of the estate, which otherwise by law she might have, she also in court refusing to relinquish her said jointure or dowry."[54]

Early American word choice and sentence structure make the passage difficult to interpret. It does seem clear, however, that the widow Button, by refusing to relinquish either her jointure or her dower right, had subverted the law. Perhaps she knew that by choosing either dower or jointure, she could not live comfortably, and she took control of her life, with or without the approbation of the legal system. Given the context in which the court presented the ruling, the magistrates made a point about the power of widows. They wanted to make it clear to other widows in the community that Button's actions were unacceptable—and illegal—and should not be duplicated.

While some widows unsuccessfully pressed the courts for what they perceived as their right to dower or jointure (or both),[55] other widows, if they were persistent enough, won their cases and received their due. Martha Ely petitioned to have her dower from land her husband, Nathaniel, had previously sold to George Colton. Her petition did not stipulate whether her husband sold the land without her consent, but the court ordered the parties to come to an agreement between themselves. In case they could not, the magistrates appointed three men to "determine what may be her Right according to Law of Dowries as wel as they can."[56] By appointing this committee, the magistrates implicitly recognized that Martha was not going to settle for less than her dower rights in one-third of her husband's land. They also signaled that they agreed she was entitled to payment equal to one-third the value of the land sold to Colton. In a similar case, when Eunice Porter sued for dower rights in land that her husband had sold to Osman Trask, despite testimony that she knew about it and "manifested more willingness to sell than did her husband," the magistrates ruled in her favor.[57] In both cases, the magistrates recognized that the community might be responsible to care for these widows if they could not provide for themselves.

Some widows successfully turned to the court to recover dower rights that had been falsely or mischievously denied to them. In suing Philip Nelson for title to land in her husband's estate, Susanna Rogers of Newbury convinced the magistrates that she held the morally (if not legally) correct position. She, like other widows relying on a well-understood gendered cultural identity, claimed she was a poor widow whose husband left her little but the land in question, "whc [her four] poore Children was put out prentis to pay for." According to Rogers, Nelson (who subsequently gave deed and possession of some of the land to other men) never pressed ownership of the land until she "desired to them my thirds of that they bought." She believed her claim was "just and righteous," and she proved her contention by claiming that they did not need to "gitt from mee that which is my right, for its knowne they have litle neede of it but it is my livelehoode."[58] When reminded—sometimes delicately and sometimes forcefully—by widows, lawmakers and justices came to understand that full dower rights provided economic support for widows without making them a burden on family or community. Even in rural areas, where economic survival and family maintenance especially depended on access to and control of land, male ownership of property did not always take precedence over widows' rights and needs.

Widows sometimes negotiated their own dower rights with the court, as did the widow Susanna Saben on April 4, 1737. After refusing to administer her husband's estate, Saben asked the magistrates to grant her two loads of "good Mowing Grass," use of the orchard for the "Sustenance of one Cow" in the winter, and some pasturing land. All of this was "far Short of [her] Said Thirds," but if the court would grant her request, she would "Rest Satisfied." If it would not, she requested they lay out her thirds.[59] Because she did not want to get stuck administering an estate that was likely debt-ridden and that would be hers only for her lifetime, she asked for control over what she believed would provide sufficient support. Yet, she was no fool; if the court would not assent to her request, she would revert to her legal rights.

In losing their husbands, poor widows lost even the meager property and power of their deceased husbands. American colonists familiar with the Bible knew that the scriptures always modified the word "widow" with the paired adjectives "poor, helpless." Poor widows were "everyday sights that cry 'have pity on us,'" and sermons urged both family and community members to be "charitably & mercifully affected" by such sights. But poor widows also had a responsibility to their family. Although the prescriptive literature never specified those responsibilities, court records did. In their public as well as private activities, poor widows were expected to wait patiently, "like the Widow of Sarepta," to be "almost miraculously provided for,"[60] and to be supplicants to their superiors and to the paternalism that marked widows' reliance on men for their support. When poor widows found it impossible to support themselves, they were forced to turn to others to do for them what their husbands had previously done. For example, in 1684, the Hampshire County Court recognized that the widow Horton,

> In as much as . . . her self pleades infirmitie & weakeness of body to what she hath beene besides the great Care yt will unavoydeably be upon her to bring up the Children many of them being Small & one of them something impotent & helpless this Courte judge and have allowed sd Widdow out ye sd Estate, to her Own absolute right One Hundred Poundes to be fixt Set out to her as forsd and ye use of the Remainder to ye Estate belonging to ye Children till they Come to be of age.[61]

Alice Thomas's petition to the General Court demonstrated how widows themselves perceived their rights and responsibilities under dower law. In the winter of 1662, Evan Thomas died, leaving a house, a brew house, and land to his widow. He also left her exposed to "many troubles & losses & uncomfortable distractions" because of several outstanding debts.[62] She asked the magistrates to give her what legally belonged to her according to "a law Intituled Dowyres" that "doth Allow unto [widows] the thirds of whatsoever houses & lands their husbands had in possession at their decease" so that she "may not bee left in a worse Condition then shee was In before shee was marryed" to her husband.[63] Unfortunately, she had also entered into a prenuptial agreement with him and by law could not claim both dower and jointure.

Thomas skillfully laid out five justifications for her request. First, before she married Thomas, she lived comfortably with her children; on marriage she "prudently" made an marriage contract with her husband that would look after her children "should matters fall worse." Second, through careful management of both the estate she brought to the marriage and her husband's estate, the whole "was much ye better preserved

& Increased above what it might have beene otherwise." Third, she contributed at least £100 to her husband's estate. Fourth, she is "now putt out of a Comfortable way," her houses were going to ruin, and the comfortable life she lived before marrying Thomas was so drastically changed that she could not rectify the situation and "shall be a great sufferer both her selfe & children." Last, she took care of a husband much "afflicted with Infirmityes & Maladyes," which she bore with great pain even though she "did it not for to gayne by him." In closing, she argued that because she was a good wife, she should not be debarred from that which "her husband would willingly have given her & ye law also hath provided for her." After reviewing the marriage contract and Alice Thomas's petition, the court granted her request on May 13, 1662. Thomas's petition reveals that widows believed dower, regardless of previous prenuptial agreements, was supposed to compensate them for the money, work, and caring they had contributed to their marriages. The court's decision confirmed that belief.

Colonial husbands could, of course, bequeath to their wives more than their thirds if they wanted. Thomas Brown of Ipswich, Massachusetts, although he had three sons and three daughters, bequeathed his wife his entire estate "in consideration that she hath spent so much of her time & strength in my service and good care that she hath taken in Nursing me in my old age."[64] A husband could also negotiate his wife's dower rights through his will. For example, William Partrigg of Hadley, Massachusetts, bequeathed to his wife, Mary, "in addition to her thirds in the entire estate, . . . the new roome or addition to his house," *if* she agreed that the house would not be counted as part of her thirds.[65] More often, husbands maintained a balance between their wives' and their children's economic well-being. The balance was often difficult to maintain. Thomas Banister explained his bequest to his wife, his "Dear Companion & Yoke fellow":

> It much Affects me, and draws Tears from mine Eyes, To think of willing you nothing but what the Law . . . gives you, but I knowing by Discoursing this matter with you that you desire nothing more, as also That your Thirds will be Ample provision for you. . . . And, altho, if you and I were to live together to the longest Age of man I should not fear your wronging our Children, unless by your overkindness & Tenderness towards them, Yet it often falls out otherwise . . . as Experience daily shews[.][66]

In a codicil to this will, Banister noted that, after friends told him that he had "not made that provision therein for my Dear Wife, as I intended," he bequeathed her £1,000 over and above her dower. Because of such attempts to balance rights, the issue of fair dower rights remained contentious in Massachusetts.

As in England and Maryland, the treatment of dower in personal property changed repeatedly in Massachusetts. On May 2, 1649, the General Court repealed the clause in the 1648 dower law that gave "a wife a third part of her husbands money, goods, and chattels, reall & personall," declaring that the "printed law concerninge dowries, upon second view and examination, appeares not so convenient as was formerly conceived, in every perticuler thereof."[67] Thereafter, dower rights attached only to a husband's real property. The magistrates gave no reason for changing the provision for personal property so quickly, but the inconvenience would not have been to the widow but to the legal heirs. It is likely that the magistrates feared that widows would take advantage of the generous dower law and jeopardize their children's future. A case brought before the Court of Assistants several decades later highlights the ongoing legal and cultural issues over dower.

In a petition presented on May 29, 1679, Frances Quilter asked the court to grant her a share of her husband's personal estate.[68] Quilter claimed that her husband died with an estate valued at £600, "a considderable parte wherof was mony." She attributed the large size of Mark's estate[69] to three causes: "the product of whatt [she] brought to her husband," "her owne & her husbands labour for the space of about Twenty three years that they lived together," and "the extreame penurious sparing kind of life that wee did live denying ourselves and famyly what was meett for us to have." She also pointed out that her husband "turne[d] what wee could gett into mony." Mark Quilter made a deathbed will that she categorized as "irationall inconsistant with itselfe & with the mynde of the testate" and that witnesses termed questionable, if not illegal. The probate court declared that Mark Quilter died intestate and named Mark's brother, Joseph Quilter, administrator.

According to Frances Quilter, Joseph came upon her "in her griffe & through her Ignorance drew her into sum inconvenience" and carried away "the greatest parte of the estate." As a result, she suffered "many sorrofull daies in getting of" her share of her husband's estate. Without legal remedy and because she was without "parents, husband, or children," the traditional means of support for widows, she was "in danger of coming upon [her friends and family] or the Towne wher she lives for her reliefe." It was unjust that she who had contributed her "constante dilligence day and night" should be denied a comfortable existence because her husband's estate consisted mainly of personalty. She asked not for her dower rights (why would she, since dower law gave her almost nothing?) but for a just share of the estate. By appealing to the justices' sense of responsibility, she relied on long-established values of caring for "poor, helpless" widows. By reminding the magistrates that the town would be responsible for supporting her if they left her destitute, she relied on well-known fears of indigent widows. The day after Frances Quilter presented her petition, the court awarded her Mark's entire estate for her lifetime.[70] In cities like Boston, widows were much more likely to need dower rights in personal goods, such as the £600 Frances Quilter sought, than in landed estate. When the technicalities of the law denied them what they saw as just, they fought for their rights.

Although intestacy rules in Massachusetts were much less specific than English law, the colony did open the possibility of widows receiving an estate share in this way. In the May 2, 1649, ruling regarding dower, the magistrates ruled that if a husband died without leaving a will, the courts had the "power to assigne to the widow such a part of his personall estate as they shall conceive just and equall." This act was echoed in the revised 1660 *Booke of the General Lawes and Libertyes*. Because the law stated only that the magistrates had "the power to assigne," but were not required to lay out, a portion of the estate to the widow, *they* retained the flexibility, authority, and paternalism inherent in the 1641 law regarding the disposition of a decedent's estate.

The rules regarding children's rights in their parents' estate were much clearer than widows' rights under dower and intestacy law. Magistrates believed strongly that children's economic futures had to be secured by their parents and protected by the court. In 1642, the magistrates ordered that, when "Parents dye intestate, the eldest sons shall have a double portion of his whole estate reall, and personal." If there were no male heirs, then daughters inherited "as copartners."[71] Massachusetts magistrates apparently conceived of real property as normally men's property, for they used the pronoun "his" in discussing the disposal of the parents' real property. Although they knew better, the lawmakers did not conceive of—or at least did not write into law—a widow's leaving an estate to divide among her children. Again appearing to ignore the role widows played in the family economy, in 1649, the court claimed the right to "devide and assigne to the children . . . their severall partes and portion." Lawmakers repeated the law in 1660 and again in 1692.[72] Such laws, however, contributed to tensions between widows and their children and between widows and the magistrates.

On January 26, 1653, the Suffolk County Court proved John Glover's will in which he stated that Ann Glover, in "relinquishing her right of Dowre in England," was to have all the rest of his goods and the profits from two farms in Dorchester and half the "house yard houseing & tanpits in Boston" for her lifetime. Several of his children disputed Ann Glover's management of the estate. Acknowledging that she was frugal and pious, they were careful not to insult their mother. But, to their "amazment," Glover sold all the stock and moveables of one farm. They lost the share of the estate that they would have received on her death. When asked why she sold the goods, Glover claimed that she needed money to pay outstanding debts. Her children were not convinced, arguing that the debts never appeared in the inventory and that she certainly would have known if there were any debts to include in the inventory. The children implied that the son who lived with Glover had coerced her into selling the goods for his benefit. A witness not only denied this but also claimed the son had adamantly opposed the sale. According to witnesses, Ann Glover pretended there were debts to be paid in England so that she could sell the goods.[73] At issue was Ann Glover's power to control her estate—which she did without consulting any of her children. Through her actions, Ann Glover jeopardized her children's well-being. The outcome of this case is unknown, but clearly the court could have used the 1649 law to redistribute the estate as they saw fit.

The extent to which intestacy laws and customs permeated the community is evident in an agreement signed between Tamsen Buffam, her sons, and her sons-in-law. Robert Buffam died in 1669, and, according to two neighbors, on his deathbed he gave his entire estate to Tamsen. This testimony was "not attested upon oath," and his widow never filed the nuncupative will. Ten years later, Tamsen and her children signed an agreement giving all the land to her two eldest sons, £16 in silver to her sons-in-law, and one-third of the produce and wood from the "ground at Castle Hill" to Tamsen, who also had the remaining estate at her disposal.[74] This agreement reveals that members of the community understood the boundaries of widows' rights and put pressure on widows to adhere to them. For whatever reason, after ten years of controlling her husband's entire estate, Tamsen conceded much of that control to her sons and sons-in-law (presumably for her daughters). She remained in control of what would have been hers according to intestacy law.

Other cases were not settled so amicably. On January 30, 1672, the Suffolk County magistrates granted Justine Patten administration on her husband Nathaniel's estate.[75] They also granted her permission to dispose of half of the estate; they gave the other half to her husband's nephew, Benjamin Beale, at her death. Two years later, Nathaniel's brother, John Patten, the self-proclaimed "Lawfull and proper heire" to Nathaniel's estate, sued Giles Dyer, a tenant in one of Nathaniel's houses, for "refusing to deliver possession & rent for one yeare or thereabout." Patten never denied that the court had a right to assign Justine her share of the moveables and her dower in the landed estate, but he adamantly denied them the power to "alienate houses or land of an intestate from the heirs." Any lands given to a widow were to be assigned from the heir, not the court. Here the vagueness of the law—the right of the court to assign the widow "Such A part of as they Shall Judge Just & equall"—created problems for the would-be heir, the widow, the court, and the community. Patten reminded the magistrates that the heir and the widow "are two Distinct persons—ye widow is not ye Heire—the Heire is to Set out to ye widow of ye Intestate the Just 3d part." He claimed that Justine Patten's share of a "very Considerable [personal] estate" and her thirds of the realty would provide her "a Comfortable maintenance." John Patten believed that dower provided widows with an adequate living; receiving more would be illegal and selfish.

Giles Dyer agreed that Justine Patten was not a legal heir of Nathaniel but asserted the court's right to give her whatever it thought was just, including houses and lands. Moreover, he argued that such housing and lands were given not by the heir but by the court, with the remainder given to the heir. In closing, he stated his hope that Justine Patten and Benjamin Beale would not be at John Patten's "Disposall," implying that John could not be trusted to look after the widowed and orphans of the community as was every man's responsibility. Although the court found in favor of Dyer (and Justine Patten), the widow never argued on her own behalf. She was at the mercy of men arguing over their share of her estate.

Commonly, however, widows looked after their own rights. When Frances Axey presented James Axey's inventory in Essex County Court on June 29, 1669, the magistrates appointed Frances Axey administrator. At the time (and again when Frances Axey's will was presented), several members of the community testified about the distribution of the estate and the reason James did not leave a will. In trying to allay the condemnation of the community, James had told his friend, if "anybody should ask why he did not make his will to say he would have done it but his wife would not let him." Samuel Tarbox and Andrew Mansfield swore to the truth of this statement. Mansfield then explained to Frances that "it was an Apoyntment of God for [James] to sett his house in order." Nonetheless, she told James "you will give awaye all" and then adamantly proclaimed, "I will not nor can not consent to it." Frances opposed her husband making a will because she believed he did not love her as he once did and she would suffer because of it. Although James Axey claimed he would never "give nothing from you whilst you Live except" some small legacies, Frances Axey seemed to fear that he would give her less than she would be given by intestacy law, especially since she believed he wanted to give most of his estate to John Pearson. James tried to reassure her that, in giving his estate to Pearson, he meant that "he [Pearson] should looke after it for you." Others testified that when James Axey gave his land to John Pearson, "his intent was that his wife should have liberty to sell part or the whole for her comfort if needed."[76] However, Francis Axey knew better than to put her trust in someone else to look after her. The court upheld her wishes.

Massachusetts lawmakers in 1692 and again in 1699 clarified the rights of a widow in her husband's intestate estate. In addition to their dower, widows were to receive one-third of their husbands' personal estate forever if there were children and one-half if there were no children. A notable aspect of the 1692 law granted that administration was "unto the Widow or next of kin to the Intestate, or both, as the Judge for Probate of Wills and granting of Administrations shall think fit." Although the judge had discretion to appoint single or joint administrators, the law insisted that the widow play a major role in overseeing her deceased husband's estate. The law portrayed widows as capable of fulfilling their financial responsibilities, and, if appointed joint administrators, at least they had a partial voice in the process.[77] When Katharine Belcher's husband, Gregory, died intestate, the Suffolk County Court gave her all his personal estate forever and "that part of the dwelling house & appurtenances which Shee now enjoyes to live in during her life." The court also permitted her to sell any part of the real estate to pay his debts and to maintain herself during her lifetime. What is unique about this case is that the Belchers had sons among whom the estate could have been divided.[78] It may be that the sons had received their portions on their marriages, because they approved of the settlement. It also seems likely that the court wanted to ensure that creditors would not suffer by the settlement when it (and her sons) gave Belcher permission to sell her real property. The confluence of the law and local customs is also evident in the agreement between Mary Pepper and her father-in-law disposing of her husband's estate. She gave her daughter twenty-one acres of land valued at £60, keeping the rest of the estate for her use. She agreed to pay all of her husband's debts and to bring up her daughter until she "comes of age or marries." In return, they agreed that Mary Pepper could plant a fruit-tree orchard, half of which was to be given to Bethiah Pepper at age, and could have the use of her daughter's portion until she reached maturity.[79]

Taking advantage of the law, Mary Veazey of Suffolk County presented her case before the county magistrates in 1700. According to Veazey, her husband wrote a will before he married her. Shortly after their marriage and before he could amend his will to provide for her, he went on a voyage and died at sea. She requested that his estate be distributed as if he had died intestate; she demanded her thirds. Samuel Veazey's executors and heirs objected to her request, claiming that it would be not only "much to Our Damage" but also "Contrary to any Law or Custome in New England." They argued that Samuel Veazey had left a will, which was proved in court, and that, although he did not mention Mary Veazey in this will, "he did provide honnourably for her out of his Estate." The court was apparently persuaded more by the widow's plight than it was by the arguments of the executors and heirs: they granted Mary half of Samuel's personal estate and a third of his real estate for her lifetime. This court was not alone in giving the widow more than her minimum rights in her husband's estate.[80]

But a widow was at the mercy of the legal heir of her husband's estate—usually his son. The widow Sarah Burnell petitioned the court for her share of her husband's estate because her son "refuseth to releive her or yeild her any Succor or maintenance therefrom." The court did not appear to grant her full dower rights, but it ordered that until all parties could be present at the next court she be "put into possession of the Chamber Shee formerly had in her Son's house . . . and bee paid five Shilings in money per weeke by her Son." At the next court, the magistrates ordered Samuel Burnell to pay his mother £4 16s. a year for her lifetime "in lieu of her thirds of Land sold by him." The court also ordered him to give his mother the room she formerly lived in his house "unless hee provide other to her content."[81] Possibly Samuel Burnell was Sarah Burnell's stepson, but nothing in the court records indicate that he was.

. . .

The complexity and detail of probate law and the court cases in South Carolina, Maryland, and Massachusetts reflected the complex circumstances widows faced. In all three colonies, dower and intestacy law, drawing heavily on English common law, decreed that widows were to receive support so that they did not become a burden on the community, but not so much that they took away from their children's fortunes. Granting widows power and independence was certainly not a goal of the lawmakers. Yet, in all three colonies, widows used the courts to ameliorate their condition and to garner a certain level of power and independence. Widows in Massachusetts, Maryland, and South Carolina fought hard, and often successfully, against the claims of male heirs or their decreased husband's wishes.

Case law suggests that magistrates in colonial Massachusetts were less willing to grant widows discretion than were magistrates in Maryland or South Carolina. Through most of the seventeenth and early eighteenth centuries, Maryland and South Carolina lacked stable communities. Frontier conditions skewed sex ratios, while exploitive economic practices mitigated communal restraints on property holders, whether males or widows. Because of the late date at which South Carolina was settled, its dower and intestacy law changed little before 1750. That was not true for Maryland. As society stabilized in Maryland and the economy became less volatile, more like that of Massachusetts, Maryland laws that regulated widows' lives became more detailed and rigid, tying widows' hands. The law not only assumed male authority and power but also assumed women's greater responsibility for their children's welfare. In a dispute between a male property holder and his children, the male property holder frequently triumphed. In a dispute between a widow and her children, the widow triumphed only if the courts believed that her children were cared for, and many widows found the law inadequate to protect their rights and provide for their needs. Personal, professional, legal, and economic ties among men remained strong, and those ties greatly affected widows who no long lived under the immediate governance of a husband. Still, in all three colonies, on the deaths of their husbands, many colonial widows like Elizabeth Schenckingh and Rebecca Holmes Amory were determined not to acquire a new master and to create new identities for themselves. They sought to resist the reimposition of male authority over their lives, whether in the form of a new husband, an eldest son, or court magistrates. In the seventeenth and eighteenth centuries, control over property, especially land, gave individuals a measure of autonomy. At their husbands' death, colonial widows struggled to gain title to their husbands' estate and thereby to secure their share of that autonomy. Many successfully manipulated the ambiguity of both intestacy and widowhood to their best advantage, however variously they defined advantage.

Having made the choice to remain widowed and having learned to negotiate the legal system, widows found that the most important role they had to undertake was that of head of household and that the most important realm they oversaw was the home. It was here that widows intimately and concretely faced the reality of their lives, the reality that they had suddenly become masters of their ships. It was here that widows began to understand their anomalous position with respect to their own households and the wider community. Part of the responsibilities entailed in the masculine roles assumed by widows was raising the children and looking after their fortunes. As we have seen, this could be problematic for the widow and her community. However, as the following chapter reveals, widows took on these tasks in large part through their literal and figurative wills.

3

"To the Tenderness of a Mother Add the Care and Conduct of a Father"

Widows and the Household

On August 14, 1649, John Bateman and the widow Margarite Perry, both of London, signed a marriage contract under which Bateman promised to bequeath his intended wife, Perry's daughter Mary, £1,000 sterling for her own use. To ensure compliance with this agreement, Bateman bound himself to Perry for £2,000 sterling.[1] Such marriage contracts were not common, but neither were they unheard of.[2] John Bateman, having moved his family to Maryland, died without fulfilling his obligation to Mary and her mother. In his will, Bateman bequeathed land and other goods to his "widdow and Relict" Mary and named her as executrix. He also left an estate burdened with debt that exposed Mary to the "trouble and disturbance of many persons" and to the danger of losing both her bequest and the £1,000 sterling he promised her in the marriage contract. Legally, the deceased's estate was liable for all debts before the estate could be distributed.

Mary Bateman, instead of renouncing John's will and claiming her dower right, acknowledged her husband's marriage contract as a legal debt for which the estate was liable. In 1664, Margarite Perry shrewdly demanded £2,000 from the executor of John Bateman's estate. Perry produced Bateman's bond in court and Mary confessed judgment for the £2,000, making her mother the preferred creditor. The Provincial Court ordered an execution against the Bateman estate for the amount to be delivered to Margarite Perry. Perry, in turn, transferred her claim in Bateman's estate to her daughter.[3]

Her satisfaction was brief. On January 15, 1665, Henry Scarborough, a London merchant and Bateman's major creditor, petitioned the court. He claimed that Bateman had left an estate large enough to satisfy his creditors and that Mary Bateman had undervalued the estate to "defraud" them. The court appointed new auditors, who gave Bateman the land and goods bequeathed to her to the value of £1,000 sterling, instead of the £2,000 sterling owed Perry. Mary died in 1667 and bequeathed her entire estate to her infant daughter.

As this case suggests, widowhood redefined a colonial woman's economic and familial relationships. The demands on women as wives and as widows could be quite contradictory. Being a widow was not simply a matter of no longer being a married woman. Widows were at once never-married women, married women, and men. Widows resumed all the legal rights of *femes sole* and assumed male rights and responsibilities within an intricate web of communal standards of gender, wealth, and status. Their identities were forged dialogically. Prescriptive literature advised widows to select—and widows indeed selected—aspects of masculine and feminine, paternal and maternal roles. Widows thus crossed gendered boundaries to fulfill their responsibilities or to take advantage of the ambiguity inherent in those roles. The cases of Mary Bateman and Margarite Perry underscore the importance of widows' actions as legatees, legators, and executors. They reflect the meanings of family as widows constructed them within the constraints of law, custom, property, and the competing wishes of their kinfolk. These women responded to their familial responsibilities by engaging in economic battles generally reserved for males. They symbolized the ways widows, often described in English law as "relicts," could manipulate the system to their and their daughters' advantage.

The English settlers brought with them traditional beliefs about the economics of the family. Inheritance provided productive wealth for the next generation, preserved the household, controlled the family structure, and transferred authority from one generation to another. In economies of scarcity, English inheritance law sought to perpetuate male lineage, and male testators often used their bequests to maintain a "traditional social structure" based on male control over land and its resources. This meant granting all land to the eldest son. When men possessed sufficient land, custom encouraged them to bequeath it to all their male heirs and their personal property to their daughters. In the early stages of colonization, the abundance of land allowed patriarchs to ignore the custom of primogeniture and to bequeath to all sons land sufficient to support their families and to maintain their class standing. Indeed, at times, estates were large enough for wives and daughters to receive landed bequests along with their personal goods—although that occurred infrequently. If men lacked extensive land, the women likely only received personal goods.[4] Moreover, in cities, land lost much of its family significance as other forms of property became critical to family sustenance—money, personal goods, stock, and lease holds—property not traditionally associated with male ownership.[5]

A close reading of the language used in early colonial laws reflects the assumption that testators were male. Widows could devise their estates, and the 1692 *Acts and Laws* passed in Massachusetts recognized that proprietors could be male or female. Yet, they declared that any person, "in his own proper right in Fee Simple," can devise by "his Last Will and Testament . . . all such Lands, Tenements and Hereditaments to and among his Children or other, as he shall think fit at his pleasure." Additionally, when Massachusetts lawmakers explained how the unbequeathed surplus of an estate would be distributed among the heirs, they described what wives and children—not husbands and children—would receive.[6] They stated that "it is found by experience that some Men dying, having made their Wills, . . . that the wills are Concealed" and that their wives and children therefore suffer. Finally, a 1700 act providing for children who "not having a Legacy given them in the Will of their Father or Mother" insisted that such children receive their lawful portion of the estate "provided, Such Child or Children have not had an equal proportion of his Estate bestowed on them by the Father in his Life-time."[7]

Yet, women's control of wealth was not entirely dependent on male relatives. Widows not only improved the value of the estate their husbands left them but often had their own estates to bequeath, even if small. Such wealth may have motivated, even compelled, widows to execute their own wills. Widows helped to actively produce and reproduce the economy through their bequeathing patterns. They did not simply react; rather, they actively structured the family and the family economy in particular ways. In distributing property from one generation to another, colonial widows put an ambiguous female imprint on a decidedly paternal society.

Recall that John Bateman referred to Mary as his "relict." The *Oxford English Dictionary* defines that word in several ways, and each definition signifies how Anglo-American authors defined widows' place in society. The first use of "relict" as "a widow of a man" appeared in 1545. Beginning in the mid-fifteenth and early sixteenth centuries, the nuclear family began replacing large kin networks just as private property and household production began replacing the communal enterprise. Thus, the individual family and its head assumed new standing, and English women's roles within the family became increasingly constricted, with women identified primarily through their relationships to men.[8] The head of the household represented the family in all matters economic as the family became the model for the well-ordered and hierarchical social structure. The husband ruled the unified household as the king ruled the country.[9]

However, "certain things in the house" pertained "to the authority of the husband" and in "other things" he gave "over his right unto the woman."[10] The specific tasks they performed enabled the household to survive as an interdependent unit. As Thomas Tusser, author of one of England's most popular books on the household, penned:

> Take weapon away, of what force is a man?
> Take housewife from husband, and what is he then?[11]

Wives fulfilled necessary and important roles as helpmeets to their husbands. When death disrupted the complementary relationship, some of those ideals changed as other, more complicated meanings of "relict" suggest.

Widowers were never referred to as relicts of their deceased wives, because their wives' death did not alter their status. Men remained heads of households, property holders, and, often, citizens.[12] There was no need to advise them on how to manage their passage from one marital state to the next because the death of a wife, at most, inconvenienced a widower. The definition of relict as a "deserted or discarded person" (1592) or "the remains of one deceased" (1649) signaled a profound transformation for a woman subsumed into the person of her husband. A widow was not a whole being but a fragment. Yet, Tusser's belief that "If widow, both housewife and husband may be,"[13] turned the legal construct of a masculine unity of person into a cultural construct of a feminine unity of person. The important responsibilities thrust on English wives by their husbands' death meant that widowhood signified a change in a woman's very being. As titles in English society separated the elite from the ordinary and the superior from the inferior,[14] so, too, did "relict" separate widows from other women—and men. Defining that role concretely proved as elusive as did determining whether a widow should remarry or not.

While widows were expected to display their grief at the loss of their "honoured Companion and guide,"[15] the prescriptive literature established a fine line between mourning too much and mourning too little, linking both to gender and sexuality. The image of a widow's tears falling "not like a hasty Shower, but a still Rain" portrayed an acceptable manner of grieving.[16] The latter ensured that a widow would be "serene and sorrowful."[17] However, ardent weeping suggested that a widow who could not control her emotions could not "so well secure the Chastity of her proper estate." Simply put, she was too sensual.[18] Excessive tears also indicated that a widow was not "manfully" bearing the cross God had presented to her.[19] The use of the word "manfully" suggests that mourning was, indeed, gendered. Men, too, grieved the loss of their wives, and they turned to others who had experienced a similar loss for emotional support. But ministers advised widowers that they "must be resigned to it" and that they should "bear this chastening of the lord."[20] A widow with the social and financial freedoms of widowhood was expected to display the masculine virtues consistent with those freedoms.[21] If she did not, she was suspect. While most writers sought to limit the violation of gender boundaries, all emphasized the importance of widows behaving as their husbands would have. Heywood's compendium of "illustrious" female exemplars idealized the widow Artemisia because she became "the living sepulcher of her dead husband," Mausolous. A popular advice book written in 1673 advised widows to "represent him so to her own thoughts, that his life may still be repeated to her."[22]

Cotton Mather, in the funeral sermon preached for Sarah Leverett, the widow of the former governor of Massachusetts, commented that "in her own House, the Lively Concern that she Expresed, for the serving of Her God, and the saving of her Soul, gave a lovely Representation of Christianity to the Life."[23] Most sixteenth- and seventeenth-century advice books voiced similar sentiments about "the Life." Widows, especially older widows who had "little worldly Business and Care to take [them] off, or being past Labour," were supposed to withdraw from "the World" to the solitude of their home and "put on the Ornament" of prudence."[24] By confining themselves to the household, humble and pious widows conformed to the role ascribed to them as wives. Such advice made sense if people believed, as numerous authors did, that, when a woman's husband dies, "her intellectual part is gone, the verie faculties of her soule are . . . benummed, dimmed and dazled so that she cannot thinke."[25] In 1718, Cotton Mather described widows as unable to speak for themselves, "as their husbands could."[26] Mirroring this sentiment, the Englishman John Dunton described the widow Brick of Boston as "a Gentlewoman whose Head has been cut off, and yet she lives and Walks."[27] These images hardly inspired trust in widows who were undertaking new responsibilities as heads of their households.

Wives acting as "deputy husbands" assumed male roles "sometimes by choice and sometimes by necessity" but usually at the behest of their husbands. It was, however, a carefully delimited realm, and wives who overstepped their boundaries were charged with being "masculine women" or "man-woman," with "acting more a husband than a wife," and with "unmanning their mates." Wives who assumed these notorious roles turned the social order upside down.[28] Didactic authors, however, recognizing that, on the death of her husband, a wife became "father as well as mother to the orphans with whom she is left entrusted,"[29] in essence gave widows permission to take that crucial step toward assuming masculine roles. Colonial funeral sermons asserted that a man's responsibility was "in his ship as in his house"—that is, he was to command "good order [and] wise government." Ministers urged men to manage their families with "exactness" by seeing that each member read the Bible and kept prayer meetings.[30] Because wives became masters of their ships and of their households at their husbands' deaths, ministers likewise expected widows to "supply the place of both parents." Madam Brick, understanding her new role, claimed that she must "put on the Affections of both; and to the tenderness of a mother, . . . add the care and conduct of a father."[31]

When St. Paul wrote, "If anye widow have children, or childrens children, let her first learne to handle her owne house vertuouslye, and do for her progenitors againe,"[32] he honored a long tradition of widowed mothers caring for their children. As the women of each generation assumed that responsibility, they repaid or rewarded their maternal ancestors. Such a role expanded the widow's rights. It also placed her in an anomalous position with respect to her own household. Acting as a father meant that a widow had to put aside her emotional attachment to her children and order her family strictly.[33] One funeral sermon even praised the widow who "Rul'd among her Children like a Queen," recognizing female competence and power in a decidedly paternal society. This admiration of queens was not lost on Anne Bradstreet. She particularly admired Queen Elizabeth and set her up as the exemplar that proves that all women have intellect of their own and can rightly (lawfully) assume the role of head of household. She wrote:

> Now say, have women worth? Or have they none?
> Or had they some, but with our Queen is't gone?

Nay masculines, you have thus taxed us long,
But she, though dead, will vindicate our wrong,
Let such as say our sex is void of reason,
Know 'tis a slander now but once was treason.[34]

While funeral sermons almost never addressed a man's economic roles within the family, nearly every one praised a widow's responsibility for "the uncommon prudence of her Oeconomy."[35] "Economy" meant managing the expenses of the household, which would have been women's responsibility. It also meant administering the economic resources and orderly productiveness of the family at large, which would have been men's responsibility. Ministers honored men's economic roles through references to their public service and relegated widows to their role as overseer of the household's economic well-being. As heads of household, however, they assumed the male responsibility, and, by praising women's competent management of the household economy, authors educated other widows of their responsibilities.

That women of the community understood these responsibilities becomes clear with the case of Hannah Sharpe. When the widow Sharpe died, her son-in-law presented an estate £23 in arrears, thereby suggesting that Sharpe was an inadequate head of household. Mary Sharpe of Jamaica, incredulous, argued that it "seems very Improbable that a Woman of Mrs. Sharpe's frugality & Carrecter who always lived in very good Credit & Reputation, her house well furnished . . . should die & leave among all hir household stuff not a plate, dish or anything Else of pewter."[36] As Jane Kamensky argues, "in this face to face world, stories about one's neighbors constituted a vital form of social currency,"[37] so Mary Sharpe fought to ensure that her widowed relative would not be thought of as a spendthrift or as irresponsible in the way she fulfilled her role as mother and father during her widowhood.

Another indication that widows understood their maternal and paternal roles was their relatively high rate of testation.[38] Like early American lawmakers, advice book authors also conceived of property as masculine and the giver of that property as male. *The Whole Duty of Man* instructed the wealthy parent to "distribute [his estate] to his children, remembering that since he was the instrument of bringing them into the world, he is, according to his ability, to provide for their comfortable living in it." Although writers admonished both parents to nourish their children's physical and spiritual well-being, they advised the father to bequeath his wealth to his children. Writers ostensibly gave this advice to both mothers and fathers, but they directed it primarily to fathers, often conflating "he" and "the parent."[39] Such authors assumed that parenthood was a masculine responsibility and that the male head of the household would determine his children's financial future. Widowhood challenged those assumptions and put economic power in the hands of widows, for, in reality, many testators were widows. Their wills reveal the ways widows conceived of their families and their responsibilities to their sons and daughters. Just over 50 percent of the widows in Massachusetts, Maryland, and South Carolina whose estates went through probate died leaving wills.[40] It unclear why some widows left wills and others did not. But high rates of widow testacy suggest widows' dissatisfaction with the way their intestate estates would be divided and their desire to exert control over their families.[41] Luckily for us, a few widows left explained their motives.

Widows like Joanna Newman asserted that "the frame and Constitution" of her "husbands' will" required her to "Sett my house in order."[42] Other widows acknowledged—according to Scripture—that "he that provideth not for his own family, is worse than an infidel."[43] Other widows left wills because of the problems an intestate estate created. Mary Ward lamented "the trouble I have mett with & been put unto" because her husband died "before hee setled his Estate." She wanted to settle her estate "for peace sake that my Sonn & sonn in Lawe & grand-children may live in love & peace." Margaret Haugh wrote her will (which ignored her son) because she had "expended the whole of his Father Johnsons Estate in bringing him up & . . . and because I have suffered him to Enjoy a House and Land at Charlestown, which his said Father dyed Seized of, and never demanded my Thirds or Dower."[44] She did not want her son to get any more of the estate. All these widows acknowledged their responsibilities to their family as head of the household and demonstrated their ability to step beyond their rigidly defined roles as wives.

While writers portrayed daughters as "Comfortable Companion[s]" to their poor mothers, they portrayed sons as their mother's "Main Support" who would "Supply of her Necessities." Daughters provided emotional sustenance, sons economic sustenance;[45] indeed, many men's wills reflected this belief.[46] John Clark, a tallow chandler from Boston, put an intriguing twist on this ideology. He stipulated in his will that his wife, Rebecca, should "Continue in the possession of the House I now live in with my two [widowed] Daughters." This suggests that he turned to his daughters for their mothers' economic sustenance. However, his widow was to assist them in carrying on his business and in "getting in my Debts for payment of" the cash legacy he left her. Clark insisted that Mary remain with his daughters for eighteen months "Rent washing Lodging & Diet free." If Rebecca could not raise the £500 legacy by the end of that period, he directed that she "Continue in possession aiding & assisting my said Daughters aforesaid till" she could raise the money.[47] Ultimately, his daughters were not responsible for their mother's economic security; his widow was to earn her own legacy and freedom. Despite prescribed male support, many widows declined it. When Mary Talbot of Ann Arundel County, Maryland, became widowed, her son argued that if she came to live with him—and brought her estate with her—she could live a more secure widowhood. The widow Talbot "resolved to abide by [her husband's] will," which gave her "the Use of all my Land at West River during her Widowhood and after one third part During her Life her Right."[48] She steadfastly refused to give up her independence, even if it meant living less comfortably.

When necessary, widows took control of their lives and used their testaments to encourage their children to look after them in their old age or infirmity. Mary Barker and her son signed an agreement in which he promised "to provide for her during her naturall life, food rayment & attendance necessary in her age and all times to supply what physick she shall stand in need of" because she bequeathed him her entire estate. Similarly, Hannah Beadle did likewise because her daughter and son-in-law loaned money to repair her "homestead" and "for what they . . . shall advance toward my support" during her sickness. And Experience Miller and her sons agreed that in exchange for £5 paid annually plus all the personal estate her brought to her marriage, Miller gave them her dower rights in her husband's estate.[49] Widows at times also punished bad behavior. Sarah Button of Boston gave her son Robert only five shillings because he "hath taken no care of me in my Widowhood." She gave the remainder of her estate to her daughter Ann, "who has always lived with me and is now about to be Married with my Consent & good liking."[50] Such agreements and bequests belie the seemingly natural construction of sons as their mothers' main support.

But instances of such punishment were rare. In fact, the opposite was true. Of the widows (and male testators) who explicitly specified a favored heir in their wills, nearly a third of them claimed that a child cared for them in myriad ways and acknowledged that support with their power of the purse. Sarah Pemberton of Boston, Massachusetts, in 1709, bequeathed to her daughter Mary the household goods Sarah had purchased by her "own Industry since my husbands Death," thereby rewarding Mary for the "Tender care . . . of me her Aged Mother all along to this day."[51] These personal comments were not aberrations. Widows frequently noted that daughters and granddaughters cared for them. In fact, contrary to ideology, widows claimed that daughters and granddaughters cared for them three to four times more often than did sons and grandsons. Intriguingly, again contrary to ideology, male testators noted that sons had cared for them three times more often than did daughters. However, they denoted favoritism more often by granting a double portion than they did by noting that someone had cared for them, suggesting that men believed they did not need to turn to their children for help—or, at least, that they should not publicly admit that they did.

Three wills in particular further illustrate the ambiguity of and tensions around female bequeathing patterns. Sarah Burnham gave her estate to two sons, thereby ignoring her other two sons and her two daughters because they had been provided for in their father's will.[52] Mary Root divided her estate evenly among her sons and daughters, but the probate judge did not "wholly approve thereof" and gave Root's eldest son a double share and the reversion of her husband's land to the other three sons, who were then in turn to pay their sisters' portions in money.[53] The magistrate ensured that one son would be privileged over the daughters and that the landed estate would be distributed according to colonial gender norms. Mary Fisher gave her daughter Abigail all the estate she "had gotten since the death" of her late husband, as well as her remaining personal estate; she gave a son the remaining stock. Three other daughters (and their husbands) objected to the will. They claimed that their father had given Mary Fisher his whole estate for her lifetime only, which prohibited her from bequeathing it. Although Fisher was "very Diligent and Industrious" and thereby free to dispose of her own hard-earned estate, she was also "very often weak and infirm of Body and for the most part Stood in need of being Nursed." The expenses of nursing Fisher offset whatever estate she might have earned. They claimed there was, ultimately, "no addition made by Her to the personal Estate" and thus nothing to bequeath.[54]

When it came to dividing an estate, an individual's and a family's place in the life cycle mattered a great deal. Widows tended to be older than male testators. The latter typically established their sons' economic independence by giving them a landed estate, often at the expense of their daughters (who at best received a portion of their personal estates). In turn, having independent sons freed widows to be more generous to their daughters—but that generosity was never to come at the expense of sons. While they controlled less wealth than men,[55] they were neither "widowarchs" nor economic dependents. Relatively few widows possessed estates valued at less than £299. Indeed, the mean value of the estates of Massachusetts widows was £1,017, of Maryland widows £1,016, and of South Carolina widows £1,307.[56] The mean wealth of urban widows was significantly higher than that of rural widows (£1,143 to £895)—and nearly 70 percent of bequeathing widows lived in urban areas. Widows had real and personal estates to bequeath, and they bequeathed them with a precision that reflected their ambiguous relationship to the prescriptive literature, which positioned them as both mother and father, as constrained and unconstrained will makers. My analysis of widows' wills groups the types of bequests into two broad spatial and cultural locations: "out of doors" (real property and slaves—typically gendered masculine) and "within doors" (household goods and personal goods—typically gendered feminine).

While men were two to three times more likely to bequeath realty than widows, fully one-third of testate widows bequeathed real property. This is startling, given that previous studies suggest that real property belonged primarily to men.[57] Adhering to a belief that real wealth was masculine, in the aggregate widows named sons as recipients of real property twice as often as they did daughters.[58] However, across time, widows increasingly bequeathed more equitably to daughters and sons (and especially to granddaughters and grandsons) than did male testators. The more settled the community, the more likely women were to have secured control over land. Population growth, increased economic activity, falling mortality rates, accumulated realty, and expanded literacy all favored the growing control of American women over property—the material prerequisite of authority and freedom—especially for those of middling or elite status.

Looking more closely at the specific content of real property bequests reveals subtle differences, differences that reflect geographic location more than different constructions of widowhood. Massachusetts testators, male and female, who possessed only land were nearly five times more likely to give such land to sons than they were to daughters. When the bequest of realty included a house, however, widows changed that pattern dramatically. They favored sons only two and a half times more often than they did daughters. They bestowed upon the next generation of women independent access to real property; men never wavered in their bequests.

Massachusetts mothers, most of whom lived in urban areas such as Salem but especially Boston, understood, in a way that men did not, the importance of houses to their daughters, either as a way of earning a living (as I discuss later, most female "businesswomen" ran shops, taverns, or schools out of their house—or they took in boarders to supplement their income) or simply as a way to ensure they would have a place to live after their mothers' deaths, without or without a husband.

In Maryland, land played a much more important role in bequests. Nearly 70 percent of widows gave daughters land alone, about four times the rate at which they gave daughters a house. On the other hand, only 40 percent of male testators bequeathed land alone to daughters, and 60 percent bequeathed a house to daughters. Maryland men signaled that, for daughters, a house and land were more important than land alone. They may have thought about houses much as Massachusetts widows did. However, Maryland widows understood the longstanding relationship between land and economic survival in the Chesapeake. A house alone or even a house with a small plot of land attached did not provide economic security in a colony that relied almost exclusively on agriculture.[59] By bequeathing land to daughters, widows in Maryland, like widows in Massachusetts, sought to ensure their daughters' economic security and, perhaps not coincidentally, their independence.

South Carolina—like Massachusetts a colony dominated by a large city but, like Maryland, dependent on agriculture—showed traits of each. Deep South widows gave their daughters a house slightly more often than they did land alone, and they gave sons a house only slightly more often than they did daughters. South Carolina men overwhelmingly favored sons over daughters in both. Men, controlling great wealth and often hundreds of slaves, were particularly sensitive to notions of male hierarchy. Land assumed the continued wealth and power of their heirs, and they used it to sustain their lineage. Widows in South Carolina distributed their bequests of real property much more equitably than their northern and Chesapeake counterparts—and far more equitably than men in their own locale. Living in an area both heavily urban and heavily dependent on rice production and possessing greater resources than other colonial women, they had the flexibility and freedom to more generously provide their daughters with domestic and productive realty. But how are we to interpret these bequests? Cara Anzilotti argues that women "were not only tools of patriarchy but also its steadfast promoters." Culturally conservative, they "groomed their sons to become successful landowners and their daughters to become the wives of wealthy men" and then "retreated into the background." Lorri Glover asserts that as women struggled to "balance competing family obligations," they embraced both deference and cooperation—and in turn "constructed relationships based on mutuality and interdependence."[60] The widowed testators I examined neither overturned the male-dominated hierarchy nor firmly shored up an entrenched patriarchal structure. They provided their daughters with a measure of wealth and power, a situation with the potential to radically disrupt the paternalism so important to South Carolina culture.

Despite the longstanding association between prosperity and power (and the desire to control women's power), colonial testators generally passed realty on to their children free of encumbrances, and, while daughters received bequests of real property less frequently than their brothers, the property they received came with fewer strings attached. When they did impose conditions, fathers did so more often than mothers, and they typically required sons to provide goods or services to another. Unlike male testators, no widow required her daughters to perform similar services. Widowed and male testators who worried about what would happen to their daughters' land once they married bequeathed it for only so long as they remained single. Men might have wanted the land to remain in the nuclear family, and widows might have assumed that once their daughters were married, they would no longer need the land as an economic resource. Women especially wanted to keep the land out of the hands of unscrupulous husbands, for many widows stipulated that the realty—and, as will be evident later, other forms of property, as well—they bequeathed to their daughters not come under the control of their husbands.[61] Thanks to the efforts of their mothers, many daughters enjoyed new freedoms.

The paradox was that the property that formed the basis of freedom for many American whites required the enslavement of American blacks. Because of the paucity of slaves in New England, very few Massachusetts estates contained bonded property. In South Carolina and Maryland, however, slave property was nearly as important as landed property. If slaves are categorized as gendered property on the basis of who bequeathed slaves, slaves in South Carolina and Maryland were clearly female property. In both colonies, more widows than men bequeathed slaves. If slaves are categorized as gendered property on the basis of who received them, the picture becomes murkier. Male testators overwhelmingly (at a nearly six to one ratio, in fact) favored sons over daughters and never bequeathed slaves to grandchildren. Rather than improving for daughters of male testators, the situation grew steadily worse over time. In stark contrast, Maryland and South Carolina widows bequeathed their slaves approximately only one and half times more often to sons than to daughters—and, as time passed, they increasingly bequeathed more slaves to daughters and fewer to sons, reaching near-parity after 1720. The third generation lost out, as widows bequeathed slaves less often to grandchildren as they bequeathed slaves more often to daughters.

These bequeathing patterns reflect not only gender role expectations of male testators but widows' direct challenge to those expected gender roles. Widows bequeathed slaves to daughters twice as often as male testators did, while male testators bequeathed slaves to sons twice as often as widows did. Widows apparently understood the importance of securing their daughters' futures. They also believed in securing the future of successive generations more than men did. Widows' concern for "generational depth"[62] declined over time as the means to work the land became more valuable and as the pressure to look after their children increased. "After 1710 slaves began to equal the value of all other elements of an estate in the southern colonies, including land, and became the most important determinant of an individual's wealth."[63] As Maryland widows bequeathed land with increasing frequency to their daughters, they also more frequently bequeathed their daughters the slaves with whom to work that land.

South Carolina widows, who bequeathed on average 15.5 slaves, vigorously looked after their female heirs' future. They slightly favored daughters over sons and overwhelmingly favored granddaughters over grandsons in such bequests. Like men in the other colonies, men in South Carolina named sons as recipients of slaves more than twice as often as they named daughters. They did not bequeath slaves to grandchildren at all. As in Maryland, the gender differences are revealing. South Carolina widows did not simply bequeath slaves differently from men; they reversed the pattern set by men.

Widows in both Maryland and South Carolina—but more vigorously in South Carolina—secured the future of their daughters and granddaughters, even at the expense of their sons and grandsons. While both South Carolina women and men assumed that daughters would marry and that husbands would care for them, widows were more reluctant than men to leave their daughters' lives solely in the hands of their spouses. As recent studies suggest, two inextricably linked principles explain this pattern. First, widows understood that, in a society sustained by slavery, access to bonded labor meant that their daughters would have time to "read, write letters, attend prayer meetings, and do benevolent work"; that is, their daughters would be able to assume their role within the plantation hierarchy. Second, widows "actively participated in the slave marketplace, buying and selling laborers, used them as a source of revenue by renting them out, and expected these slaves to further their relatives' economic welfare."[64] Widows gave their daughters the means to secure a better marriage or to survive should their husbands be neglectful or die. Well into the eighteenth century, the nuclear family remained more unstable and less highly developed in South Carolina than in Maryland, and widows' concern for their daughters and granddaughters was particularly acute—and understandable.

The widow Henrietta Fisher's sale of two slaves to her daughter Elizabeth Petrie indicated that slaves belonged most appropriately to women and that they provided an important source of support for both generations. While it appears that Henrietta profited little from the sale (she charged her daughter only ten shillings), she knew how much income they could provide for her daughter.[65] Although the number of urban testators bequeathing slaves before 1720 was small, widows bequeathed slaves to daughters three times more than to sons. After that date, urban widows' bequests of slaves to children increased markedly and they bequeathed slaves nearly equally to daughters and sons and overwhelming favored granddaughters over grandsons. Urban widows defined slaves as female property, especially for the third generation of women. By contrast, both widows and men across time in rural areas saw slaves as masculine property by favoring sons and grandsons over daughters and granddaughters as recipients of slaves. It may be that slaves were largely field hands in rural areas, essential to the efficient operation of farms and plantations. But slaves were more than agricultural workers.

In cities, slaves were likely to be household servants working with women and doing traditionally women's tasks, which explains why, over time, widows defined slaves as more properly female property. "Elite southern women delegated their most onerous household chores . . . to a growing corps of domestic workers," using slaves to "facilitate the formation and management of increasingly complex and comfortable households. . . . Slaves enhanced the style and comfort of domestic life and allowed elite women to spend more time with their children or pursuing leisure activities." Ultimately, the ownership of slaves accorded women in South Carolina a degree of economic freedom and autonomy. "For some women that meant substantial legacies for children and extended families. For other women, it meant a choice of whether or not to remarry."[66] According to the historian Walter Johnson, "the social relations that defined slaveholding households . . . were made material in the shape of a slave." They certified status ("in a social sense, one could not *be* without" slaves), and both southern and northern widows used their bequests to ensure that their daughters and granddaughters retained their upper-class standing.[67] Urban widows, especially, understood that, in a slave society, slaves as much as land determined social status. Widows sought to guarantee that their daughters and granddaughters would retain their ancestral gentility.

On March 18, 1684, Elizabeth Carr of Salisbury, Massachusetts, left a will "that soe there may be no trouble among my children about it after my decease." Her caution arose from the multiple court appearances she had made after the death of her husband.[68] In the final division of his £1,100 estate, the administrators each received £180; his six other children each received £90, and his grandson received £20. Seven weeks later, Elizabeth's son-in-law James Bailey, husband of her daughter Mary, petitioned for their fair share of the estate.[69] Eight months later, two other sons-in-law and a son added their signature to Bailey's petition. After refusing to take what they perceived as unequal shares, they "made severall [unsuccessful] propositions for a peaceable agreement." The court appointed a committee to settle the issue, but its final ruling is unknown. However, Elizabeth Carr's will provides some clues about the dispute. After bequeathing money to daughters Sarah Baker and Anna Putnam, two sons, and a grandson, Carr left the remainder of her meager £65 estate in equal portions to three other sons. She left nothing to her daughter Mary Bailey, whose husband created all the trouble over George Carr's will in the first place. That her inventory mentioned no real estate and still her children fought so persistently over her estate suggests that historians—unlike colonial Americans themselves—have tended to devalue the significance of personal estates to the economic survival of the family.

At the most basic, bequeathing a locket, a gold necklace, or a watch symbolized a testator's love and affection. However, these personal goods represented more than sentiment. Jewelry, especially for women, displayed affluence, the family's standing in the community, and gentility. Moreover, "purchasing, selling and giving," not to mention receiving, jewelry empowered women. While jewelry might be women's only material possession (what one historian has called "portable wealth"), it more importantly reflected women's "social and economic networks."[70] In addition, books could provide much-needed practical and ideological knowledge—knowledge that was often gendered by subject matter and recipient.[71] Before 1720, widows in Massachusetts—more than a fourth of whom did leave personal goods—favored sons roughly twice as often as daughters as recipients of those goods. Thereafter, widows gradually but steadily increased their bequests of personal goods to daughters and granddaughters. Male testators in Massachusetts always favored sons over daughters by a two-to-one ratio as recipients of their personal goods. While widows did not ignore their daughters' access to books (indeed, an earlier chapter discussed the importance of prescriptive literature for women), the percentage of Bibles and other reading materials bequeathed by Massachusetts widows declined significantly between 1633 and 1750. At the same time, the percentage of precious metal items bequeathed increased threefold. When widows bequeathed books, they were 50 percent more likely to leave them to sons than to daughters, but when widows bequeathed mourning rings and other various precious metal items, they were twice as likely to leave them to daughters as sons. Male testators completely reversed these patterns. Widows in South Carolina—a third of whom bequeathed personal goods—favored sons over daughters by a slim 20 percent and granddaughters over grandsons by 50 percent. Male testators bequeathed evenly to daughters and sons and ignored the third generation. About six out of ten widows bequeathed reading material, and they bequeathed it nearly three times as often to daughters as to sons, suggesting that they were passing on advice literature and that they believed strongly their daughters should inherit the cultural identities and gendered ideologies presented in those books. No male testators bequeathed reading material. Widows in Maryland—a fifth of whom bequeathed personal goods—favored daughters nearly three times as often as they did sons. They only rarely bequeathed personal goods to grandchildren, and none bequeathed reading material. Male testators in Maryland rarely bequeathed personal goods, whether books or jewelry. That Maryland widows bequeathed personal goods slightly less often than widows in Massachusetts or South Carolina suggests that women in that colony did not necessarily measure their place in society by prescriptive standards or measure their wealth by participation in the market for consumer goods, likely because both cultures reached rural areas later than it did urban areas such as Salem, Boston, and Charleston.[72]

These patterns reveal that widows chose to provide security for their children and grandchildren in gendered ways. They preferred to give their sons access to educational materials, which in turn could provide them with a means of wealth and self-sufficiency, and to give their daughters access to items that they could use as a small measure of economic support, as a means of carving out a public identity for themselves as women of status, and as an entry into the world of a burgeoning consumer culture. More important for that world, however, were household goods.

Nearly 60 percent, more than 65 percent, and just under 50 percent of widows in Massachusetts, Maryland, and South Carolina, respectively, bequeathed household goods (including bedding and linens, furniture, and cups, bowls, and plates made of ceramic, silver, brass, pewter, or wood). Sometimes widows bequeathed those goods along gender lines, as did Sarah Morse of Newbury, Massachusetts, when she left her sons "the tools and tackling of husbandry" and her daughters "such goods as belong to huswifery."[73] Perhaps not surprisingly, widows bequeathed household goods at approximately twice the rate of men. In those bequests, Massachusetts widows consistently favored daughters over sons. Initially, they bequeathed household goods equally to granddaughters and grandsons, but their preference for granddaughters became pronounced after 1690. Widows seemed to be publicly declaring that second and third generations of women needed and should have the family's household goods. Male testators altered this pattern in a striking way, and this at a time when the supply of movables was increasing.[74] Prior to 1720, they, much like widows, favored daughters over sons as recipients of household goods. After 1720, they overwhelmingly favored sons over daughters as recipients of household goods. Men appear to have tried to ensure that their sons would have the material structure in addition to the physical structure to establish an independent household.

The same pattern holds, albeit not as rigidly or as consistently, for Chesapeake and Deep South testators. Maryland widows favored daughters over sons as recipients of household goods by about two to one. As granddaughters lost ground in the shift over time, sons gained ground. As the economy became more unsettled and goods of all types gained in value, widows focused their efforts on the second generation. Male testators favored their sons as recipients of their household goods. South Carolina widows, too, favored female recipients of their household goods, naming daughters about twice as often as sons and granddaughters seven times as often as grandsons. Men bequeathed their household goods equally to daughters and to sons and rarely to the third generation.

Urban widows favored daughters over sons as recipients of household goods. They also steadily increased the proportion of bequests to their granddaughters. Widows accomplished this by gradually decreasing their bequests of household goods to sons and dramatically decreasing their bequests to grandsons. Like Massachusetts male testators, urban male testators shifted their bequeathing priorities in the late period. Before 1720, they defined household goods as female property, but afterward they overwhelmingly named sons over daughters as recipients of their household goods. As male testators constricted their bequests of household goods to daughters, widows made up for the imbalance by bequeathing household goods more frequently to daughters and granddaughters. Widows in rural areas consistently favored daughters over sons and granddaughters over grandsons as recipients of household goods. However, after 1690, they decreased such bequests to granddaughters to the benefit of sons but to the even greater benefit of daughters. Rural male testators always favored sons over daughters and never named grandchildren as recipients of household goods.

As male legatees after 1720 shifted their bequests of household goods from daughters to sons, widows shifted their bequests of the same from granddaughters to daughters. This suggests that widows absorbed the notion that things "within doors" belonged to women. But, before we dismiss these bequests as inconsequential, we must recognize that, while household goods may not have supplied daughters with substantial real wealth, at a deeper level, they endowed daughters with the means to establish and maintain a viable household in a changing and sometimes unstable economy. The literature on an early American consumer culture is vast and still growing, but bequests of household goods also suggest that widows "found themselves teaching their children how to be successful consumers" in a burgeoning commercial culture. Eighteenth-century mothers, especially southern mothers, expected their daughters "to have the leisure to cultivate polite accomplishments, exhibit their virtues . . ., and preside over genteel households." As Cynthia Kierner argues for South Carolina, women played a crucial role in the "public culture" of hospitality. Performing in "hospitality rituals," women straddled the boundaries of private and public, not only acting as benevolent caregivers but also upholding a refinement that demonstrated their authority and power.

Widows, thus, provided their female heirs visible markers of gentility and ambition, as well as a personal and cultural identity.[75]

A stunning essay by Laurel Thatcher provides another way to think about these bequests. She argues that we must understand that culture was expressed not only in sermons "but in things," and this was especially true for women whose "identities were built from selective fragments [that is, material objects] of the past." In the context of those women's goods, she explains that we will find the meaning of women's household goods in "the small politics of everyday life," rather in a broader analysis of emulation and cultural diffusion. Women's goods provided "crucial props in unobserved, intimate rituals." Accordingly, she argues that, while "women might use goods to assert status and define relationships," they more importantly used lockets, books, beds, cups, plates, and furniture "to create a world of meanings and ultimately to transmit [their] history." Perhaps most important, in the process they established *their* lineage through their daughters' and granddaughters' inheritances.[76]

A final point about bequests: testators rarely named children by law (stepchildren or in-laws—it is almost impossible to distinguish the two in the legal records) as recipients of any type of property. When they did, in all categories and across time, widows named sons by law much more often than daughters by law. It is not clear why, but several explanations are likely. As Sarah Howard explained, she gave her husband's son a bequest because he "has received no Satisfaction" of the bequest his father left him, thereby fulfilling her paternal duty.[77] Johannah Davis offers yet another possibility. In her will, Davis noted that she had been supporting her son-in-law Richard Knight by:

> dealing out . . . many good Sumes of money, etc. . . . besides One hundred pounds in money which I Lent him towards the purchase of Mrs. Scotts house and Twenty Seven pounds in money more . . . when he began to keepe Shope . . . . And also Sixty odd pounds more in money that I paid . . . for goods for his accot. Also a debt due to me from him by Said Son Knight by book.

Then Davis formally bequeathed him what she had informally given him throughout the years.[78] Yet, as her will also suggests, widows granted such largesse to sons by law because they were the husbands of their daughters—whom English and colonial law placed under male authority. Testators may have felt more comfortable improving the material conditions of their daughters' lives indirectly through their sons-in-law. This is quite likely, given that most such bequests occurred before 1689, when the testators had recently lived under English testamentary law and custom, which adhered strictly to the notion that land and its appurtenances were masculine property. Widows understood that their daughters' husbands would control the property their daughters inherited and eventually pass on to their grandchildren. As the colonies developed their own legal structure and customs, and as various categories of goods, especially land, became more plentiful, testators may have felt freer to bequeath property directly daughters or granddaughters than had the generations before them.

Bequests to stepchildren raised other issues, such as the melding—albeit not always easily and peacefully—of two families and two estates. It was here that widows' testamentary power generated the most contention; while they might ensure economic security for some, they threatened that security for others. Shortly before his death, in 1639, Richard Haffield of Massachusetts wrote his will, naming his wife, Martha, as the executrix and bequeathing £30 to each of his five daughters—two by his first wife and three by Martha.[79] Richard expected Martha to divide the remaining estate among them at her death. However, when Martha wrote her will twenty-three years later, she left her house, lands, and most of her clothing and household goods to her unmarried daughter, Rachel. The difficult years between Richard's and Martha's deaths explain why.

In September 1666, the General Court declared Martha Haffield "non compos mentis" and appointed her son-in-law Thomas White her guardian, which gave him complete control over her estate. White became angry because Rachel Haffield had used money from Martha Haffield's estate to buy her husband's freedom from indentured servitude. Witnesses testified that Martha gave Rachel the money because White "had her [marriage] portion in his hands and she doubted whether she should get it." Witnesses also claimed that Thomas "went about to undue [Rachel] in every way," even though she had lived with and cared for a mother who was unable to care for herself and who supposedly had given Rachel the right to dispose of all her money as "she saw occasion." Rachel testified that "the household stuff and the cottage which was built for her mother and herself" and given to her by her mother's will "while she was in her right mind, had been unlawfully sold and the estate disposed of as White pleased." The court found the testimony in Rachel's favor convincing and ruled in her favor.

The conflict did not end there. A month after Martha Haffield's will was probated, the two daughters from Richard's first marriage petitioned the General Court for the £30 their father left them and the full share of Martha Haffield's estate that they were to inherit on her death. They claimed that Martha had given her own children the £30 as well as £50 more, while she had given them only ten shillings each. In a second petition, Richard's daughters claimed that they could "shew a considerable part of the estate came with their own mother" and sought to have Martha's will declared null and void so that they could receive their share of an estate valued at £349. Seeming to agree with Martha Haffield that a mother should first look after her own children, the court ruled against them.

Like the Haffield case, in a petition to the Massachusetts General Court on May 18, 1667, Mary Ward (widow of Benjamin Ward of Boston) answered unspecified charges made by her stepchildren. At issue was the manner in which Mary Ward had disposed of her husband's (their father's) estate. Ward claimed that Benjamin had wanted to show his love for her son, but beyond that he wanted to reward him for "all his faithfull & diligent service." She asked that the court grant her half at "her dispose" and grant the other half to Benjamin's grandchildren. The court awarded the entire estate to Mary Ward. Two months later, she wrote a will, in which she named her son and his children as her primary heirs.[80] She reiterated that, because her son had been helpful to Benjamin Ward, he had intended to give Stephen "a Considerable part of his Land & Estate." Because Benjamin Ward had died intestate, Stephen received nothing from the estate. Mary Ward's will made up for that unhappy circumstance. She closed her will by saying that she hoped "for peace sake that my Sonn & sonn in Lawe & grand-children may live in love & peace." They did not. After years of squabbling, on July 27, 1680, Benjamin Ward's grandchildren finally won their suit against the estate.

As these complex cases demonstrate, children of melded families competed with each other for their parents' assets. Widowed testators not only brought the conflicts to the surface through their individual bequests but often exacerbated the conflicts by purposefully neglecting stepchildren. Martha Haffield showed that she did not approve of the way her husband had devised his estate when she wrote her own will devising the estate differently from the way he wanted. Mary Ward exerted her legal and economic power by making her own son the primary heir of her and her husband's estates. Like Haffield and Ward, colonial widows often stepped in to construct and restrict the family structure as they saw fit.

As we saw earlier, Mary Fisher's children bitterly disputed the bequests she made in her will. Unfortunately Fisher also neglected to name an executor.[81] As a result, Margaret and Nathaniel Gay, Mary's daughter and son-in-law, petitioned to be granted administration of Mary Fisher's estate. Although the other children objected, the Gays took control of the estate—an action revealing the importance of naming an executor. The executor was responsible for probating the decedent's estate and presenting a "true inventory of all the known lands, goods, & debts" within a specified time frame. In addition the executor had "to collect in all the goods and chattels so inventoried," which often meant the executor had "very large powers and interest conferred on him by law; being the representative of the deceased, and having the same property in his goods as the principal had when living, and the same remedies to recover them." If executors did not complete their tasks within the deadline, they could be fined or their executorships taken away. As soon as an executor took possession of an estate, she or he was immediately responsible for repaying the decedent's debts. This worked in the favor of Mary Bateman but it put many widows in a vulnerable position.

Executors sometimes found it difficult to pay off the debts of the deceased, and Mary deBourdeaux of Charleston, South Carolina, renounced executorship of her husband's will in favor of the "principal creditor of the testator." A law passed in Maryland protecting executors from "double paying of debts, and limiting the time for payment of obligations" suggests that unscrupulous creditors took advantage of the situation. Throughout the colonies, executors initially could not use real property to pay the debts of the deceased, but, in 1692, Massachusetts reversed that law, decreeing that it was injurious to creditors since "the Estates of Persons within this Province to chiefly consist of House and Lands." In Maryland, executors could not use slaves to pay the debts of the deceased unless all other personal property had been exhausted and outstanding debts still remained.[82] Nonetheless, executors had at least limited control over the estate's real and personal property. Therefore, whom testators named as executors of their estates truly mattered and symbolized their beliefs about and strategies for structuring gender roles within the colonies.

Historians tell us that in mid-eighteenth-century Pennsylvania, male testators never named daughters "sole executors and only three were co-executors with other males." In late-eighteenth and early-nineteenth-century Virginia, "People of both sexes had their doubts about the capacity of women to make independent financial decisions and transactions. Women, however, had fewer doubts than men did." Male testators nominated their executors "more or less according to stereotype, women acted according to their own lights."[83] They acted similarly in Maryland, Massachusetts, and South Carolina before 1750.

When John Saffin testified about Esther Houchin's management of her late husband's estate, he placed her in direct opposition to most women in his community by claiming that she was never "in a capacity Lawfully to act as an Executrix or indeed to order her Domestick Affaires as other Women ordinarily are.[84] Reflecting a similar belief in female competence, nearly 7 percent of early American widows named female executors, and that was eight times the rate at which male testators did. Widows named joint male and female executors twice as often as male testators. This might have been a measurement of widows' willingness to be egalitarian; more likely, they were demonstrating their faith in their daughters' ability to handle the estate without creating a sensation in the community or without creating an undue or unfair burden on their daughters.

Before 1690, Massachusetts widows named sons as executors nineteen times more often than they did daughters. After that point, the rate dropped dramatically to five times more often. Factoring in those who named joint daughters and sons, the ratio across time dropped to approximately three to one. Across time, Maryland widows named sons as executors seven times more often than daughters, but after 1720, as they named daughters and sons as joint executors more frequently, the ratio of sons to daughters dropped to 3.5 to 1. South Carolina widows diverged from widows in the other two colonies in that they named sons as executors only slightly more than four times as often as daughters. And if we factor in those who named joint sons and daughters—over a one-fourth did so—the ratio drops to about two to one.

Widows did not say why they named executors as they did, but their reasons might be inferred from other comments they made in their wills. Mary Baker of Boston noted that she had not received the thirds of her husband's estate; nonetheless, with the help of her daughter, she had worked hard in her business to pay off her husband's debts; she left a sizable bequest to her daughter. We do not know who the executor of her husband's estate was, but, given how often men named their sons as executors, it was probably her son, William. That Baker named her daughter as her executor suggests that her experience taught her not to trust her estate to her son or another male executor. Sarah Bragg, also of Boston, maintained that the executors of her husband's estate, her sons John and Thomas, had not given her the remainder of £50 her husband bequeathed her. Like Mary Baker, Sarah Bragg left her entire estate to her daughter and named her daughter's husband as her executor. Bragg did not trust her sons to administer her estate fairly and properly.[85] One way around this problem was for widows to name their sons-in-law as executors in the belief that this was one way their daughters could at least indirectly control the estate left to them—and, in fact, widows in all three colonies frequently named sons-in-law as executors or co-executors.

Similarly, the widow Frances Quilter complained that "the greatest parte of [her husband's] estate" was "carried away" by Joseph Quilter, her brother-in-law and executor of the estate. She charged him with presenting a fraudulent will to the court and of taking "bages of mony out of ye thatch of ye house" without giving her any account of the estate and without presenting a true inventory that included the money in question.[86] As executor, Joseph Quilter had considerable power. The way he exercised that power put the widow under great financial and emotion strain. Widows likely named daughters as executors more frequently than male testators did simply because they knew only too well the problems unscrupulous male executors could cause. The rate at which widows named sons as executors of their estates suggests they felt pressure to conform to prescribed gender roles. However, and more important, they also felt strongly enough about their negative experiences with male executors that they—at first reluctantly, then much more willingly—circumvented the ideology by handing over control of their estates to their daughters. In all three colonies, as male testators circumscribed the responsibility of their daughters over time (if they gave them any at all), widows increased it.

The scarcity of productive land and constricted economic conditions, as well as a more even balance between the sexes (if not a surplus of women because of declining mortality rates and the large number of young men migrating west in search of land or employment), led to changing testamentary behavior.[87] After 1720, the rate of permanent widowhood increased, more extensive kin networks were built up, and women found their social and economic freedom constricted because of the "increasing pressures on family resources."[88] During this period of economic stagnation, inheritance was a crucial factor in determining children's economic success.[89] According to Allan Kulikoff and Philip Greven, the colonies were able to develop a "domestic patriarchy" in the late seventeenth and early eighteenth centuries because fathers began living long enough to assert their authority over their wives and children. Within this so-called developing domestic patriarchy, when economic resources, particularly land, became scarce, fathers tended to bequeath all of their land to their sons and a small amount of personal goods, such as livestock and slaves, to their daughters.[90]

Despite the intervention of the courts, family, and community members, widows' bequests indicate that colonial widows learned to deal with a changing social and economic structure that affected them and their daughters. Like Mary Bateman and Mary Fisher, who walked a fine line between what society expected them to be and what they knew they could be, eighteenth-century widows did not leave complete power and control over the family to their husbands' literal and figurative wills. Widows controlled more wealth and asserted themselves over their families, frequently in ways at odds with male bequests. Bequests of either real or personal goods to daughters did not necessarily provide the daughters with independence or power, because once the daughters married, their husbands managed or absolutely possessed those bequests.[91] Colonial widows, however, pursued two different strategies for empowering their daughters.

First, although most widows did not give such bequests directly to their daughters, they gave the estate indirectly to them through their daughters' husbands. While widows may not have foreseen their bequests solely as instruments of independence and power, they seemed to believe they could help their daughters achieve a better life by providing them with an estate that enabled them to marry well and start out their lives in more economic security than their husbands had previously provided. In the eighteenth century, widows began to protect and provide for their daughters even if their husbands had not. Their bequests enabled their daughters to participate in a genteel consumer culture built around the possession and display of goods; at the same time, those bequests led to the creation of a female identity and female lineage.

Second, widows made sure their bequests remained under their daughters' control. In 1654, Elizabeth Hardy of Salem gave her daughter, Elizabeth Hascall, real and personal property with the provision that it was "to be at her proper disposing without having any Relation to her Husbands Leave in it." Similar bequests became more frequent after 1700. Although Elizabeth Walker of Boston technically bequeathed all her movable estate to a good friend, it was for the sole use and benefit of her daughter. She specifically noted that she bequeathed the goods this way so her daughter's husband could not have use of or interest in them. Similarly, Martha Clark stipulated that her daughter's estate was to be in the hands of three male overseers and "the Profits arising there from shall be paid for her sole & separate use exclusive of her Husband." That widows wanted to ensure that the rents and income from the land went directly to their daughters is revealed in Susanna Condy's will. She stipulated that her son pay such money "into her [Elizabeth Russell's] own proper Hands, and not into the Hands of her said Husband Thomas Russell . . . for her sole & separate Use and her said Husband to have no medling with the same."[92]

Suzanne Lebsock argues that women in the early nineteenth century bequeathed to other women because of the influence of the doctrine of separate spheres, which defined women as inherently different from men and prescribed a female world in which women were "deeply engaged in the lives of other" women.[93] William Flint's will suggests that might have been true for the eighteenth century, as well. He stated in his will that he left his daughters nothing because he had given them something already; he left it to his wife to "doe well for her daughters," while he would do "well by" his son. Although the widow Alice Flint did not leave a will, she indeed looked after her daughters. Twenty-four years after William Flint wrote his will (which remained unsettled for legal reasons), Alice Flint petitioned to have "an equal distribution of the estate" so that her four daughters, who were left nothing in the will, "may have their share." She was successful. After giving the widows her thirds for her lifetime and the eldest son a double portion, the court divided the remaining estate equally among the Flints' daughters.[94]

Nevertheless, colonists did not expect widows to look after only their daughters. Elizabeth Phelps felt completed to explain her bequests. She knew that some in her neighborhood would think it "strange that my son Nathaneil ye Eldest Son should have no more given to him in my Will." She—and they—understood that, standing in lieu of a father, she should look after that son. She stated her reason clearly: "his father in his lifetime did considerably more for him" than he did for her two sons and her daughter. Still, widows assumed responsibility for their daughters when their husbands did not. The widow Elizabeth Woodward of Northampton, Massachusetts, declared in her 1685 will that she left what "smal mattr [she had] to dispose off" to her daughter because her son had already received his portion of "his fathers" estate. Elizabeth Rozer of Prince George's

County, Maryland, similarly bequeathed her daughters two slaves each because their father had inadequately provided for them in his will.[95]

Across all categories of property, mothers did not correct the inequity between sons and daughters. To do so would have ignored their paternal responsibility to ensure their sons' futures. More so than fathers, however, they looked out for their daughters. The shift of widows' bequests to daughters began in the early eighteenth century. Facing changing economic circumstances, they used the family's estate to secure the well-being of the entire family, not just the male lineage. Widows defined their world in neither patriarchal nor egalitarian terms but in family terms. Their children required economic support regardless of gender. Widows acting as fathers and mothers used their estates to preserve the entire family, not just the male stem. In doing so, they subtly and unintentionally changed the character of American families.

Vested with significant property, colonial daughters gained authority within their families. Colonial husbands no longer completely absorbed their wives' personalty at marriage. Instead, increasingly, they found themselves sharing the marriage bed with a fellow property owner who happened to be a female. While colonial wives found themselves constrained by their husband's name and authority, their ownership of property gave them a degree of independence. In the north, by the 1820s, sons and daughters had become virtual equals in their parents' wills, and daughters were just as likely as sons to be able to read and write. The resources that undergirded these changes were early American widows' legacies to their daughters and granddaughters.

In their ambiguous roles as male and female or as mother and father, widows frequently left the household and entered the wider world of the neighborhood, a world of sometimes complicated relationships. Because the necessity for widows to conduct business went beyond tending to their own household, widows assumed new, more encompassing roles as both recipients and providers of charity, as friends, as neighbors, as female support networks, and, finally, as citizens in the polity who assumed both rights and responsibilities of citizenship even if they did so within the domestic realm broadly defined. As the following chapter argues, such different roles were not always easily reconciled in the give-and-take of prescribed behavior and the quotidian realities of the world beyond the household. However, they influenced the debates about how to sustain the life of the community and its individual members, and they helped bring those deliberations forward as interests for public action.

4

"Tho She No More Increase One Family, She May Support Many"

Neighborly Widows

Part of the responsibilities entailed in the masculine roles assumed by widows forced them from the household and into the wider community. The necessity for widows to conduct worldly business went beyond tending to their own households. However, because the prescriptive discourse portrayed men as innately rational, clear-headed public individuals and widows as innately sentimental, "benummed" private beings, the widow who entered the world of the community threatened the natural order—as the complicated lawsuit Widow Mary Smith initiated against her son-in-law, Richard Rowland, demonstrates. On September 30, 1662, Smith complained to the Essex County Quarterly Court that Rowland "tooke a sticke & strucke her upon her arme and her legg." The direct cause of Smith's alleged abuse was her refusal to give her son-in-law passage through her Marblehead property. The part the neighborhood community played in this saga began when three men testified in court about the incident. John Bartoll asserted that the way Smith and Rowland "have lived severall yeare[s] is well knowne to all that live nere them." Samuel Cutler claimed he "was in the widow Smithes howse falling into discourse" about Rowland's "violent carriadg." Francis Johnson swore that Rowland asked him and Samuel Ward to go with him to hear what Smith had to say, and "they went into the chamber." This testimony suggests that it was not unusual for neighbors to go into one another's house to settle disputes and that the knowledge gained within the privacy of the house often became public knowledge.

A similar confluence between household and community arose when witnesses recounted the Mary Smith's physical abuse. Cutler avowed that Rowland had called his father-in-law, James Smith, an old rogue, "threw him downe, took him by the neckcloth, & held him so strictly that . . . [Smith was] hardly able to speake." Rowland's abuse of his mother-in-law continued that behavior, at least according to Mary Smith, who claimed that "if she should die, [Rowland] would be the cause of it." That Rowland assaulted Smith appears clear from testimony by four neighbors, Mary White, Mary Treuett, Goody Gatchell, and Elizabeth Legge. Testifying to the extent of Smith's injuries, all four women claimed that they found her lying in the field and that they had had to tie their aprons around her to carry her back to her house. Goody Nicholson, who tended Smith's injuries, noted that there was "something black there." Yet, George Emery and Dorithy Crumwell, who searched Mary Smith's body four days after she was hurt, "could find none, neither any evidence that any had been there." Nicholson, who understood the seriousness of such charges, advised Smith "to be careful what she said against her son, because it would be blazed abroad to his disgrace." She took this advice to heart, for, while never explicitly denying Rowland's abuses, Mary avowed that "what was don, was don p[ar]tly by my one [own] haste disposition." She then relieved Rowland of all guilt "yf I dye tomorrow night."[1]

Nine male and seven female witnesses disputed whether Rowland had assaulted his mother-in-law. The magistrates discharged him of his bond for good behavior and ordered both Richard and Mary to appear at the next Salem Court. On November 13, 1662, the court ordered Mary Smith to pay the costs of the lawsuit because she was unable "to clear herself of causing much trouble to the court and diverse persons by her passionate distempers in difference" with Rowland.[2] She was a relatively wealthy widow. As executor of her husband's estate, Mary controlled land, houses, and personal property valued at £421 (only 30 percent of Massachusetts widows under study here died with estates inventoried at £400 or more); moreover, he left her his farm and ten acres attached to it, as well as his house and land in Marblehead. He also bequeathed her all his household goods and four cows. Her status did not protect her in this case. Although friends and neighbors tried to help Mary Smith, the justices disapproved of her making a domestic dispute public.[3] She had used her control over her land to the detriment of her son-in-law, but, more significant, her outbursts pitted neighbor against neighbor. Mary herself seemed unsure about her position. In the end, she took an equivocal pose that did not fully absolve Rowland but that restored peace to the community.

That colonial communities were small and neighbors not only *watched* one another but also *watched out* for one another is revealed in this newspaper announcement by Elizabeth Hill: "Dropt betwixt my House and the Town, a silver snuff box, marked EH 1715. Whoever finds it and bring sit home shall be well rewarded." In an "intricate network of neighborly swapping," men and women frequently visited each other's homes, offering advice, caring for the sick, assisting at harvest time, helping deliver a child, or sharing food. They ignored or challenged each other only at their peril. Yet, as this case (and the necessarily fragmentary evidence I use throughout the chapter) suggests, widows had to be very careful when they stepped into the public role of head of household. The colonial neighborhood was a mediated space between the private realm and "the sphere of public authority" and a place of conflict.[4] Mediation, an act of crossing the borders, especially ambiguously gendered borders, suggests dependence but also interdependence.

Community members expected widows to adhere not only to commonly accepted norms of behavior deemed appropriate for the role but also to widely accepted norms of female behavior. As previous chapters suggest, such different roles were not always easily reconciled, and for many widows, like Mary Smith, stepping into the world beyond the household engendered disapproval. However, many widows played an important role within the community, and they often forced community members to acknowledge that they relied heavily on them. In the negotiation between prescribed behavior and the sometimes brutal realities of day-to-day life, they created an identity that gave them "stature in their own eyes . . . and in the wider community."[5] Widows frequently left the household and entered the neighborhood, the world of "small politics," to present petitions to magistrates, to dispense charity, to create female support networks, to adjudicate community disputes, and to be active in the civil polity.

In arguing that widows negotiated a space between the household and the community, I do not mean to re-create a false dichotomy between a male public sphere and a female private sphere. While one looks in vain for evidence that widows played a significant role in the masculine civil polity, Laurel Thatcher Ulrich suggests that religious injunctions for women to share in the "defense of the land" as "Handmaids of the Lord" opened up the possibility of women participating indirectly in civil society. Linda Kerber offers a more inclusive way to explore widows' role in the polity by arguing that we must "broaden the discussion and recognize that citizenship involved wide-ranging issues of claims of rights and of political behavior, as well as matters of allegiance, support, and analysis."[6]

Although both Ulrich and Kerber focus on women in the Revolutionary era, their perspectives can be applied to community-centered colonial America where political society "function[ed] for a definite purpose, with all parts subordinate to the whole, all members contribute[d] a definite share, every person occup[ied] a particular status." Land may have given both men and widows a degree of social economic independence, but, according to John Winthrop, the people of the community were to

> be knit together in this worke as one man, we must entertaine each other in brotherly Affeccion, wee must be willing to abridge our selves of our superfluities, for the supply of others necessities, we must uphold a familiar Commerce together in all meekeness, gentleness, patience and liberality.

When Winthrop used the phrases "one man" and "brotherly Affeccion," he did not intend to exclude women from this community, for, he proclaimed:

> Now when the soule which is of a sociable nature findes any thing like to it selfe, it is like when Eve was brought to [Adam], she must have it one with herself . . . [,] she conceives a greate delighte in it, therefore shee desires nearenes and familiarity with it: she hath a greate propensity to doe it good and receives such content in it, . . . she will not endure that it shall want any good which shee can give it.[7]

He and other leaders conceived of the polity in broad terms. Men and women may not have contributed in the same way to civil society, but they both played an important role in its survival.

A much later political theorist, Jurgen Habermas, seemed to elaborate on Winthrop's definition in arguing that it is possible to recognize civil society in the relationships created for sustaining life and to bring them forward for public discussion or action.[8] In breaking down the opposition between private and public spheres in the eighteenth century, Dena Goodman argues, "the 'authentic public sphere' articulated by Habermas was "constructed in" and was a part of the private realm. He distinguished this authentic public sphere, where "private people com[e] together as a public," from the "the intimate private sphere" of the bourgeois family.[9] The town—and, I'd argue, the neighborhood—"was the center of civil society, . . . the public face of the private realm." Goodman convincingly argues that "the eighteenth century was the historical moment . . . [when] no stable distinction can or could be made between [private and public]—a moment in which individuals needed to negotiate their actions, discursive and otherwise, across constantly shifting boundaries between ambiguously defined realms of experience." Thus, the authentic public sphere was not masculine—it was not the public sphere of the patriarchal state authority—and women did play a recognized role in it. Widows in particular "functioned within a private realm that had a public face" as they fulfilled their civil responsibilities and pressed their demands for certain rights. At two different but complementary levels, widows exerted a degree of authority and thus carved out a place in the colonial community.

Funeral sermons preached in part an ambiguous message about widows in the neighborhood community, although no such ambiguity arose in sermons preached for men. Above all other characteristics, ministers praised male community members for their service to the community.[10] Public service was the "ornament men wore most proudly and visibly." As ministers, merchants, and civil rulers, they displayed their "justice," "skill," "wisdom," "experience," and "valour."[11] In their capacity as "fathers of the people," they earned the honor and respect of "their children," the townspeople. In showing this respect, the people simply followed the Fifth Commandment, which required children to honor their Father, especially if they had been "nursing Fathers to them."[12] Such fatherly exemplars commanded authority, not only within their own families, where "everyone mov[ed] in a known sphere," but especially in the community, where they maintained "good order."[13] Men were active, "vigorous," and clear-headed. These qualities made a man "well form'd for government" and likely to be remembered for his public usefulness.[14] As the creation of seventeenth-century Maryland orphan's courts to stand in as "fathers" made clear,[15] authorities did not necessarily expect widows to fulfill a comparable role.[16]

Widows should never "thrust" themselves into "resorts of men and gathering of people" because these places brought them "afoare many mens eies," thereby jeopardizing their honesty and tempting them to turn away from a life of religious contemplation. The problem was widows' independence and the association of that independence with a wantonness that could potentially disrupt the community as much as if not more than Mary Smith's dispute with her son-in-law did. A sixteenth-century English minister claimed that, upon her husband's death, a widow became "sequestered from much conversation."[17] An ideal widow lived a solitary, private life.

Ministers and advice book authors largely saw sexuality as an issue for young widows. "Antient" widows posed their own problems. They suffered from decayed bodies and from "neglects, disesteem, insignificancy; or which are yet worse, ingratitude, undutifulness, and wrongs." Some family and community members treated widows irreverently by, at best, disdaining them, seeing them as insignificant members of the community, and, at worst, ignoring them. As a result, older widows acted discontented and "forward." They spoke their mind and vented their anger at pain and injustice, especially when meted out by their family and community.[18] Benjamin Colman, minister of the Brattle Street Church, in Boston, claimed that "it is eminently the duty and the honour of Aged women, that they be in behaviour as becometh holiness." He particularly focused on "all that appertains to [their] *Publick* [emphasis added] Appearance & Conversation; Garb, Dress, Gate, Countenance, Speech, Silence, [and] Gesture." Elderly widows who did not adhere to the standards of behavior he set out were more "odious" and "scandalous" than men who did not adhere to appropriate standards of behavior. Indeed, Mary Smith was fifty-nine when her son-in-law assaulted her and the court found *her* guilty of causing trouble in the neighborhood. Colonial ministers emphasized the proper behavior of aged widows because they served as models for younger women for how to behave. They set "Examples & Patterns, teaching and living Rules" for their juniors.[19] This positioned widows in a passive relationship within the community; it was a position more rhetorical than real, however, for widows were not passive—nor did their neighbors expect them to be—at least not in certain circumstances.

In 1643, in England, a petition entitled *The Widowes Lamentation for the Absence of Their Deare Children, and Suitors*, presented women's concerns to Parliament during the English Civil War:

> Before these warres . . . there was not a widow amongst us, from the old crooked beldame of fourescore and fifteen, to the young buxome widow of twenty, but had some hope . . . to have her sorrowes wiped away by the succession of a young lusty husband, that might cherish and administer both to the necessities of her body and her soule. . . . We have no man that will rub up our memories, or delight our senses, which have quite lost their feeling for want of bodily exercise; we being growne meer toothlesse mumping things, having no body to arme our frosty constitutions.[20]

While the satirical petition reduced widows' complaints about the very real and severe disruptions of the English Civil War to a plea for more sex and belittled the trauma they suffered,[21] it also demonstrated an important way widows entered into the public discussion of not only their responsibilities but also their rights.

Both the setting for presenting petitions and the instrument itself reflected important aspects of widows' place in the neighborhood community. The courthouse "defined social relationships and carefully guarded boundaries of status." For rich and poor, male and female, this "familiar and formal" ritual space became a place of public performance, a "dramaturgical exercise" that established one's position in the neighborhood, reaffirmed collective values, and judged communal conduct.[22] In the seventeenth century, courts held sessions in meetinghouses; in the early eighteenth century, they moved into taverns, both "primarily male spheres of authority and sociability." Around 1720, when towns began constructing separate courthouses, the architecture visually reinforced the power of the magistrates. The impressive raised bench where the justices sat at the front of the structure spoke volumes to the women who walked into and up to this seat of authority.[23] While women likely experienced a greater sense of awe and intimidation than did men, colonial courtrooms provided a space in which they "did not find it incongruous with their subordinate social and political status to claim the right to be heard or to be given their due."[24]

In Anglo-America, the acceptable way for generally disenfranchised people, but especially women, to complain of wrongs—and to seek redress of those wrongs—without questioning the rulers was through the petition, what Edmund Morgan calls the "fiction of the people's capacity to speak for themselves."[25] Because married women were legally subsumed in the person of their husband, their voices were infrequently heard. Widowhood provided new opportunities for them to speak out. Yet, they could as easily be praised for their masculine conduct as derided for their unfeminine demeanor. This question posed by Jay Fliegelman perfectly illustrates the complexity and ambiguity of this relationship: "do widows transcend their female nature or perfectly embody it . . . or are they a combination of compensating passive and aggressive postures?"[26] The answer is equally ambiguous. That women felt compelled to justify their actions suggests they understood that they were "encroaching a long way into men's territory."[27]

As widows exposed their private lives to the gaze of the public, the language they used was crucial. As did all petitioners, widows simultaneously reaffirmed their loyalty to their protectors and demonstrated their subservience, gratitude, and obligation in the act of seeking help. Female petitioners wore the "humble" guise well. In the words of Amanda Vickery, this constructed helplessness brought out "the benevolent paternalist lurking in almost any patriarch." Nevertheless, petitions legitimized female power and authority and "turned gender roles upside down" because the inherent contradiction was that the ruler was obligated to meet the needs of the petitioner. Petitions gave women a voice they could use to make demands of (or, less frequently, rebuke) the rulers.[28] Although petitioners stood in relation to the court as children to their fathers, colonial widows actively if cautiously made demands in order to look after themselves, their families, and the community, much as men would have been expected to do. While widows—especially poor widows—often relied on the mercy of their neighbors and community, through petitions, which ultimately proved more fact than fiction, they exerted a degree of public authority.

Widows' petitions to courts and letters they wrote to friends at one level attest to their miserable conditions. Often, widows had to sue to secure even the most basic necessities, such as bedding, pots and pans, and clothing, from their husband's estates. When this failed, they turned to others for help. When the widow Catherine Prichard asked Daniel Dulany for help in 1751, she adopted the typically deferential stance of all petitioners:

> If my Present Condition were not Insupportable to me, or if I knew any one person that would give me Relief under my Present Melancholy Circumstance I would carefully avoid giving you the Least trouble . . . but I have no prospect of receiving the Least consolation or any assistance whatsoever unless you will Vouchsafe to Commisserate Me.[29]

In closing, she pleaded, "I hope for God Sake that you will take a poor forlorn widow's Case into Consideration and grant me all the help & Comfort you may think fit." An examination of the more than fifty requests to the Scots Charitable Society of Boston reveals a similar use of language. These widows presented themselves as "object[s] of Compassion," humbly *begged* for help, and abjectly expressed their appreciation for the assistance they received.[30]

Alice Thomas's petition to the Massachusetts General Court in 1662 clearly established such paternalistic relations. Thomas initially declared that "god hath made you the fathers of this Common Wealth . . . & your petitioner being Confidently perswaded of your Care & Compassion toward ym that are under your charge & do stand in need of your help as in a spetial manner fatherless & widdow doth."[31] In seeking her rightful thirds from her deceased husband's estate, Thomas referred to the justices' paternal wisdom and prudence. She claimed that the "ye honoured Court knowes better then your poore petitioner" the law of dowries, but it was clear from her reference to the law and the specific page number of the law book that she knew full well her legal rights. Thomas understood that if she appeared knowledgeable, forceful, or independent, the court would not grant her request. She closed by claiming that she did not want to "bee further burthensome to ye honoured Court," and so her "humble request" was that they would take the matter into consideration and order that she receive her portion of her husband's estate. Thomas created an identity as a poor—that is poverty-stricken—widow, but also as a poor—that is, helpless—widow in need of fatherly care. On April 29, 1662, the General Court granted her petition.

The widow Ann Sheffield Perry similarly petitioned for financial relief. Although the facts of the case remain unclear, what is important is the language Perry employed in pressing her cause. She noted, "as is well Known"—here suggesting the *public* recognition of her circumstance—she had been forced to rely on the Bounties and goodness" of her "Christian Neighbors." To minimize the burden she placed on her friends and community, she asked that she "might first Spend what is my own, in the hands of Mr. Joseph Holmes," and, as many widows had been forced to do, resorted to asking the magistrates to "bee Helpers of the pore widdow & fatherless and Such as are opressed."[32] She asked to possess and then sell a share of her husband's estate so that she could live independently and not be a burden to her neighbors.

On June 30, 1718, five men signed a petition to the selectmen of Boston. They wrote on behalf of Mary Durant, recommending her "with all freedom" to continue her deceased husband's license for a "House of Publick Entertainment." The five, who lived in Durant's neighborhood, noted that she had "Good Conveniences for Entertaining for man & horse." More important to them and to this chapter, however, was the fact that she was "a person as far as we know or have heard, that keeps good Order in Her house and may also be usefulll in the Neighbourhood."[33] Four of the men labored in the neighborhood; one worked as a leather dresser, one was a blacksmith, one was a cordwainer, and one was a cooper/wine cooper. They understood the contributions someone like Mary Durant could make to the community—and they did not fear her independence.

Martha Cogan's petition to the Massachusetts General Court in 1658 indicates the consequences when widows forcefully demanded certain rights.[34] Cogan had earlier addressed "the honoured Court," requesting that £200 belonging to her "by the law of God Nature and Nation" (but given instead to William Ting's children) be returned to her. The Court refused, which led her to petition the magistrates again the next year. Cogan declared that, since the death of her husband, she lived "otherwise by the will of her husband . . . but from hand to mouth, being also left alone by the other executors who for reasons best known unto themselves doe refuse to accept thereof." In closing, her "humble petition therefore of your most humble desolate and disconsolate petitioner" was that "the dyeing declaration of her late deere husband . . . may by this honoured Court be duly weighed & prudently considered, so as your petitioner may be timely repayed & releived according unto the loud crie of her present condicon."

Cogan presented herself "most humbly & hartely as duty binds her" and promised to "dayly pray for your [deputies'] happinesse." Yet, however humble and desperate Cogan tried to appear, she could not sway the Court. She had, in fact, apparently petitioned the court once too often, because the deputies did "well remember that much time have bin spent referringe to this case" and saw no "reason (as yet) to recede in" their earlier decision. They declared that Cogan "should rest satisfyed with reference to the consent of our honoured magistry hereto." These men did not like being told by a woman that they had misjudged a case. Martha Cogan had challenged their authority and thus had not behaved like a proper "poor, helpless" widow; she did not gratefully accept the previous judgment, and she did not display enough deference to the deputies. She paid the price for her impertinence. In a visible display of male power, the magistrates not only rejected her second petition, they chastised her.

Martha Cogan died intestate two years after presenting this woeful petition to the magistrates. With an estate valued at more than £1,000, she was not poor. Her inventory included a wide variety of household goods, books, foodstuffs, money, and gold rings, as well as a house, a shop, and more than one hundred acres of land.[35] It is not clear why she presented her petition in the first place, but it is clear that even a wealthy widow was expected to behave in deferential manner appropriate for a woman. Money gave some widows male freedoms, but within limits. Widows routinely presented themselves publicly as "humble," "poor," living in "melancholy circumstances," "destitute," and "forlorn." Undoubtedly, many of these widows were poor and needed financial assistance, as the swelling rolls of contemporary charitable societies indicate. But the language used by both lower- and upper-status widows in addressing benefactors also reveals the status they had to accept if they wanted help.[36] The way in which these widows presented their cases conforms to the language used in other cases in which women were given or took the opportunity to express their opinions before a male-dominated body for the first time. But, the ambiguity remained as widows like Cogan presented themselves as meek and demanding, feminine and masculine.

Others also assumed both roles when the community took over the court's role in easing widowed poverty, a problem that increasingly faced Anglo-American colonists throughout the seventeenth and eighteenth centuries. This was especially true in cities like Boston and Charleston, which suffered from hurricanes, earthquakes, and fires. However, poverty knew no geographical boundaries, and a lack of formal poor-relief institutions meant that neighbors cared for the poor either by boarding them in their home or by providing charity. As poverty rates increased, providing relief to the poor became increasingly difficult for all communities. According to Gary Nash, this poverty "almost always seemed to be the result of ill chance within a social system fundamentally based on family and kinship"; widows were especially vulnerable in such a system.[37]

One unique approach to helping poor widows was mentioned in the *South Carolina Gazette*: "For the Benefit of the Widow and Children of the late Mr. Cook. On Friday the 10th of June next, at the Play House in Queen-street, will be a Concert of Musick. Tickets to be had at the House of Mr. Isaac Holmes on the Green at 40 s. each."[38] Most often, however, ministers and justices instructed neighbors to offer assistance to needy widows.[39] Aiding needy widows was not necessarily an altruistic activity. To pray for and to give sustenance to widows not only helped the widows, it also benefitted their benefactors. Ministers asserted that by easing the suffering of "poor, helpless" widows, a patron might be more likely to receive divine sanctification.[40] Such religious bribery implies that family and neighbors often abandoned or ignored poor widows. To allay communal fears, Cotton Mather told his audience that, although there was "a multitude of Widows" in Boston, "they are all provided for. None of them are starved; They live; They get along; They find succour; Supplies are sent in unto them."[41] Succor did not come as easily as the ideology suggested, however. If widows had neither family nor neighbors who would or could support them, churches and clergy were expected to supply their needs. Throughout his diary, Cotton Mather noted the meals, money, and comfort he gave the poor widows of his neighborhood.[42] In turn, ministers relied on private contributions, contributions that were often insufficient to meet the needs of the poor. To that end, the prescriptive literature suggested that, while the community had a responsibility to look after widows, widows had an equal responsibility to the community, especially the sick, poor, and homeless among them.

According to Mather's *Ornaments for the Daughters of Zion*, a widow's "exercises of Charity toward her needy Neighbours[,] . . . her visits, her Bounties, and her Succours to the Poor are now increased rather than abated, with her New Leasure for them." Because widows had to account to no one for either their activities or their possessions, such pious actions ideally filled their spare time and reined in their independence.[43] Often, ministers likened widows to the biblical exemplar Anna, who did "in the Temple Dwell So zealously Devout, So Examplarie."[44] But, also like Anna, an ideal widow was "full of good works and alms-deed" and "cloth'd the Naked as far as her Ability permitted."[45] While widows could and did support many families through their bequests of realty, household goods, and slaves to friends and neighbors,[46] the prescriptive literature advised them to show their commitment to the needy through their charitable bequests. This generosity left a "greater exultation and transport in the Giver then it can ordinarily raise in the Receiver."[47] In his funeral sermon for the widow Abigail Foster, Increase Mather publicly pointed her out as an exemplar of civic responsibility in both life and death. He noted in that "In her last will and testament she has considered the Poor as indeed God expect that They who have considerable Estates should devote Part of them to His Poor."[48]

The widow Hannah Harris of South Carolina resisted this altruistic role. According to the executors of Captain Richard Harris's estate (who made their complaints public), Harris gave "1000£ to the Ministers and Vestrymen of the Parish of St. Thomas, for the Maintenance and Education of the poor Children," he gave his widow Hannah "7 Negroes . . . and half of the yearly Profits of all his Estate during her natural Life," and he gave "Elizabeth Baker, his Wife Hannah's Granddaughter, all the Residue of his Estate, real and personal, of a very great value." Apparently, her husband's wishes angered Hannah, for she, "having obtained Liberty . . . to peruse the said Will, did tear the same to pieces, and hath since sold and made away with great part of the Stock of Cattle, and other personal Estate . . . to the manifest Prejudice and Wrong of the said Parish of St. Thomas, and all other Legatees."[49] She apparently believed that her needs outweighed those of the community poor and her granddaughter—and she acted on those beliefs. Yet, she proved to be the exception to the rule.

The widow Hannah Boulton of Newbury, after dividing her real estate evenly among two women and two men, gave the remainder of her meager estate (£28) to "charitable uses" and her remaining "Canadian land grant" for the poor.[50] Mary Sanders of Charles County gave five hundred pounds of tobacco to the poor out of an estate valued at well over £500. On average, widows in Massachusetts and South Carolina gave approximately 7 percent of their monetary bequests to the poor and to their church or minister. The generosity of male testators in both colonies never equaled that of widows.[51]

A few widows in Massachusetts and South Carolina earmarked their charitable bequests of intangibles for other widows. Elizabeth Cushing of Boston gave £5 to the "poor widdows," Madam Elizabeth Gerrish, who was a shopkeeper in Salem, gave £10 to the poor widows in her neighborhood, and Mary Combassye of South Carolina, after leaving a yearly legacy of £30 to the minister of the Parish of St. John, ordered that her entire estate be sold and the money used to "support and maintain the widows of the ministers of the Church of England in the several parishes of the province."[52] These bequests were rare, but they point up the fact that poor widows were a visible and vexing problem throughout the colonies. Widows well understood two ideological pillars underlying their communities: women alone in a society built on the male-headed household were especially vulnerable; and men, who had more alternatives for economic survival than women, were expected to exhaust those means before turning to charity. Reflecting the reciprocal nature of community obligations, much as neighbors helped needy widows, widows helped needy neighbors. More important, they stepped in to create a gendered support network.

By acting as agents of charity, widows, through their generosity, "eased the costs and consequences" of a poor-relief strategy that at best worked inefficiently, but, unlike nineteenth-century benevolence, it did not provide them with explicit formal power.[53] Ideology suggested that danger lurked even in the most benevolent corners. On the one hand, widows' fortunes were not to be "assign'd to vanity and excess" but instead were to be used for charity and alms giving. Frequently, such charitable activities were associated with the maternal role: "She may be a mother when she ceases to bear; and tho she no more increase one family, she may support many."[54] A widow was once again fulfilling her responsibilities as a wife by caring for the needy "children" of the community. The maternal aspects of a widow's entrance into the wider community made such public activities more palatable to that community, but especially to the male elite. On the other hand, because widows had to account to no one for either their activities or their possessions,[55] what limited their power within the community? Prescriptive literature played a key role here. For example, Thomas Fuller chastised a widow who gave so much to the poore that she "neglect[ed] those at home." In that case, she carried the power of her purse to extremes.[56] Widows walked a fine line between private and public; when a widow's feminine and masculine responsibilities clashed, the feminine gave way. If a widow began looking out for the welfare of the wider community to the neglect of her own family, she was expected to return to the rules that governed her duties as a "father." I analyzed such duties to the household in a previous chapter, but it is worth reiterating that men provided for their families; not only did society expect as much, but "a man felt a unique obligation" do so.[57]

Despite such constraints, widows who left charitable bequests were not alone in living up to their civic responsibilities. Sometimes the altruistic nature of widows' activities hid their tangible place in the community, yet, in life as in death, their activities in the neighborhood often became the crucible where ideology and reality met. For example, in 1662, Anne Gillam's four female neighbors testified about her recent absences from public meeting. Ministers expected widows to be "constant and diligent" attendees at the meetinghouse, and when they were not, ministers expected clear explanations for their absence. In this case, Gillam's neighbors pointed out that she was sick and weak and that her family had "extreame need of her at home." More important, they added that "she was very helpfull to us in times of sickness and weakness . . . [and] if she should bee absent we should have great loss of her."[58] As this female network suggests, widows in the public realm were important to all other women, not only those who were poorer and younger than they were.

Widows' wills provide added evidence of a female network in the community. While not explicitly performing acts of charity, widows across the colonies looked after neighborhood women. Nearly 20 percent of Suffolk County widows and nearly a quarter of South Carolina widows bequeathed various goods to other women, yet what is more interesting is the size of these networks. While almost half bequeathed to only one woman, two-thirds bequeathed to between two and ten women—and Susanna Oxenbridge (the widow of John, minister of the First Church of Boston) named fourteen other female friends and neighbors. A smaller and more intense widows' network existed within this female network: nearly a fifth gave part of their estates to other widows. While admonitions to widows to show beneficence toward their needy neighbors and the widow's eager response to those calls suggests there was an economic divide between women, it was a divide easily bridged. For example, in Boston, Sarah Harris bequeathed goods to her servants, Mary Blakely, Mary Coxcroft, and Sarah Ripley; Margaret Claxton did the same for her maid, Ann Cox, and Mary Norton for three maids; in Hadley, Mary Barnard bequeathed goods to her maid, Jane Williams, and Sarah Fenwick of Berkeley County, South Carolina, did the same for her slave, Judith.[59] It was not atypical for women to live with their female relatives or for widows to provide hospitality to other women.[60] However, this explicit female network, openly expressed and acknowledged in their wills, likely gave widows a strong sense of accomplishment, independence, and influence within the community. They found themselves in the position not of seeking support but of giving it freely and willingly to others. They used their benevolence and patronage to help other women.

Like other widows, Rebecca Amory contributed £49 to the building of a house "for the Publick Worship of God." Moreover, she agreed to help support the ministry and to give the land on which the church would stand in common to the Proprietors and their successors. What made this "gift" unique is that, in return, the church granted her pew number 35.[61] Amory's was not as much a charitable donation as it was a purchase—in its dual meaning of acquiring by payment and a leverage. Between 1728 and 1743, five other widows in Suffolk County had pews in their inventories valued from £30 to £50. It is unknown if they bought the pews themselves (men did bequeath pews to their wives), but it is noteworthy that pews appeared in inventories only when they had attained a clear monetary value. Once pews became valuable possessions, they became controversial. For example, the pew in Sarah Middlecot's inventory created some heated discussion. Her son, William Payne, claimed that the administrator, Mr. Cooke, had omitted items from the inventory (thereby diminishing what each heir would receive of her quite substantial estate), including a pew he valued at £30. Mr. Cooke responded, "As for the Pew at the North Church, If the Gentlemen of that Society think Mr. Payne ought enjoy Mr. Middlecotts Pew . . . they may so do, but to put it into the Inventory of Mrs. Sarah Middlecott [*sic*] ought not to be."[62] Middlecot's heirs could sit where they (or the churchmen) wanted, but they could not claim the pew's monetary value.

However, evidence that pew ownership went beyond monetary value appeared throughout the century, particularly in a complex dispute "concerning Mr. Sheafes Right to his pew in Controversy with Mrs. Gibbs." Although specific seat assigning practices varied from colony to colony, in general the seating committee based seat assignments on criteria relevant to widows: age, wealth, reputation, marital status, community service, family connections, and gender.[63] Pews were a different matter. In assigning pews, the committee primarily considered a person's real and personal estate or subscription to the cost of the new meetinghouse. Once pews replaced seats in the meetinghouse, wives and other female relatives sat with their menfolk. In an attempt to preserve "order and decency," the elders ruled that pews could neither be transferred or nor sold without official permission. Individuals generally abided by the rules and tried to maintain harmony. For example, the widow Rebecca Flavel of Charleston, South Carolina, perhaps to forestall turmoil among her heirs, demanded that her pew in the Church of St. Philips be "reserved for the use of my family and not sold." People unhappy with their assignments had several options: they could convince the committee to reassign them; a husband, like the merchant Thomas Banister, could skirt the rules by bequeathing his pews to his wife so that *she* could "Order who shall set with her in it"; or they could simply sit where they wanted. When all these failed, disgruntled church members took their disputes to the committee, as did Mr. Sheafe.[64]

The "Mr. Sheafe" in question was Sampson Sheafe, and "Mrs. Gibbs" was his niece Mary Gibbs, widow of Robert Gibbs Jr., who died in 1703. Like others, this dispute involved issues of status within the neighborhood. More significant, however, it revealed widows' role in the creation of the community's public memory. As research suggests, memory is power not only because it reflects a shared ideology of the neighborhood's quotidian life but also because those who control memory control that ideology.[65] In 1719, six women—three of them prominent widows—and two men recounted their understanding of who had the right to the pew in question. Perhaps the most prominent of the widows to testify was Madam Katherine Winthrop, whom we met in chapter 1. In this instance, she "remember[ed] the pew being Mrs. Thatchers" (Widow Margaret Sheafe Thatcher, Sampson Sheafe's mother-in-law). According to Winthrop, after Mrs. Thatcher's death, in 1694 (twenty-five years earlier), the pew was given to Sampson Sheafe.[66] She also remembered, "Mr. Corwin and wife [Margaret Thatcher's other daughter, Elizabeth Sheafe Gibbs Corwin] were gon to Salem before Mr. Sheafe had the pew and that whenever Mr. Corwin or family came to town that they never Satt in the sd pew." She hints that rights to sitting in the pew should have fallen next not to Mary Gibbs but to Elizabeth Corwin, who was married to a wealthy New England merchant and judge.[67] Theory suggests that people mobilize memory when they are threatened by the passage of time or by social changes. The widow Winthrop likely reflected communal fears that social conventions would be subverted unless the pew passed to Elizabeth Corwin. Then she eased those fears by testifying that the Corwins had exhibited no interest in the pew, and thus it became acceptable for Mary Gibbs to sit there. More important, she "heard by sundry persons" that Mr. Sheafe had invited Robert Gibbs Jr. and his wife, Mary, "into the Pew." That she relied on the stories of many different people reveals how individual memories are intimately linked to a collective memory of the community—and she played a crucial role in that memory by assuming a crucial role in garnering the facts and exerting her power within the community.

The widow Miriam Tyler also remembered key events, specifically the "sitting up of the pew" and Mr. Sheafe's purchase of it for £20. Mrs. [Mary] Gibbs told her that "she satt there upon curtisie and that it was Mr. Sheafes pew." The widow Mary Alden, who lived with Doctor Nathaniel Williams, claimed to know Mrs. Gibbs "at the time" she "was first married" (in 1692—her memory went even further back than did the widow Winthrop's) and stated that she had *heard* Robert and Mary Gibbs claim that the Sheafes gave them "leave to sett in there pew." As with the widow Winthrop, the widow Alden's testimony uncovered key relationships among people in the community, relationships that constructed the way events were recounted. Her statements also reveal how certain emotional events—in this case, the marriage of Mrs. Gibbs—took on particular significance for the community. As with the widow Winthrop, the widow Alden exerted her power within the community. Of the two men who testified, one simply "saith the same" as the widow Winthrop, and the other merely remembered "the fitting up said Pew."[68] Ultimately, the committee determined that it was Mr. Sheaf's pew. While he triumphed in this case, three prominent widows contributed a public voice, a voice that shaped neighborhood values. They may have selectively told stories of the community, but their particular accounts of the past circulated in public among family, friends, and neighbors.

The last example, and perhaps the most noteworthy example, of the public recognition of widows' place in the community arose in a more formal venue. On August 5, 1715, the Salem selectmen granted the widow Elizabeth Mackway a license to sell beer, cider, and ale "in Consideration of her keeping a victualling house for Entertainment of Strangers and others." On the surface, this action does not seem worthy of note in a discussion of widows and the neighborhood community, for the selectmen regularly granted such licenses to widows. However, another decision made by the selectmen reveals the significance of their action. In response to the continuing danger the town faced from the many sick and infectious people leaving Boston for Salem, they appointed people to investigate such "strangers" and established a house for "the Entertainment" of them. To this end, they authorized the town treasurer to pay the widow Ashley for the "use of her house for the Sick of the Small pox the last Winter."[69] While most historians assume the private realm to be irrelevant to politics, faced with threats to the colonial community, commonplace domestic duties took on new meanings and revealed that widows' private actions had public consequences. The minister Jared Eliot publicly praised widows for lodging strangers and relieving the afflicted, much as Salem widows Mackway and Ashly did during the smallpox epidemic in Massachusetts.[70] The civic polity under discussion here reflects widows' roles in neighborhood writ larger. Widows who entertained strangers or used their house for the sick performed services for the town, which defined them as citizens and thereby signified their important position within the community.[71]

The traditional definition of citizenship entails a wide range of civic obligations, such as patriotic loyalty, economic independence, the payment of taxes, and service to the community, usually through jury duty, office holding, or military duty. It also involves claims of certain rights, particularly the right to vote. Historians have argued that, in early America, these rights and responsibilities belonged to men because women, most of whom were wives, were loyal to and coerced by their husbands—that is, they were not free agents and thus owed no obligation to and received no rights from the polity. However, these gendered definitions of citizenship changed subtly but significantly when a married woman became a widow and assumed the traditional male role as governor over the family and its real and personal property. As Daniel Defoe's eponymous Roxana claimed, "while a Woman was single, she was a Masculine in her politick Capacity . . . [;] she was a Man in her separated Capacity, . . . and was In Subjection to none." In many towns, widows owned land shares that often had rights and responsibilities attached to them.[72] Indeed, in 1636, the Salem selectmen gave freeman land grants to the widows Mason, More, Felton, Skarlet, and Higginson, and they admitted the widow Keniston as an inhabitant.[73] Moreover, when the town's marshland was divided among the heads of households in Salem, ten widows were given their proportionate share.[74] Widows also paid taxes and contributed their share to maintaining the highways. Between 1718 and 1750, at least twenty-three widows contributed time, money, goods, or teams—and many of them did so repeatedly. For example, the widow Hannah Pickering was paid for wintering the town bull for two years. Perhaps the most consistent contributor to the welfare of her community was the widow Ginger Andrews, who contributed eight days and her team for two days and a hand for two days in 1730; one day and her team for half a day in 1743; four days and her team for two days in 1745; and one day and a hand for half a day and her team for four days in 1748.[75] Even operating a "public house of Entertainment" could take on broader civil significance, as the Salem selectmen revealed when they granted the widow Sarah Ellis a license to do so because they "judge[d] it needful at this time, the Widdow Dean & Widow Beadle having both laid down."[76] These actions made widows at least partial participants in the polity in the traditional sense.

Although Winthrop's ideal polity was rarely achieved, aspects of his beliefs appear throughout the colonial era. While, as I argued earlier, the maternal aspects of a widow's entrance into the wider community made such public activities more palatable, the focus on helping the poor was more than a reflection of individual good works or women's traditional domestic duties; it was a public responsibility which was "profoundly local." There were almshouses in Salem, but it was usually cheaper for the community and a more effective way of maintaining the ideal social order if the poor were supported in other ways.[77] A widow who assumed that duty without overburdening the local treasury or the church coffers fulfilled a significant civic responsibility for the community.

Concrete evidence of this responsibility to the community, of widows' freely chosen obligations to the public good, can be seen in the Salem town records between 1634 and 1750. In at least seventy distinct instances, the selectmen of Salem made agreements with widows and granted them payment from the town treasury for caring for others in the community—and they often continued such agreements and disbursements of the public funds for many years. This is the key here—the act of discussing, planning, and contracting highlights the public authority they could exert. Although these widows cared for both men and women, they were much more likely to care for children and other women, reflecting the gendering of community roles. For example, in 1713, the selectmen ordered that town funds be given to the widow Henfield for "keeping ye Widdow Wadling," in 1718 to the widow Lockyer for "keeping" Mary Elson, in 1721 to the widow Procter for "keeping a poor child," and in 1724 to the widow Elizabeth Frost "to keep the Wido Bethia Peters at her house for the space of one year . . . [and] she to find her with all needful meat drink lodging fireing and attendance." In 1725, the selectmen ordered that the widow Simson, "being ailing and very weak [and] she remaining in ye Alms House under ye Nursery of the Widow Chanterlin and she to provide all." In 1732, they paid the widow Elizabeth Wilson for keeping Abigail Burch; in 1746, the selectmen dispersed funds to the widow Silsby "for attendance on the Widow Small"; in 1746, they paid the widow Driver for "keeping the Widow Silver and her Daughter"; and in 1747, they paid the widow Jean Flint for "nursing the Widow Franks when sick of ye Smallpox" and for keeping John White "when sick ye same distemper."[78] Not only did such widows perform an important civic responsibility to the community by agreeing with the selectmen to provide for their needy neighbors, but they created female support networks whose importance was officially recognized time and time again in the public ritual of the selectmen's meetings.

To claim that definitions of communal responsibility and citizenship were gendered in early America is not to say that widows had no role within the realm beyond the household. Indeed, they assumed both rights and responsibilities of citizenship, in various guises. On one side of the equation, widows like Mary Smith, Alice Thomas, and Martha Cogan visibly and ardently demanded of the leaders the rights they assumed to be theirs as citizen of their local community, to be recipients of the public good through their petitions. On the other side of the equation, widows like Hannah Harris, Rebecca Amory, and Katherine Winthrop openly, willingly, and publicly negotiated with the leaders of the town in order to fulfill their obligations. They helped the ministers and the selectmen provide for the public good, especially a female public good, by being supportive neighbors and generous testators. Widows did not play the same role within civil society as men did, but, both informally and formally, they contributed a powerful female voice to the discussion of how to sustain the life of the community and its individual members, and they helped bring those discussions forward as interests for public action as they merged a domestic culture with a civic culture.

Widows took their experiences with the civic community in the world of the marketplace. Embracing their masculine responsibilities as heads of household, they actively pursued overlapping and increasingly public strategies for ensuring their own, their families', and their female neighbors' economic survival. They opened shops, they borrowed and loaned money, and they rented, bought, sold, and bequeathed goods or property. In the process, they created new identifies as influential, even powerful, businesswomen and shaped the world of money and commerce in ambiguously gendered ways.

5

"Through Industry and Care Acquired Some Estate of My Own . . . Much Advanced the Same"

Widows in the Economic Community

In her will, proved October 13, 1742, Benedicta Netmaker bequeathed her estate to six female friends, including Anna Wroe, the daughter of her "much Esteemed Friend Mrs. Magdalen Wroe," whom she named as one of the executors. Wroe also had two sons, both of whom Netmaker ignored both in her will. Just three days later, Magdalen Wroe's executors proved her will, in which she named Benedicta Netmaker as the executor of her estate. Coincidentally, earlier that same year, the widows had written their wills less than a month apart.[1] Or was it coincidental? The sources that would answer that question do not exist, but it appears they made a pact to look after each other's estates, for the close relationship between these two widows had begun decades earlier. As shopkeepers in Boston, they supported themselves, each other, and other women in the community.

On April 28, 1735, Magdalen Wroe advertised for sale "fine Florence Oyl, all sorts of Cambricks, Tea, Coffee, Chocolate, and all sorts of Grocerys." Her shop was "at her House adjoying to Dr. Gibbon's House." In November, she increased her stock, selling lace, "all sorts of Fringes, best and most fashionable" ribbons, children's caps, material "for Head Dressing, Fans, Gloves, Patches, and other Millinary Wares." As a good businesswoman, she enticed customers into her shop with the simple phrase "All at a Reasonable Rate." Two years later, she imported from London a more complex array of luxury goods, including gold and silver lace, "new fashion ribbons," "best double glaz'd Stamp Gloves," superfine thread hose, "newest fashion stone necklaces with Lockets & Solitares set in Silver," "new Fashion best French Necklaces and Earings, best brocaded Gawze Handkerchiefs," "rich new fashion'd Silver Ribbons and Girdles," and "best London pins." She advertised these items for sale several times between May and November.[2] In April 1741, she once again advertised more prosaic but essential groceries and household goods, adding that she would sell them at "either at Wholesale or Retail at reasonable Rates," which suggests a growing business adventure. At the same, she also announced that she had moved her shop to "the three Sugar Loaves and Cannister in King-street." King Street, lined with wharves, merchants' warehouses, taverns, lawyer's offices, a dancing master, shoemakers, goldsmiths, bakers, barbers, wigmakers, and various other retailers, buzzed with economic activity. This new location would bring in more customers. After announcing her new location, she listed goods "To be Sold at the same Place by Mrs. Netmaker, Imported in the last ships from London."

Benedicta Netmaker had been advertising goods for sale since 1738, and the two women shared a shop long before 1741. Like Wroe's, Netmaker's shop was initially "next door to Dr. Gibbons." She, too, imported luxury goods, including goods that sounded remarkably similar to those offered by her friend: "rich Silver and gold Ribbons and Girdles, Silver and Gold Lace," a "variety of new Fashion Fringes," gloves, "fine Stone Necklaces, . . . Earings and Pendants of the newest Fashion, fine Stone Girdle Buckels, French Sizars, best London Pins, Needles and Patches, Artificial Flowers." In 1739, she advertised a similar list of items that would "be sold by Mrs. Netmaker at Mrs. Wroe's"—two years before Wroe announced that they shared a business address. Moreover, in early 1741, like Magdalen Wroe, she proclaimed that her goods were "to be sold . . . at the Three Sugar Loaves and Cannister in King Street near the Town House Boston."[3]

In a path-breaking book exploring domestic in preindustrial America, the historian Jeanne Boydston analyzes a conceptual shift regarding work that began in the early eighteenth century. She argues that, as men's wage earning became more important in the market economy, the value of women's work diminished; as colonists valorized male economic agency, they divorced women's work from the "real economy"; as "incursions of cash relations" encouraged individual gain, focus on the community declined.[4] However, as the title of this chapter and the deep and ongoing relationship between Wroe and Netmaker suggests, widows (unlike the wives Boydston analyzed) created an important place for themselves in the economic life of the community *and* in the wider market. These women embraced old and new economic values, assumed male and female economic agency, and pursued individual and communal economic goals.

The deaths of their husbands, unexpected or not, brought widows face to face with the reality of being financially on their own and needing to provide for their family on a daily basis. Widows in the countryside, in small towns, and in large urban cities assumed the role of provider, as their husbands had done. Because there were few guiding principles about this aspect of their lives, widows stepped cautiously further into the public realm. They took with them their household, legal, and communal experiences, as well as the lessons about the behavior of proper widows taught to them by prescriptive literature. As they transformed customarily noneconomic sites into a source of financial survival, as they entered the market economy of money and credit, as they put their reputations on the line, widows created another new identity. Using their rights and responsibilities as both male and female, widows pursued a variety of overlapping and increasingly public strategies to ensure, if not success, at least their survival and the survival of other widows around them. These activities in the economic community extended beyond shopkeeping or tavern keeping to selling their husbands' estate, bequeathing and being bequeathed goods, renting and selling property, and lending and borrowing money. Widows' involvement in the economic community[5] brought the ambiguity of assuming male and female roles full circle.

Advice book authors and ministers infrequently addressed the issue of women's economic roles outside the household simply because they could not ideologically conceive of this reality—despite the evidence all around them.[6] However, two eighteenth-century works did address widows in the marketplace and highlighted their ambiguous gender roles in the economy: Daniel Defoe's manual *The Complete English Tradesman* and Susannah Centlivre's play *The Basset-Table.*

Through sayings, amusing anecdotes, and constructed dialogues, Defoe advised men on how to be wise and profitable mechanics. As he glorified trade, Defoe advised men to teach their wives how to run the shop, keep the books, and treat customers. By implication, a wife who understood her husband's business not only would be a valuable helpmeet but would also be able to carry on after his death. In acknowledging that women could take on male responsibilities, Defoe directed some of his sharpest criticism and utmost esteem at tradesmen's widows. While he was sympathetic to their plight, Defoe also sternly chastised the widow who did not make "the best of things that are left her, or to preserve herself from being cheated, and being imposed upon." He argued that "weak and foolish" widows get what they deserve: nothing. By contrast, he valorized widows who thought "fit to rouse up themselves to their own relief," claiming that they "are not so helpless and shiftless creatures as some would make them appear in the world; and we see whole families in trade frequently recovered by their industry." This was high praise, indeed, but, for those widows who might not have gotten the point, he ended his discourse with this warning: the necessity of running a shop "will humble the minds of those whom nothing else could make to stoop; and where it does not, it is a defect of the understanding, as well as of prudence, and must reflect upon the senses as well as the morals of the person."[7] Only sensible, well-behaved, and hard-working widows could protect their reputations.

A widow's economic reputation was at stake as well for Susannah Centlivre. However, she presented a different picture of the working widow, the Lady Reveller, "a Coquetish Widow, that keeps a Basset-Table."[8] The very naming of this widow is illuminating: she was a merry-maker, a flirt, and a gambler. Any one of these roles would make her suspect; the three combined doomed her to failure, as four key moments in the play make clear. The first comes at the beginning with a visit from her uncle at 4:00 a.m. In the eighteenth century, gaming became fashionable, and Lady Reveller has been working hard all night. He complains that "your Apartment is a Parade for Men of all Ranks, from the Duke to the Fidler" and he implores her to "give over, for Shame, and marry." She defiantly establishes herself as a self-sufficient and independent widow when she replies, "I'm resolv'd to follow my own Inclinations." At the second critical moment, her "sober" friend, Lady Lucy, warns the Lady that if every woman followed her example, "the Order of Nature would be inverted, and every Good design'd by Heaven, become a Curse; Health and Plenty no longer would be known among us." In the third, to the turn the world right side up and put Reveller back on the right path, Sir James Courting sexually accosts her. An intriguing conversation between the two reflects gendered concepts of money. She implores, "how has my Carriage drawn this Curse upon me?" He rhetorically asks, "Can a Lady that . . . takes as much Pains to draw Men in to lose their Money . . . boast of innate Virtue?" He then triumphantly exclaims, "we never part with our Money without Design." Finally, in the fourth critical moment, Lord Worthy redeems this working widow when he proposes marriage—which she readily accepts, crying, I "hate myself for all my Folly."

Any widow who had both works on her bookshelf—or had read both—would clearly understand the options available to her. But was the tension between two competing ideologies and the realities of widows' lives that easily resolved? Ann Pollard of Boston proudly declared, "the Estate left by my said Husband is Considerably Advanced and bettered by the Disbursements, I have made thereon, and . . . payd for out of my own proper gettings by my Labour and Industry." Other widows noted they had "gotten and Acquired" landed and personal estates since their husbands' deaths through their own "hard and difficult" endeavors.[9] That diligence is evident in their wills. Nearly 10 percent of all widows in Massachusetts and 2 percent in Maryland bequeathed a shop, and nearly 5.5 percent of South Carolina widows identified in some fashion as shopkeepers. Newspaper advertisements from the *Boston Gazette* and the *Boston News-Letter* reveal a much higher number of widowed shopkeepers: between 1711 and 1750, ninety different widows advertised a wide range of goods and services for sale. Likewise, between 1732 and 1750, thirty-eight widows did so in the *South Carolina Gazette*. These shopkeepers attest to the influence of Daniel Defoe's advice—and reflect a powerful female agency in the pursuit of economic gain.

In 1720, the Bostonian Sarah Cross, who lived in "Elliston's Corner House at the lower end of Cross-Street [which, while not as economically vibrant as King Street, was lined with a number of taverns, inns, coffeehouses, and small shops]," announced that she kept "a Shop and Publick House." Beyond this, we know only that the selectmen approved the widow Cross as a retailer in July 1719 and that they, on January 4, 1720, licensed her to sell strong drink as an Innholder. The merchant Thomas Amory sold her numerous hogsheads of rum and wine between August 2, 1722, and July 27, 1724, when he simply noted, "Settled Accompts this day with Sarah Cross and the Balance due to me on her Accompt am to pass to her husband Sam[u]el Mattocks acct." She had married him on July 8, 1723. She apparently worked hard and lived quietly; that final entry in Amory's account was the last evidence of her independent economic activities. In the words of Laurel Thatcher Ulrich, "well behaved women seldom make history." This, of course, is not entirely accurate, as the growing body of work on early American female shopkeepers makes clear,[10] but most surviving documents, especially court documents, focus on women who crossed the line between respectable and disreputable economic activities, as did the Lady Reveller.

In her petition to the Massachusetts General Court for a license "to sell "wines & some other Liquors out of doors, to Accommodate strong & Seafaring men," the widow Elizabeth Hall noted first that she was impoverished by her husband's sudden death in Jamaica and was caring for five children; then she assured the magistrates that she sought "all Lawfull & honest means for the procuring & providing a competent maintenance." Widows frequently ran inns or taverns to the approbation of the community.[11] However, when that same community deemed a widow's behavior questionable, it swiftly rescinded its approval. For example, Alice Thomas, whom we met in the previous chapter diffidently seeking help from the magistrates, less carefully constructed an identity as a shopkeeper and innholder.[12] Before her husband's death, in 1662, Thomas ran a coffee or cook shop. The brewhouse left her by her husband led to Thomas's troubles, and not just because of the many debts he also left her. In January 1672, Suffolk County magistrates convicted Edward Naylor of frequenting the widow Alice Thomas's "bawdy house," convicted Mary Moor and several other women of fornication, and convicted and imprisoned Thomas for the "shameful" crimes of abetting a burglary, of "giving frequent secret and unseasonable Entertainm[en]t in her house to Lewd Lascivious & notorious persons of both Sexes, giving them oppertunity to commit carnall wickedness," of selling wine and liquor without a license, and of "profanation of ye Lord's day." In addition to imprisonment, the court sentenced her to "stand [on the gallows] one hour with a rope about her necke, one end fastened to ye sd Gallowes," and "alsoe to be carried from the prison to her one [own] house and brought out of the gate strip't to the waste, & there tyed to a Cart's Taile, and soe to be whip't [thirty-nine times] through ye Streete to the prison."

Six months after Thomas's harsh public punishment, in response to what they deemed an alarming number of "Stews, whore-House[s], or Brothel House[s]," the magistrates enacted a law establishing the same punishment for all like crimes. In the same month, the court granted Thomas liberty during the daylight hours and then her complete freedom in exchange for her leaving Boston. On October 15, Thomas petitioned the General Court for permission to return to Boston. According to her, the injunction was "very much to her damage and inconvenience" since she was unable to improve her house and she was "exposed to many inconvenient and uncomfortable journeys over the water." Because the magistrates prohibited Thomas from selling or renting her "living in Boston," she claimed she was unable to support herself or to pay her debts.

Such an appeal to self-support normally would have been enough to move the court to rescind its banishment.[13] However, the magistrates did not allow Alice Thomas to return to Boston for another three years. The male authorities and Thomas perceived her role as an economic provider markedly different, but they apparently reached an accommodation because after her return she seems to have become a well-behaved, hardworking member of the Boston community. When she died, in 1697, she left an estate valued just over £863, which she divided among two daughters, two sons-in-law, seven grandsons, and eleven granddaughters. Despite her generosity, a widow who provided for herself and her family in a troublesome manner represented a potential economic threat to the community. Alice Thomas was not a unique example.

In 1677, the Suffolk County Court fined Abigail King for "entertaining Strangers" and admonished her "not to entertain any lodgers in her house without" approval of the selectmen.[14] The court expressed concerns that were even more clearly stated in its charges against Elizabeth George.[15] On October 29, 1678, the court convicted and fined George for selling "Strong drinke without licence." The magistrates had renewed her license for the previous two years but declared that the license had allowed her only to "keepe a house of publique Entertainment & to Sell wine beere & Sider." What happened in those two years? On April 30 and July 30, 1678, Charles Lidgett and Edward Pegge, respectively, were presented for "being unseasonably at the house of Widdow George Ordinary Keeper." Although the magistrates did not bring charges of sexual misconduct against the men or against George, clearly they believed the three had behaved inappropriately. To punish the widow George for overstepping her bounds, the magistrates revoked her license. Nonetheless, she continued the business (even though the court imposed numerous fines on her) because she needed to support herself and her family. She was, if nothing else, a hardworking widow, but she also proved to be a weak and foolish widow. Although many married women ran inns and taverns, so-called public houses, with their husbands, they were predominantly male gathering places where men could avoid communal restraint. Widows who inhabited this male-dominated and disreputable space faced suspicions of unsuitable, likely sexual, conduct.

These concerns were not necessarily unfounded. The Hampshire County Court presented the widow Kellum of Enfield, Massachusetts, for "Lascivious carriages in that she was found . . . under the bed cloathes with a man who was a Stranger." The Suffolk County Court charged Sarah

Buckminster of Suffolk County with fornication and with having a bastard child. The Maryland General Court presented Susanna Dunn of Charles County, Maryland, for living "as man and wife" with Philip Carey for two years, as well as for having a bastard child. These incidents might not have occurred in taverns (the records do not say), but they do suggest the social and economic consequences of widows' inability to support themselves. The case of the widow Hannah Hownsell makes the point more clearly. In 1683, the Suffolk County Court charged the "poore distressed" widow with fornication. In trying to defend herself, Hownsell explained her plight and asked the magistrates to consider "the Povertye of Me." She had "Nothing to live on butt What I Gitt by hard Labor." Sometimes working diligently was not enough; some widows who could find no other way to support themselves and their family stooped to prostitution. Unmoved, the court ordered Hounsell whipped and placed "into some good Family where shee may bee under Government."[16]

Widows revealed little of their tavern-keeping activities in their wills; in fact, only six Suffolk County widows (and none in any other county in Massachusetts, Maryland, or South Carolina) indicated that they operated taverns. Perhaps it was because, as the evidence suggests, "taverns were the headquarters of the classic lower-class vices—cursing, fighting, lewdness and drunkenness."[17] What widow, "Being weak of body but firm of mind and memory,"[18] desired to be remembered the way Alice Thomas and Elizabeth George were? Yet, clearly some did, for historians tell us that those numbers grossly underrepresented the number of reputable widowed tavernkeepers. Moreover, advertisements from South Carolina reveal that even though tavern keeping remained a suspect way for widows to earn a living, they found a way around the dilemma. Mary Bedon addressed her business to "Gentlemen that will be so kind as to be Customers." She assured them that they would "meet with the best Reception and Entertainment in her Power." Several years later, Anne Shepard declared "those that please to favour her with their Custom may depend on having the best entertainment and the civilest Usage from Their most humble Servant." In an intriguing note, she declared that, "in order to have the best of every thing to furnish my Guests, as reasonable as possible, I am determined to deal for ready Money only."[19] These widows constructed their establishments and themselves as orderly and respectable by aiming their advertisements at "gentlemen," by calling their services and their behavior "the best," and by conflating the domestic and public—again, acting as male and female.

The wealthy and much-respected widow Rebecca Holmes owned and operated the Bunch of Grapes in Boston for ten years. Advertisements by Massachusetts officials in the *Gazette* constructed her tavern as sanctioned by the government: they [re]presented it as the place at which the Collector of the Excise demanded "innholders and Retailers" pay their "half Years Excise" and then, two years later, as the location for "the Commissioners appointed to Receive and Examine the Creditors Claims . . . Represented Insolvent."[20] The boundaries between the domestic and the public became blurred as Holmes's tavern served an economic, social, and political function. In a similar fashion, the widow Peach of Charleston, South Carolina, advertised the multiple uses of her tavern: she sold shop space it in, she sold goods from it herself, and, more significant, she (and not colonial officials) publicly constructed it as both domestic and commercial space when she advertised a "choice and curious collection of pictures" from "her house, the New Tavern on the Bay." Ultimately, Defoe's valorized widow took center stage.

Another strategy widows employed for economic survival was their testamentary power. Here they embraced individual *and* communal economic values; they controlled cash and consumer goods, items that suggested that they actively participated in the market economy, but through their bequests they ensured not their own survival but that of other women. Historians argue that early modern English widows bequeathed their property (sometimes real property, but more generally personal property) to nonkin much more often than did men. It may be that, as heads of households, those men had already provided for their children in their wills, leaving widows, particularly older widows, free from such parental responsibility.[21] As I demonstrated in the previous chapter, in the colonial American context, widows, like men, assumed and carried out their testamentary duties as household heads. Yet, some widows' bequests, unlike men's, did encompass a wide array of legatees. For example, in 1654, the widow Rachel Bigg of Dorchester, Massachusetts, named thirty-two heirs in her will—fifteen females and seventeen males. She disposed of her estate among immediate family, distant relatives, the poor, a minister, and, more important, eight women who were not kin. Similarly, in 1745, Rebecca Flavel of Charlestown, South Carolina named fourteen heirs and of that number, eight were female nonkin.[22] Most of these bequests consisted of personal property. Like men, widows tended to bequeath real property to their immediate kin, recognizing that land was key to establishing their children's and grandchildren's security. Nevertheless, that did not diminish the significance of other bequests. Indeed, some historians argue that previous "androcentric" studies place too little value on the personal property that widows bequeathed and too much value on "male land." Widows' bequests of household goods and slaves to friends, neighbors, and near kin reveal another avenue by which they extended their economic power among community, becoming increasingly less concerned with land and more concerned with commercial capitalism.[23]

Where paired gender differences could be determined—sisters/brothers, nieces/nephews, female nonkin/male nonkin, and female servants/male servants—widows everywhere and at all times primarily gave their household goods to other women. Gifts of household goods often consisted of a silver bowl, a pair of sheets, or a kitchen utensil. As such, these gifts could be seen as merely simple gestures. Nonetheless, even if only symbolically important, they acknowledged an earlier kindness, rewarded some attention given to the widow, or visibly demonstrated a friendship. Yet, these bequests were not trivial and suggested that widows understood them as one strategy women employed to survive financially. Widows understood that, as female property, household items enabled women to run their homes more efficiently and more effectively. Moreover, these bequests created strong female networks beyond the family, since many recipients were not relatives. In a concrete way, widows repaid those who had helped them in times of need, and they sought to help others in their times of need. Because the contents of wills were often public knowledge even before the testator died, such bequests could cement ongoing networks or educate others about the proper way for widows to look after friends and neighbors.

An equally, if not more, significant bequest made by widows was of slaves. Throughout the colonial era, widows bequeathed slaves to immediate family members in rural colonies significantly more frequently than did those in urban areas. Maryland widows largely bequeathed slaves to sisters, brothers, nieces, and nephews (only 7 percent left any to nonkin), indicating that they believed slaves were critical to the survival of family farms or plantations. Not surprisingly, few Massachusetts widows bequeathed slaves. Yet, the advertisements in urban newspaper suggested slaves were important to city dwellers. The mere number of these advertisements indicated that widows understood slaves as a significant source of income for themselves. However, the wording of the advertisements also revealed that they believed slaves could make another woman's domestic life easier or could assist her in running a shop or tavern. Between 1706 and 1750, twenty-eight widows advertised slaves for sale in the *Boston Gazette* and the *Boston News-Letter*. For example, Rebecca Amory advertised, "A Likely Negro Man born in the country and bred a Farmer, fit for any Service;" the widow Bond advertised "a very likely Negro Woman . . . fit for any family business;" and the widow Lydia Vial advertised a "negro used to the Business of a Baker."[24]

Like widows in Massachusetts, widows in South Carolina perceived slaves as a form of female property, bequeathing them to sisters twice as often as brothers, nieces four times as often as nephews, and female nonkin three times as often as male nonkin. Moreover, not all bequests of slaves were linked to the land.[25] South Carolinians relied heavily on slaves to run the household or used them as skilled laborers. Also like widows in Massachusetts, southern widows frequently sold or rented out slaves. Slaves provided not only a ready source of cash but also, as I will explore a bit later, an entrée into the lucrative debt network. Twenty deeds of sale in which a widow sold varying numbers of slaves entered the probate records between 1720 and 1750. The widow Magdalen Evans of Berkeley County sold nine slaves for £1,000; Mary Lesur of Berkeley County bought a slave for £200 in April 1744 and a year later sold that same slave for £300, thereby making a 50 percent profit in twelve months. In addition, between 1732 and 1750, fifty-one widows advertised slaves for sale in the *South Carolina Gazette*—either as "a parcel" (the widow Martha Sillevant advertised "23 choice Negro Slaves") or as individuals suited to leather dressing, gunsmithing, butchering, cooking, cleaning, needlework, or washing. Elizabeth Hawkins of Charlestown sold Benjamin Perry and Ralph Taylor, Charleston merchants, three slaves for £400.[26]

At the time that networks and communities began to flourish not only in Massachusetts but in Maryland and South Carolina as well, conduct-book writers and ministers told widows that, although their primary responsibility was to their children and grandchildren, it was still their responsibility to "support many" beyond their immediate family.[27] Colonial widows used the various forms of personal wealth, especially household goods and slaves, at their disposal to secure the well-being of female friends and neighbors. Widows' determination to look after other women reflects a genuine concern with women's needs and a desire to respond to those needs, particularly in time of economic stress.

. . .

Beyond running a shop and bequeathing their personal property, widows pursued yet another seemingly mundane strategy for economic survival—selling or renting their estates, which took them visibly and decisively into the wider market of individual gain. Elaine Forman Crane claimed that widows' petitions for permission to sell their realty—which "increased dramatically" in number after 1720—revealed a profound poverty among widows.[28] This was true in part, but her argument reflects the legal documents she used; exploring colonial newspapers north and south suggests another interpretation. Sarah Lloyd placed the following announcement in the *South Carolina Gazette*:

> TO BE SOLD at publick Sale . . . , the House and back Houses wherein I now live, also the Wharff that lies before the said House, And some good House-Wenches; . . . If any Person is inclinable to Purchase . . . [these items] before the Time mentioned, they may agree with me at the said House. The Conditions of the Sale may be known of me at anytime.[29]

Although it is unclear how much land the widow Lloyd had for sale, her statement that interested parties could learn the conditions of the sale from her suggests that she knew very well the value of the estate and how to sell it—and her advertisement was not usual. A look at the *South Carolina Gazette* reveals thirty-two widows who sold land and large town lots. The amount of land they sold ranged from 44 acres to 2,860 acres; only three widows advertised lots smaller than two hundred acres; and the average size was 564.5 acres. Four widows sold two lots totaling 662, 2,100, 1,034, and 1,500 acres; one sold three properties totaling 1,324 acres; and one sold four lots totaling 1,350 acres. Widows with that much land might not have wanted to take on the burden running a plantation, but they were not "needy." They participated in a booming market that saw land prices increase "nearly 1 percent per year" between 1724 and 1750. According to economic historians, "These long-run gains proved land to have been a better investment than slaves, whose prices spiked upward only at the end of the colonial period."[30] In addition, thirty widows sold houses, and nine sold town lots. In addition to attempting to sell nine hundred acres of plantation land, Elizabeth Hill also advertised a "very commodious new Cypress-house, well finish'd with a handsome large Hall & four rooms on a floor, each a Chimney, very good under ground Offices and Pump, also a pleasant Garden, the Land well fenc'd in." If that were not enough, several months later she attempted to rent out "Hillburrough, containing about 300 Acres (under good Fence) of which about 200 Acres is excellent Pasture, pleasantly and advantageously situated about 4 miles from Charlestown, having a convenient landing place [on the Ashley River], dwelling house and other Out-houses, with a good Orchard." Sarah Lloyd similarly put her estate to good use by renting out rooms.[31] In all, twenty widows rented out houses, three rented out rooms, four rented out plantations, and five rented out business enterprises—two taverns, a wharf, a tanyard, and a bridge. They chose not to or could not afford to carry on their husbands' businesses, but they found a way to profit from them, nonetheless. In fact, cash often proved more valuable than real property; in the new market economy, money provided widows with freedom and flexibility.

Enterprising widows in Boston similarly demonstrated command of both the urban and the rural economies; they knew how to phrase their advertisements to their advantage. For example, the widow Abigail Bart advertised "a Farm lying in the West Part of Woburn about two Miles from the Meeting House, and nine Miles from Charlestown Ferry, has on it two Dwelling Houses, two Barns, several Orchards." She then astutely noted that the orchard "in a good Year" produced "100 Barrels of Cyder" and that her meadow land was "well Wooded, and well watered at all seasons, and a good Soil both for Grain and Grass." The widow Elizabeth Porter advertised "A Certain Tract of Land [in Salem Village], containing about 200 Acres, well wooded and water'd with a Brook fit for a Saw or Grist Mill, good Meadow and other accommodations fit for a Farmer." All interested parties were to "inquire of the said Porter, at her House in Charter-Street Boston."[32] Twenty-seven widows sold houses with land attached. In addition, two widows sold town lots, and eight widows sold land ranging from 115 to 215 acres. Only two widows rented out land. In an urban area like Boston, it should not be surprising to find Elizabeth Pitts advertising a "Dwelling House & Land and brew-house" in 1725 and Deborah Warner advertising "a Fish Warehouse, Cooper's Shop and Blacksmith Shop, with the Wharf and Land" in 1748.[33] That only one widow in the intervening twenty-three years specifically enticed potential buyers of her house by proclaiming the presence of a shop was surprising. However, eleven widows rented out houses, four with commercial space, including a still-house and two bake-houses; four widows rented out only commercial space, including a goldsmith shop, a distil-house, and a tavern. Boston widows did not want or need to permanently give up control of their real property. They saw it as more beneficial to have the security of income flowing in on a regular basis, much like widows who participated in the debt network.

Historians argue that credit—usually supplied by merchants and wealthier planters—proved crucial for the local, regional, and transatlantic economy. Despite the economic and "psychological" risks, young men willingly participated in this debt network because it enabled them to buy and develop land, to buy slaves or hire servants, to market produce, to buy goods, to buy or build houses, and to start businesses sooner than they could have if they had had to wait until they earned enough money or until a hoped-for inheritance became reality. Debts initially came in the form of book credit—a payment that substituted for currency. Book credit had two strengths: it meant that farmers and storekeepers had "intangible purchasing power" at a time when specie was in short supply, and it neither bore interest nor required payment at any particular time.[34] As beneficial as credit was, it also created tensions within the community as people came to grips with the consequences of indebtedness.

On the one hand, despite the growing market economy, debts generally remained neighborly loans and often were not repaid until the debtor died and then only if it could be determined who the creditors were and how much was owed. The lax treatment of outstanding debts implies a high level of communal trust. On the other hand, in lending or borrowing, men explicitly put themselves at the mercy of others. Accepting this mutual obligation threatened not only the loss of money but also the loss of friendship. Therefore, neighbors and creditors looked askance at a habitual indebtedness made worse by poor judgment, poor recordkeeping abilities, and poor moral fiber. Neighbors talked—perhaps whispered—about who was going bankrupt and who needed an understanding creditor.

The widespread availability of paper money after 1690 not only made money the preferred form of credit but also created new sources of credit, such as promissory notes and mortgages, that changed the nature of the debt network. Notes required debtors to repay the loan by a certain date, and these notes could be sold to a third party, usually to someone who lived outside the community. Deborah Rosen found that it was "easier for creditors to be lenient with debtors from within their own community . . . than with debtors from outside their community." Lenders demanded timely payments where there were few customary or ongoing economic relationships. When debtors could not repay the loans made to them, creditors took them to court. This was especially true in the market economy of the eighteenth century, where interactions were more likely to be impersonal than rooted in the community.

The discussion of debt thus far has focused on men; yet, as the following notice from the *South Carolina Gazette* for March 26, 1744, indicates, widows also entered "the [public] world of men's reckonings," of unpaid debts and cash relations.

> Whereas the late Printer of this Gazette hath been deprived of his Life, by an unhappy Accident I take this Opportunity of informing the Publick, that I shall continue the said Paper as usual[.] . . . Wherefore I flatter my self that all those Persons who . . . assisted my late Husband, in the Prosecution of the said Undertaking will be kindly pleased to continue their Favours and good Offices to his poor afflicted Widow with six small Children and another hourly expected.

While Elizabeth Timothy proclaimed her husband's death more elaborately and with greater pathos than most widows did, such announcements were commonplace in early American newspapers. They reveal the varied tools with which widows navigated the turbulent financial waters many faced. The lax treatment of outstanding male debts could negatively impact widows. "Because creditors often demanded payment of overdue debts only when the debtor died, in practice the real burden of household debt often fell on [them]." Friendly creditors sometimes "freely forgave the poore Widow what [was] due to" them. But widows were not passive victims. Mary Darnall of Prince George's County, Maryland, asked "that the Creditors might take the Estate, of her deceased husband, & distributing it amongst them, might pay themselves soe far as it would amount." By doing so, she took the financial burden off herself and put it on her creditors to make sure *they* paid themselves equally—if not fully. Similarly, the shopkeeper Anna Wroe demanded that the creditors of her late husband's estate "meet together on Wednesday next . . . at the Exchange Tavern in King-Street to consult proper Measures to be taken for the Recovery of their debts."[35] Mary Roberts suggested another way widows dealt less passively with a debt-ridden estate. She claimed that, because "very little Regard has been had to former Advertisement" and because she was "unwilling to use the disagreeable Method of suing for the same," debtors "make speedy payment to her . . . (as otherwise she lays under a great Disadvantage in settling with her said Husband's Creditors)." After pleading for sympathy, she ended with a threat: if debtors refused, "she must be obliged to put the said Subscribers Names into this *Gazette*, to prevent their pleading Ignorance."[36]

Karin Wulf has argued that "the better developed a woman's personal resources [with friends and family] were, the better her chances were of surviving economically in the city. Because women had much less access to trans-Atlantic credit," widows relied heavily on local credit networks. Sometimes those networks failed. Like the administrators of Christian Herredge's estate, in 1710, the administrators of fifteen widows' estates in Suffolk County presented them as "insolvent," and the creditors fared poorly. In Herredge's case, her creditors (three of whom were women) received only "10 shillings and five pence per pound."[37] Despite the tragic circumstances such insolvent estates reflect, those fifteen widows represented only 3.5 percent of all widows' estates inventoried—hardly a number to signify the widespread suffering of widows. More often, credit networks—local or not—succeed, and widows' entry into those networks reflected their active role as moneylenders.

According to Gloria Main, widows who mortgaged their property did not need to remarry to guarantee that someone would help them run their farm or plantation. They could lead an independent ("liberating") and secure life; more important, "widows could lend assistance to other widows." She pointed to the widow Prudence Thomas of Roxbury, Massachusetts, who mortgaged her house, meadow, and orchard for fifty pounds to the widow Mary Greenhill of Boston for two years. Greenhill paid off the loan (her will did not mention any creditors and her inventory listed no outstanding debts), and the transaction benefited both women.[38] Likewise, Mary Baker declared that she had by her "Industry and care Acquired some Estate of my own . . . and not only well nigh cleared my said husbands Estate From Debts, but much advanced the same."[39] Many widows actively participated in a dynamic network of female debtors and creditors.

As widows' wills reveal, their debts were indeed more neighborly and with people they knew intimately. By far the most common debt owed was for nursing, probably during a last illness. The second most common debt was for funeral expenses, with rent, food, and wages nearly as prevalent. Similarly, the most common debt due to a widow's estate was for rent. However, while widows did not participate as frequently as men in the increasingly impersonal credit relations, engaging in local, informal lending did not preclude their getting involved in the growing realm of notes, bonds, and mortgages across town, county, and colony lines.[40] Theirs was a gendered network, however. The language of their wills, the details in their inventories, and their bequests reveal that colonial widows tended to borrow from and loan to other women.

Massachusetts and Maryland widows were much more likely than widows in South Carolina to participate in such a network—or, at least, they more often mentioned them in their wills. Fourteen percent of Suffolk County widows identified female creditors in their wills. Their female debt network was extensive, for 24 percent named one creditor, 22 percent named two, 22 percent named three, 10 percent named four, and 23 percent named five or more—and two named more than twelve female creditors. Seventeen percent of Maryland widows identified female creditors, but their debt network was less intensive than those of Massachusetts. Slightly more than half named one female creditor, nearly a quarter named two female creditors, around one fifth named three, and only one named five female creditors. Interestingly, no widows from South Carolina specifically identified female creditors in their wills. A mere 4 percent of Suffolk County and South Carolina widows identified female debtors; these networks were not extensive, with most naming one or two, but the shopkeeper Sarah Dolbear and the printer Ann Greene—both of Boston—named sixteen and twenty-seven female debtors, respectively! Eight percent of Maryland widows named female debtors, and, like indebted widows from the other two colonies, most of them named only one or two.[41] It appears that widows tended to owe more money than they lent to other women, but an examination of their inventories suggest otherwise. Approximately one-half of Massachusetts widows' inventories, a third of those of Maryland widows, and not quite one-fourth of those of South Carolina widows listed debts due to them. Because administrators usually did not name the debtors, it is impossible to determine whether they were male or female.

Bequests of money, debts due from others, and cancelation of debts due to the testator (what I call intangibles) played a significant role in all testators' lives. Across time and colonies, about two-thirds of widows' bequests of intangibles went to their immediate family. The remaining one-third went to nonkin to pay debts owed to friends and neighbors and to build economic support networks. Turning a lens on several women from South Carolina and Massachusetts makes clear the significance of intangibles (and the ability to bequeath those assets) in widows' lives. In 1744, the widow Sarah Harley left behind an estate worth £554, and, of that, £515 was in a bond due to the estate—93 percent of the total value. At her death, in 1747, Margaret Wilson possessed an estate much larger than Sarah Harley's, an estate of which 95 percent (£1,495 out of a total of £1,536) was in cash. Administrators valued the widow Mary Sumner's estate at £918, but, in order to reap the rewards of the estate, they would have had to collect £866 in debts due to Mary Sumner—that is, 94 percent of the total value of the estate.[42] Sarah Allen of Charleston, South Carolina, left an estate worth £6,956, of which £5,926 was in debts due to her (which she bequeathed to two nephews or grandnephews and six nieces or grandnieces). In addition, she left her remaining cash to five female nonkin: the two daughters of her "late good Friend Madm. Moore, dec'd Widow" and the three daughters of her "good Friend Mrs. Margaret Warden."[43] The widow Elizabeth Pierce of Boston, Massachusetts, left an estate valued at £1,365.19.02; while she owed money to two women, the bulk of the estate, £1,308.19.09 to be precise, was composed of bonds and notes due to her. She bequeathed this estate to six female friends, three of whom were widows like herself: Margaret Squire (who was integrated into a female community; the widow Pugles also left Squire part of her estate, and Squire witnessed Mary Greenhill's will), Francis Wardell, and Elizabeth Hall (the widow we met earlier as she sought a license to sell wines and liquors).[44] By bequeathing their intangible goods to female nonkin, colonial widows demonstrated their commitment to sustaining viable female social and economic networks, particularly in cities, through such bequests.

The story of Rebecca Amory provides a perfect conclusion to this analysis of widows in the economic community. A descendant's description of Rebecca is worth quoting in full because of the striking picture she paints of the widow:

> Her mother . . . and died in 1731. Her brothers were married and settled in South Carolina with homes in Charleston and valuable plantations . . . left them by their father. . . . With [her brother-in-law's] counsel and aid and that of other kind friends, she administered the estate of her husband, entangled in adventures in Carolina, the Azores, Portugal and England, and managed his property in Boson and her own inheritance with consummate prudence. About her own abode . . . were wharves and works, stills and laboratories for various commodities Mr. Amory prepared for the market, which . . . she [kept] under her special supervision. [There

> was also] a list of debts due the estate amounting to some sixteen thousand pounds. These debts scattered over the world it was no easy task to collect. Family traditions give her credit for much good judgment in discharging this difficult duty, as well as for being an excellent mother.[45]

Indeed she was. Among many other expenses, she paid £1.10.0 for "medicine & attendance for her Family," she paid a tailor nearly £6 for mending and making breeches for her sons, she paid £1.17.00 for her sons' education (including pens and books), and she paid £15.19.15 paid for Thomas Amory to attend "college" for one quarter.[46] However, the advertisements she placed in both the *Boston Gazette* and the *Boston News-Letter* indicate that she was much more than a good mother. She was an ideal Daniel Defoe widow, a successful businesswoman who employed nearly all the economic survival tactics discussed in this chapter.

Amory made her first "public" appearance in 1728, as "Administratrix of Thomas Amory," when she advertised a "still-house, with Out-Houses, and other appurtenances" for sale. Seven months later, she ran the ubiquitous request for "Any Persons who have any Claims to the Estate of Mr. Thomas Amory to bring them to her" and demanded that "all Persons who are Indebted to the said Estate" pay those debts to "avoid further Trouble."[47] From this point on, she slowly undertook more, and more complex, economic roles. As noted earlier, in 1731, she advertised a slave for sale, but another four years elapsed before she overtly indicated what she was doing to support herself and her children.

Correspondence between Rebecca Holmes Amory and her relatives in Charleston suggest her economic activities in that four-year gap.[48] To understand Amory's pursuits, however, we need to step back several decades. In October 1716, Francis Holmes Jr. wrote to his then-unmarried fifteen-year-old sister:

> Lett us not be Strangers to one another although soe far distant and lett us be still in commerce with Each Other . . . desire you to gett me . . . [a] looking glass 1 sett Tea and Coffee Cups 1 Tea table 1 tea kittle 2 doz plates 6 dishes 1 med kittle 6 Brass Candlesticks. . . . If my Money will not hold out I will punctually send itt at ye first opportunity wch service done to me [I] shall . . . lay my self under a great obligation to you.[49]

Commerce has a dual meaning that is crucial in this context. It means to converse or communicate with, *and* it means "to carry on trade" with.[50]

Thus, his letter not only reveals the growing commercial and consumer culture along the Atlantic coast but also, and more important, highlights the "obligation" to family that the commerce in those goods entailed, even for young women. As Toby Ditz's analysis of Philadelphia merchants' correspondence suggests, in the eighteenth century there was little distinction between private and public, between familial and commercial interests.[51] In a letter to his mother on April 5, 1720, Francis Jr. focuses almost entirely on issues of goods and money. After asking about "our deer family['s]" health, he wrote:

> [I] Include you a Bill of Lading for twelve Barrells of Rice ... for my Fathers and my accot[.] I begg you pay Mr. Headwine as fast as you are in Cash for our Acct ... Begg you send me some Brandy . . . with dutty to you and Love to my Brothers and Sisters.[52]

By offering his "dutty"[53] to her (and, by contrast, his *love* to his siblings), Francis publicly recognized his mother as the financial head of the family in Boston, that is, the person to whom to show deference, the person to whom he owed a moral debt, and the person with whom he was to discuss business matters in detail. These letters offer an initial glimpse of the interdependent relationships established through both women.[54] Rebecca Holmes was gaining experience in business affairs, not as a deputy husband, as many women who would become widows skilled in the ways of commerce did. She learned those skills from her widowed mother—in the absence of her male kin. She was perhaps a "deputy widow."

Once Rebecca Amory faced widowhood, her South Carolina relatives sent her a series of letters indicating that they were integrating her into the commercial family in her own right.[55] Isaac Holmes, another brother, wrote, "I am glad to hear of your welfare. . . . Mr. Allen has promised to Come to an Acct with me several times but has fail'd me but I hope soon will."[56] The reference to Mr. Allen stemmed from an earlier legal transaction. On November 19, 1723, Thomas Amory sold and Rebecca Amory renounced her dower rights in a parcel of land to Eleazer Allen of Charleston, South Carolina. Her brother helped her in what appeared to be a deal gone sour.[57]

Several months later, Elizabeth Holmes informed Rebecca that she had sent her a barrel of potatoes "markt with your name"[58] It seems a small matter, but before this point Elizabeth Holmes had written nothing remotely related to economic issues. However, upon her widowhood

(Francis had died two years earlier), Elizabeth took a part, albeit a bit part, in the family commercial concerns. Another letter Isaac Holmes wrote stressed the connection between family and commerce. In taking on the role as financial adviser and concerned brother, he wrote:

> I have rec'd your money which with the Charge that stood from the Protest is £160 which I have Shipt you … in Pork and Rice believeing that to be the best Comodity we have here[.] There is £3 this Currency due to you which I shall send in the first small parcel of silver I can get[.] I hope you will aprove what I have done it being the best secured for your interests.[59]

The gendered give and take among the Holmes/Amory family continued with these words from Elizabeth to Rebecca: "am glad to hear frankey behaves him self better then he did hope god will in abil him to se his folle and to mend he rot me he was going to Prenteis hop busnis will deuart him from folly[.]"[60] She expressed motherly concerns not only about her son's behavior but also, and more important, about his economic future. He had been living with Rebecca for at least twelve years, which meant that, as a head of household assuming masculine responsibilities, Rebecca Amory raised not only her sons but her nephews, as well.

Isaac Holmes returned yet again to the contretemps with Mr. Allen:

> [this letter] serves to Acknowlege the Receipt of … Mr. Eleaser Allens Protested Bill[.] . . . [I] should have been glad you had lett me know the Charge of the Protest that I might have demanded it of him when I took the Bill of him[.] . . . I have sent you . . . a barrel of our Potatoes . . . which I desire you to Accept of for the Entertainment [here he means providing for or maintaining] of your Children to whome give my love.[61]

Isaac Homes always signed his letters to Rebecca Amory "your Loveing Brother." Lorri Glover argues that close "horizontal ties" between brothers and sisters undermined the traditional authority of the male-headed patriarchal family structure.[62] But was it a relationship of equality between brother and sister, between male- and female-headed households? In the first letter, Isaac made the decision to send Rebecca supplies instead of money without giving her a choice in the matter; in the second, he chided her for not sending him important financial papers until after he had already made a deal with Mr. Allen—a deal in which Allen apparently bested him. However, throughout the years, she constructed an identity as a competent and powerful widow willing and able to make economic decisions about her family with or without her brother's advice.

The first outward evidence of her shopkeeping activities appeared in 1735 when Rebecca Holmes Amory advertised

> choice Mourning and Silver Crapes, the best Bombazenes . . . , fine scarlet and crimson Broad Cloths, fine Velvet . . ., black Snail and Bone Lace, Tossels for Hoods and Mantles, fine Patches, Chints, Damasks, Padusoys and Taffeties, Persians, Lutestrings and other Silks, Hollands, Cambricks, Diapers, Garlix and Prussia Linnens, Threads, Tapes, Fringes and Lace for Head Cloaks, Pound Silks, and sundry other Goods, also fine Bohea Tea and Chocolate.[63]

Like other widows before her, Amory announced that she would sell her goods "at reasonable Rates." However, she had been in business, and a very lucrative business, for at least three years prior. In settling a dispute over a bequest from her husband's English cousin, she asked to be sent "good Irish linens suitable for this Country" in lieu of a cash settlement—presumably to sell in her shop. The year was 1732. Moreover, that year, she began keeping a receipt book that revealed extensive economic activities.[64] In 1732, she paid out £825, in 1733 £1,497, and in 1734 £2,959. She actively participated in the market economy, and she continued to do for another three years; during that time, she paid out an average £3,219 annually. Unfortunately, she generally paid "on account" and only rarely noted the types of purchases she made. We know only that she paid wages and bought cocoa, tea, ale, shoes, firewood, handkerchiefs, cider, "box habadashery," milk, satin, indigo, and lamb's wool mittens. However, her progressively larger outlays suggests either that she was wealthy (which we know that, as administrator of both her husband's and her mother's sizable estates, she was) or that she had enough money coming in to pay her creditors. In the increasingly commercial economy of Boston, creditors would not have carried such large debts for long. Her receipt book also indicates that she was involved in a wide economic network, for in 1734, there were 76 different entries, in 1735, there were 100 different entries, and in 1736, there were 122 different entries. She dealt primarily with men, mentioning only ten different women in eight years of recordkeeping: Elizabeth Barnes, Mary Bulkeley, Mary Hill, Elizabeth Novel, Mary Collins, Susannah Deco, Mary Faneuil, Deborah Fraser, Hannah Willard (who was also a shopkeeper selling "Good Green and Bohea Tea, China Ware, and double refined Sugar"), and Magdalen Wroe, with whom we began the chapter. Despite the paucity of female creditors, Amory's connections to the latter two women suggests a woman-centered network of shopkeepers.[65]

Rebecca Amory's economic activities did not cease in 1737, when her receipt book does. In 1738, she advertised "Two very good Copper Stills" for sale and a "convenient Distilling House & Wharfe adjoining" for rent.[66] Two years later, she attempted to sell "a House and Land fronting Orange Street . . . with a Still House and Wharfe belonging to it, also a Copper of 700 Gallons with a Worm." She declared that she would sell them "either for Money, or Bonds with good Security." This indicated her active participation in the debt network. In 1748 and 1749, her last two advertisements (at least for the time under study here) appeared in the *Gazette*. She announced a wide variety of imported goods for sale, which she announced would be sold "by Wholesail or Retail," thereby indicating her participation in the transatlantic economy as well as the local economy.[67]

The only economic strategy not pursued by Amory was that of bequeathing (like her mother, she died intestate). Nonetheless, like Sarah Lloyd, Magdalen Wroe, and Benedicta Netmaker, she pursued a variety of overlapping and increasingly public strategies to secure her and her family's economic future. Widows, who became heads of households upon the death of their husbands, understood their masculine responsibilities. Despite advice literature that suggested they should be passive and quiescent, widows from the country, small villages, and large towns used their experiences to craft identities for themselves as creative and active participants in the commercial world beyond the family. Sometimes unconsciously, but more often consciously, widows like Rebecca Amory fashioned a vibrant female economic identity in the community and in the wider market. As hardworking (although sometimes suspect) shopkeepers and innholders, through their wills, and as consummate sellers of goods and lenders of money, widows embraced ambiguously gendered economic values.

Conclusion

"Witnesses to a Will of Madam Toys"

On July 6, 1730, Jeremiah Bumstead, Mr. Franklin, and Mr. Addison witnessed Madam Toy's will. This simple act occurred daily in early America, but there is little information about the woman. Mercy Toy—or Tay—was licensed as an innholder in 1710. John Dunton called her "a friend" and wrote of her, "she has the bashfulness and modesty of the damsel, the love and fidelity of Mrs. Green, and the piety and sweetness of the Widow Brick [whom we met in chapter 2]." He described her as "parte per Pale . . . that is half wife, half Widow, her husband [Jeremiah] . . . having been lost at sea."[1] However, there must have been some question about her mental capacity, for Bumstead noted in his diary that she had, to his best judgment, "ye use of her Reason. I haveing askt her severall Questions to which she answered Rationaly though very weak in body." He wrote down the incident in case he would be called on to testify in court.[2]

Bumstead chose to take note of the witnessing of Madam Toy's will, signaling the importance of willmaking in colonial America. It is impossible to tell from his cryptic diary entry whether he understood the significance of the widow Toy's action. She and other widows certainly did. Widows understood society's expectations of them, but they also understood how best to negotiate the sometimes rough waters of "parte per pale" that redefined their lives. Facing uncertain circumstances, they knew that there were, recalling the words of Cotton Mather, "debts to be paid, and Mouths to be fed." As willmaking suggests, many widows knew how to handle those responsibilities without remarrying. Toy probably liked being referred to a shy, faithful, pious, and sweet. After all, John Dunton (like other advice book authors) discussed women, not necessarily as they actually were, but according to how he wanted all women to behave. Yet, Madam Toy refused to let others completely define her. In her will, she publicly expressed her dying thoughts and distributed her estate as she saw fit, acknowledging a power and control over other people's lives that few women enjoyed in early America. We do not know what goods she left or to whom she left them, but the fact that she left a will suggests that she understood the importance of her ability to create her relationships with her family, kin, neighbors, and community.

Bumstead's fear of trouble over the will suggests several possibilities. It may have been that Mrs. Toy's "intellectual part" was gone and that she was so "benummed, dimmed and dazzled" that she could not think. Maybe her weakened condition reflected her age; she may have been one of the ungrateful and discontented "antient" widows who created a nuisance in the neighborhood instead of silently displaying their honor and dispensing charity to friends, neighbors, and the church. Perhaps she was in ill health and poor and thus had little to give away, offering only token rewards for the food, clothing, and housing her family provided for her in the closing years of her life. She may have included legacies of which some in her family or in the community disapproved. Perhaps she gave all of her estate to her daughters or granddaughters, as many widows did, even to the exclusion of sons and grandsons. The possibilities that lurk in Jeremiah Bumstead's brief note highlight the ambiguity of colonial American widowhood.

This ambiguity arose primarily from the nature of widowhood itself. Widows were members of several overlapping communities, and they understood the social expectation that they would conform to cultural standards made clear by the Bible, advice books, plays, sermons, and legal statutes. But the advice often failed to take account of practical circumstances. In colonial Massachusetts, Maryland, and South Carolina, the term "widow" encompassed a wide variety of women confronting different circumstances. Not only were widows different from one another, the advice offered to them was inconsistent and at times illogical.

Propertied, sexually experienced mothers without male governors, widows failed to conform to conventional notions of womanhood. Young widows were advised to remarry, while older widows were not. As mothers, widows were told to direct their concerns toward the household because public spaces threatened their virtue, but, as virtual fathers, they were also expected to venture into the community to look after their children's interests. Widows were directed to care for those weaker, poorer, and more alone than they were, even as the law, through dower and intestacy, gave widows legal control or power over the estates their husbands had bequeathed to them or over the thirds of an intestate estate. Lawmakers, as fathers to the community, established very specific boundaries around that power, especially when a widow's needs came into conflict with the community and her children. While propertied, widows rarely enjoyed the discretion of male freeholders and none of the political rights. Widows sometimes found their decisions challenged by their children and reversed by the courts. As the prescriptive literature made clear, widows had to be very careful when they stepped into the public role of head of household. Courthouses, churches, and neighborhoods, in turning the public gaze on widows, called into question their honesty, chastity, and piety. Yet, widows had a special responsibility, to the sick, poor, and homeless among them. Widows who pursued economic survival outside the household proved the most perplexing. Such widows were cast as prudent and as reckless, as hard-working and as promiscuous, and as humble and as vain.

Even so, in comparison with other colonial women, widows enjoyed great power, because, from these competing and ambiguous roles, they assumed masculine and feminine rights and responsibilities. They used the contradictions and inconsistencies to their advantage when they forged their identities as widows. They were mothers; they served as fathers for their fragmented households; and they were participants in and caretakers for their communities. Many widows, especially those who could afford it, adamantly refused to remarry even when friends, family, and neighbors pressured them to do so. They were reluctant to relinquish their freedom and independence, especially if they did not like the men who pursued them. Many decided that if they were to remarry, it would be only to a man of their own choosing, a man they loved, a man who met their standards, a man who respected their independence and who allowed them to control their own property.

Moreover, widows often determined who would receive their families' productive wealth. More often than men, widows refused to allow the courts to distribute their estate at their deaths. Widows disproportionately chose female near kin and nonkin, nieces, female friends, and sisters as beneficiaries. More so than their husbands, widows used their resources to address women's needs within their communities. Increasingly, they sought to provide female family members, especially daughters, the material means to take care of themselves both within and without marriage.

More important, colonial widows often and increasingly ignored the patriarchal presumptions of their communities by bequeathing productive property, including land, slaves, money, and debt to both their sons *and* their daughters. Colonial widows in both the North and the South bequeathed land to daughters at a far greater rate than did fathers and far more often than English testators did. By 1750, colonial widows were as likely to bequeath land to their daughters as to their sons. When colonial widows owned no land to bequeath, they gave their daughters, granddaughters, nieces, and female friends their household goods, slaves, livestock, and money. Widows well understood the constraints women faced. As land grew scarce and the legal and ideological boundaries that governed colonial families grew more restricted, widows sought to relieve the pressures on their daughters' lives. Colonial widows wanted their daughters to control the economic resources that they brought to their marriages and the economic resources that might make marriage or remarriage unnecessary. To the extent of their resources, freehold widows secured for their children freehold status, urban widows secured for sons and daughters bourgeois status, and planter widows secured their sons and daughters aristocratic status. For all their social categories, property ensured individual independence, personal liberty, and economic security.

Jealous of their privileges and property, colonial widows filed petitions and entered the courtroom as plaintiffs and as defendants. They struggled with the magistrates to maintain their economic and legal rights. Some widows chose to use their independence to become innkeepers, to take an active role in the debt network of an emerging commercial economy. Women's economic activity—the goods they bequeathed, the petitions they presented to the courts, the charity they dispensed, the place they carved for themselves in the civil polity, and the property they sold—did not necessarily imply that widows had a great deal of power. It did, however, prove that widows had clear notions about how the family and the community should be structured and how women should fit into those structures—and their roles were different from and more ambiguous than those held by men. Widowhood entailed not simply an issue of power or lack of power conferred on widows but also the issue of getting and maintaining widows' place of importance and authority within the family and within in the community. Like many colonial males, widows' self-interest, at times, took precedence over the needs of family. Widowhood provided the means for them to do so. Ultimately, it was not an either-or situation but a position mediated or negotiated between the widow and various aspects of her community.

Nineteenth-century American widows appear strikingly similar to seventeenth-century widows. For example, Joan Jensen, in *Loosening the Bonds*, argues that nineteenth-century Pennsylvania widows gave more of their estates to near kin and nonkin than they did to nuclear kin and that they did so at rates much higher than that for male testators. Suzanne Lebsock similarly claims that widows "play[ed] favorites" among a wide range of heirs, but especially in choosing daughters over sons, and that widows rewarded "loyalty and affection." Jensen and Lebsock claim that widows were freer than were men to disperse their wealth over a wider range of legatees both because they were not bound by testamentary law and because they had different social and economic responsibilities from men. Moreover, Kirsten Wood, in *Masterful Women*, argues that slaveholding widows, masters of their households and their bondspeople, were independent "to a degree usually thought impossible for women in the . . . notoriously conservative" South. Although they neither did nor could assume all aspects of masculine responsibility, they enjoyed a position of privilege over other women and nonslaveholding men. Unlike men, they drew distinctions between household mastery and their concept of womanhood; to them, they were not one and the same, so they did not suffer the psychological burdens that white masculinity entailed. Slaveholding widows received help, but they also provided help; they relied on others, yet they were strong and determined; they were both "instrumental and reliant."

Interestingly, none of these scholar views these patterns as "feminist" or as a means of ensuring that women would have power over their own lives. Instead, they argue that widows showed how well they understood the legal and economic vulnerability northern and southern women faced in nineteenth-century America and wanted simply to protect their daughters and other female kin from a harsh system. They thought of their bequests and their actions not as responses to economic constraints placed on them by individual men—which to Jensen and Lebsock would have been a feminist action—but as responses to a system that did not protect their interests—and this to them was not a feminist action. Such patterns might reveal a subtle critique of patriarchal assumptions, as Susan Amussen argues is true for English widows, but Jensen and Wood assert that American widows "played an integral role in maintaining the patriarchal family" and "in the defense of mastery."[3] They imply that widows had responsibilities to their families that were less compelling and perhaps less important than were men's similar responsibilities.

Likewise, colonial widows were neither feminist nor even proto-feminist. They were, however, willful individuals who valued their own freedom and sought to extend their "unfeminine" power to daughters, granddaughters, sisters, friends, neighbors, business partners, and customers. By the time of the Revolution, many middle- and upper-class colonial widows owned property in their own names, giving them both legal personality and economic power. The change in colonial women's status had many causes—some economic, some religious, some cultural. Taking advantage of their ambiguous status as father and mother, colonial widows exploited these opportunities to quietly expand women's access to and control over productive property. Male American revolutionaries, mindful of the stakes, carefully sought to inscribe male values in their new, republican government. They excluded women from politics and limited their power over property. But, in time, widows of the new nation followed the lead of their colonial grandmothers. By 1820, in most states, male and female testators alike bequeathed their property, including land, equally to their sons and daughters. Responding to this shift in ownership of property, pre-Civil War legislatures, one by one, granted women control over conjugal property, wages, and even children. Political equality for American women had to wait another century, but, by 1860, outside the South, Americans of property and standing were as likely to be women as men. This important fundamental change began in colonial America as the unintended legacy of colonial widows.

Notes

INTRODUCTION

1. Wills of Dorothy Upshall, proved June 17, 1676, Suffolk County Wills, 5, 291-292; Elizabeth Diggs, proved June 17, 1710, Maryland Wills, Book 13, 96-98; and Catherine LaNoble, proved March 24, 1726, South Carolina Wills, 1671-1727, 243-244.

2. Herbert H. Hyman, *Of Time and Widowhood: Nationwide Studies of Enduring Effects* (Durham: Duke University Press, 1983), 10; Helena Znaniecka Lopata, "Support Systems of American Urban Widowhood," *Journal of Social Issues* 44, no. 3 (1988), 114; Robert R. McCrae and Paul T. Costa, Jr., "Psychological Resilience Among Widowed Men and Women: A 10-Year Follow-up of a National Sample," *Journal of Social Issues* 44, no. 3 (1988), 138; and Mary L. S. Vachon and Stanley K. Stylianos, "The Role of Social Support in Bereavement," *Journal of Social Issues* 44, no. 3 (1988), 176. Today there are nearly four times as many widows as widowers. The average age at which a woman is widowed is sixty-nine; widows are much less likely to remarry than widowers; and the average duration of widowhood is fourteen years. These authors argue that widowhood is "primarily a women's issue," not only because there many widows but also because widows, unlike widowers who are independent throughout their lives, "must somehow establish a life independent of the deceased, deal with evolving family relationships and support networks, and meet emotional, health, and practical needs over the long term." They urge women to plan for widowhood so that they will not be passive victims of their circumstances but will instead take control of their lives.

3. For example, Gloria Main explained that she ignored women in her otherwise impressive study of colonial Maryland by claiming that women's records "deserve a separate study"; such statements do not solve the problem of widow's absence from current histories. See Gloria Main, *Tobacco Colony: Life in Early Maryland, 1650-1720* (Princeton: Princeton University Press, 1982), 48. The two most recent and most important books on colonial women, Laurel Thatcher Ulrich's *Good Wives: Image and Reality in the Lives of Women in Northern New England, 1650-1750* (New York: Oxford University Press, 1982) and Mary Beth Norton's *Liberty's Daughters: The Revolutionary Experience of American Women, 1750-1820* (Boston: Little, Brown, 1980), do not ignore widowhood, but it is clear that both

authors think that widowhood played a minor if not insignificant part in early American women's lives. For specific discussions of the relationship between widowhood and witchcraft, see John Putnam Demos, *Entertaining Satan: Witchcraft and the Culture of Early New England* (New York: Oxford University Press, 1982), and Carol F. Karlsen, *The Devil in the Shape of a Woman: Witchcraft in Colonial New England* (New York: Norton, 1987).

4. Cotton Mather, *Ornaments for the Daughters of Zion or the Character and Happiness of a Vertuous Woman: in a Discourse which Directs the Female-Sex how to Express, the Fear of God, in every Age and State of their Life; and obtain both Temporal and Eternal Blessedness* (Boston, 1692), 106; and Cotton Mather, *Marah Spoken To: A Brief Essay to do Good Unto the Widow* (Boston, 1718), vii, 1, 32. See also Cotton Mather, *The Widow of Nain: Remarks on the Illustrious Miracle Wrought by our Almighty Redeemer on the behalf of a Desolate Widow* (Boston, 1728), 11. For contemporary historian's general agreement with Cotton Mather, see Robert V. Wells, *The Population of the British Colonies in America Before 1776* (Princeton: Princeton University Press, 1975), 77, 96.

5. Karlsen, *Devil in the Shape of a Woman*, 295, n. 92; Lyle Koehler, *A Search for Power: The "Weaker Sex" in Seventeenth-Century New England* (Urbana: University of Illinois Press, 1980), 119; John Demos, "Old Age in Early New England," in Michael Gordon, ed., *The American Family in Socio-Historical Perspective* (New York: St. Martin's Press, 1978), 254, n. 44; Lois Green Carr and Lorena S. Walsh, "The Planter's Wife: The Experience of White Women in Seventeenth-Century Maryland," *William and Mary Quarterly*, 3rd series, 34 (1977), 555; Gwen Victor Gampel, "The Planter's Wife Revisited: Women, Equity Law, and the Chancery Court in Seventeenth-Century Maryland," in Barbara Harris and JoAnn McNamara, eds., *Women and the Structure of Society: Selected Research from the Fifth Berkshire Conference on the History of Women* (Durham, NC: Duke University Press, 1984), 25; and Edmund Morgan, *American Slavery, American Freedom: The Ordeal of Colonial Virginia* (New York: Norton, 1975), 164.

6. Douglas Lamar Jones, *Village and Seaport Migration and Society in Eighteenth-Century Massachusetts* (Hanover, NH: University Press of New England, 1981), 79; Alexander Keyssar, "Widowhood in Eighteenth-Century Massachusetts: A Problem in the History of the Family," *Perspectives in American History* 7 (1982), 88 and 93, n. 21; Allan Kulikoff, *Tobacco and Slaves: The Development of Southern Cultures in the Chesapeake, 1680–1800* (Chapel Hill: University of North Carolina Press, 1986), 192; Gary B. Nash, *The Urban Crucible: Social Change, Political Consciousness, and the Origins of the American Revolution* (Cambridge, MA: Harvard University Press, 1979), 172; Christine Leigh Heyrman, *Commerce and Culture: The Maritime Communities of Colonial Massachusetts, 1690-1750* (New York: Norton, 1984), 381, n. 13; and Cara Anzilotti, *In the Affairs of the World: Women, Patriarchy, and Power in Colonial South Carolina* (Westport, CT: Greenwood Press, 2002), 97.

7. For a discussion of the problems with using tax lists, see John J. McCusker and Russell R. Menard, *The Economy of British America, 1607-1789* (Chapel Hill: University of North Carolina Press, 1985), 273-274.

8. Kim Lacy Rogers, "Relicts of the New World: Conditions of Widowhood in Seventeenth-Century New England," in Mary Kelley, ed., *Woman's Being, Woman's Place: Female Identity and Vocation in American History* (Boston: G. K. Hall, 1979), 27, 33-34, 40, 49-50; Carr and Walsh, "The Planter's Wife," 555-557, 560. Lois Green Carr, "Inheritance in the Colonial Chesapeake," in Ronald Hoffman and Peter J. Albert, eds., *Women in the Age of the American Revolution* (Charlottesville: University Press of Virginia, 1989), 171, 186, argues that eighteenth-century widows faced a different situation. They possessed less property and power than did seventeenth-century widows for three reasons: they were less likely to receive more than their dower thirds, the land they inherited was more likely to have remarriage restrictions attached to it, and they were granted only lifetime use of personalty. As the colonial Maryland population changed from immigrant to native-born, land became scarce and more expensive, and a greater number of children survived to adulthood. These demographic changes meant that husbands were less willing to give unconditional control of property to their widows. But, while Carr acknowledged that widows' power declined over the years, her argument still rests on the assumption that economic wealth equaled social power for widows.

9. Alice Morse Earle, *Colonial Dames and Good Wives*, American Classics Edition (New York: Frederick Ungar, 1962), 30, 32, 36, and 39-40.

10. Morgan, *American Slavery, American Freedom*, 164-165. John Faragher argues that widows led more flexible lives than did widowers. He claims that widows had "economic, social and psychological support for life-options outside the nuclear family triad which granted them greater hope in facing the elderly years." Ministers, and especially Puritan ministers, expanded a widow's domestic responsibilities to include caring for the community. Widows provided a valuable service to the community and established a positive place in the social order for themselves. Ironically, because widows transcended the family, most of them could and did choose not to "resubmit to the masculine discipline of marriage." See Faragher, "Old Women and Old Men in Seventeenth-Century Wethersfield, Connecticut," *Women's Studies* 4 (1976), 27. Similarly, Linda Speth argues that southern widows achieved a great deal of "personal power and responsibility." Widows did not remarry frequently and quickly, primarily because they did not need to and often because doing so would weaken their economic position. Speth is more unwilling than Morgan and Faragher to describe a "golden age" for widows, but she is also unwilling to locate them in a "grim patriarchal milieu." According to her, although widows did not have the same power and authority that men had, they did have a great deal of power. See Linda Speth, "More Than Her 'Thirds': Wives and Widows in Colonial Virginia," *Women and History* 4 (1983), 5, 17, 22, 27, 32.

11. Elisabeth Anthony Dexter, *Colonial Women of Affairs: A Study of Women in Business and the Professions in America Before 1776* (Boston: Houghton Mifflin, 1924), 2, 19. Recent studies update or expand on Dexter's findings. The sociologists Martin Schultz and Herman Lantz examined the advertisement section of all eighteenth-century newspapers to determine women's occupational pursuits. They argue that women generally combined their traditional domestic roles with business activities because "the management of a business was frequently part of a broader integration in commercial activity controlled by the husband." They explain this preponderance of employment activity in the seaboard cities by the fact that these areas tended to have a large proportion of widows because the lure of economic opportunity drew many women from the countryside and because those who lived in the cities from the beginning tended to have husbands who had been involved in military and maritime activities, both professions with high mortality rates. The authors claim that such activity demonstrated that "widows faced broad pressures for social and ideological changes" in their lives. See Martin Schultz and Herman R. Lantz, "Occupational Pursuits of Free Women in Early America: An Examination of Eighteenth-Century Newspapers," *Sociological Forum* 3, no. 1 (1988), 97-98, 106.

12. Heyrman, *Commerce and Culture*, 381-382; Cornelia Dayton, "Women Before the Bar: Gender, Law, and Society in Connecticut, 1710-1719" (Ph.D. diss., Princeton University, 1986), 3, 39, 235. See also Keyssar, "Widowhood in Eighteenth-Century Massachusetts," 99, 108, 119; Carole Shammas, "Early American Women and Control Over Capital," in Ronald Hoffman and Peter J. Albert, eds., *Women in the Age of the American Revolution* (Charlottesville: University Press of Virginia, 1989), 137, 143, 147, 150; and Gampel, "The Planter's Wife Revisited," 23, 25, 30-31.

13. Ulrich, *Good Wives*; Mary Beth Norton, *Founding Mothers and Fathers: Gendered Power and the Forming of American Society* (New York: Knopf, 1996), 10, 139, 147,164, 403; and Laurel Thatcher Ulrich, "John Winthrop's City of Women," *Massachusetts Historical Review* 3 (2001).

14. Karin Wulf, *Not All Wives: Women of Colonial Philadelphia* (Ithaca, NY: Cornell University Press, 2000); Cynthia Kierner, *Beyond the Household: Women's Place in the Early South 1700-1835* (Ithaca, NY: Cornell University Press, 1998; Terri Snyder, *Brabbling Women: Disorderly Speech and the Law in Early Virginia* (Ithaca, NY: Cornell University Press. 2003); Linda Sturtz, *Within Her Power: Propertied Women in Colonial Virginia* (New York: Routledge, 2002), and Anzilotti, *In the Affairs of the World.*

15. Anzilotti, *In the Affairs of the World*, 3, 10, 168, 191, argues that, rather than relishing autonomy, women acted to promote the interest of their male kin and the patriarchy in general. She claims that women understood their management of family property as a necessary expedient and thus they upheld conservative gender norms. Although Wulf focuses primarily on Philadelphia, Pennsylvania,

she claims, in *Not All Wives*, 18, that "late seventeenth century Chesapeake saw vigorous enforcement of patriarchal values" and upheld the ideals of white womanhood. Sturtz, indeed, argues that women lost power—but not completely, because women with power endured in eighteenth-century Virginia.

16. For other historians who similarly adhere to this declension model see Heyrman, *Commerce and Culture*; Cornelia Hughes Dayton, *Women before the Bar: Gender, Law, and Society in Connecticut, 1639-1789* (Chapel Hill: University of North Carolina Press, 1995); Deborah Rosen, *Courts and Commerce: Gender, Law, and the Market Economy in Colonial New York* (Columbus: Ohio State University Press, 1997); and Elaine Forman Crane, *Ebb Tide in New England: Women, Seaports, and Social Change 1630-1800* (Boston: Northeastern University Press, 1998).

17. Carole Shammas, Marylynn Salmon, and Michel Dahlin, *Inheritance in America From Colonial Times to the Present* (New Brunswick, NJ: Rutgers University Press, 1987).

18. Mary Beth Norton, "Letter to the Editor," *William and Mary Quarterly*, 3rd series, 48 (1991), 639-641 (in response to Joel Perlmann and Dennis Shirley, "When Did New England Women Acquire Literacy?" *William and Mary Quarterly*, 3rd series, 48 (1991), 50-67; Mary Beth Norton, "Getting to the Source: Hetty Shepard, Dorothy Dudley, and Other Fictional Colonial Women I Have Come to Know Altogether Too Well," *Journal of Woman's History* 10, no. 3 (1998), 149; E. Jennifer Monaghan, *Learning to Read and Write in Colonial America* (Amherst: University of Massachusetts Press, 2005), 3, 11-12, 373-374. For a similar argument about the importance ofwriting equipment, albeit tied to the eighteenth-century consumer culture, see Konstantin Dierks, "Letter Writing, Stationery Supplies and Consumer Modernity in the Eighteenth-Century Atlantic World," *Early American Literature* 41 (2006), 473-494.

19. The number of female and male inventories diverges because of the nature of the sources. Although I tried to record an inventory for every person who left a will, not every person who left a will had an inventory in the court records. I did, however, record an intestate male inventory for every intestate female inventory.

20. Lisa Wilson, *Life After Death: Widows in Pennsylvania, 1750-1850* (Philadelphia: Temple University Press, 1992).

21. I have examined all published and extant manuscript colonial sermons preached at widows' funerals and all published occasional sermons dealing with or about widows and widowhood. The work of Lonna M. Malmsheimer, "New England Funeral Sermons and Changing Attitudes Toward Woman, 1672-1792" (Ph.D. diss.,University of Minnesota, 1973), 32, 114-116, proved invaluable.

22. Thomas Prince, *Be Followers of Them, who through Faith and Patience inherit the Promises. A Sermon Occasion'd by the Decease of Mrs. Hannah Fayerweather, of Boston, on January 27th, 1755. Age 53* (Boston, 1755), 22.

23. Nancy Lyman Roelker, in her introduction to a special issue on widowhood in *The Journal of Family History*, argues that we should ignore the "dire

predictions of misery, ranging from warnings that widows will be prey to all kinds of exploitation in addition to the virtual certainty of falling into carnal sin," and focus on the impressions provided by "real widows." See "Introduction: Papers from the 1981 Berkshire Conference: Widowhood and Rational Domesticity: Modes of Independence for Women in Early Modern Europe," *Journal of Family History* 7 (Winter 1982), 377. I agree that we cannot take as fact the warnings in the prescriptive literature, but I also believe that we cannot understand "real widows" unless we understand the ideological constraints on their lives.

24. Rhys Issac, "Stories and Constructions of Identity: Folk Tellings and Diary Inscriptions in Revolutionary Virginia," in Ronald Hoffman, Mechal Sobel, and Fredrika J. Teute, eds., *Through a Glass Darkly: Reflections on Personal Identity in Early America* (Chapel Hill: University of North Carolina Press, 1997), 206.

25. The literature on the Atlantic is growing fast. Here I will simply cite Elizabeth Pruden, "Family, Community, Economy: Women's Activity in South Carolina, 1670-1770" (Ph.D. diss., University of Minnesota, 1996), 289-90. In her conclusion, Pruden admits that she set up and expected to find significant differences between women of South Carolina and women from the northern and even middle colonies—but she did not. She concludes, "All of this raised a question about the relevance of regionalization as a category of analysis for the study of women. . . . regional categorization may be too restrictive and uni-dimensional. It is more effective to consider roles and economic status across regional boundaries when studying the demands and opportunities in the lives of colonial white women."

26. Bureau of the Census, U.S. Department of Commerce.

27. Jared Eliot, *The Blessings Bestow'd on Them That Fear God, as was Shewed in a Sermon Occasion'd by the Death of the Truly Vertuous Mrs. Elizabeth Smithson* (New London, 1739), 24.

28. Mather, Ornaments for the Daughters of Zion, 101.

29. Suffolk County Probate Records, 25, 118–121. She was called an "innholder" at the time an inventory of her estate was made. See Suffolk Co., 28, 413-414, February 16, 1730; and Suffolk Co., 29, 98-101.

30. *The Book of the General Lawes and Libertyes Concerning the Inhabitants of the Massachusetts Collected out of the Records of the General Court for the Several Years Wherein They were Made and Established* (Cambridge, 1648), 17.

31. Anzilotti, *In the Affairs of the World*, argues that, like migrants to Boston, migrants to South Carolina came as family groups and that they "placed familial considerations before all else," 8.

32. Carl Bridenbaugh, *Cities in the Wilderness: The First Century of Urban Life in America, 1625-1742* (Oxford: Oxford University Press, 1966), 186.

CHAPTER 1

1. I use the word "ritual" here because Winthrop and Sewell exaggerated and stylized an everyday act of romance and in the process gave it a new symbolic meaning. In doing so, they created a collective identity for widows and widowers in their community. For a similar, albeit much later, ritual between widow Frances Randolph and St. George Tucker of Chesterfield County, Virginia, see Catherine M. Kerrison, "By the Book: Advice and Female Behavior in the Eighteenth-Century South" (Ph.D. diss., The College of William and Mary, 1999), 302-306. Although it does not focus explicitly on a widow's participation in a courtship ritual, see also J. A. Leo Lemay, *Robert Bolling Woos Anne Miller: Love and Courtship in Colonial Virginia, 1760* (Charlottesville: University Press of Virginia, 1990), for a similarly lengthy and detailed description of an aristocrat's pursuit of and rejection by a wealthy woman.

2. Collections of the Massachusetts Historical Society, *Diary of Samuel Sewall, 1714, 1730*, 5th series, 7 (Boston: Author, 1882), 262-277. Waitstill Winthrop was the son of John Winthrop, Jr., and the grandson of the famous governor.

3. Edmund S. Morgan, *The Puritan Family: Religion and Domestic Relations in Seventeenth-Century New England* (New York: Harper & Row, 1966), 58-59, and Alice Morse Earle, *Customs and Fashions in Old New England* (Rutland, VT: Charles E. Tuttle, 1973, originally published 1893), 43-56, both argue that remarriage in colonial America was frequent, rapid, and based primarily on economics. In a more recent interpretation of colonial widowhood, Alexander Keyssar disagrees with the traditional interpretation of Sewall's courtship and argues that "once widowed, a woman [like Katherine Winthrop] was far more likely to die a widow than to enter into a second marriage" because of the "advanced age" at which women became widows; see "Widowhood in Eighteenth-Century Massachusetts," 94.

4. They deliberated about six prominent—and wealthy—widows in his congregation: Rebekah Dudley, Bridget Usher, Deliverance Legg, Rebekah Loyd, Lydia Coleman, and Elizabeth Bellingham. See Ola Elizabeth Winslow, *Samuel Sewall of Boston* (New York: Macmillan, 1964), 176. Of those six, we know that three of them died widows: Bridget Usher, at whose funeral Thomas Foxcroft preached the sermon; Rebecca Loyd, who left her estate to her daughter and two granddaughters; and Madam Rebekah Dudley, who left her sizable estate to two sons, four daughters, two granddaughters, and a niece—Suffolk County Wills, v. 34, 319-321, and Suffolk County Wills, v. 22, 700-702.

5. G. Winston Lane found that wealthy South Carolinian widows, especially those of Middleton family, similarly entered into remarriage negotiations that not only protected their own economic independence and power but also provided for the man in the event he predeceased her. See G. Winston Lane Jr., "Economic Power Among Eighteenth-Century Women of the Carolina Lowcountry," in Jack

P. Greene, Rosemary Brana-Shute, and Randy J. Sparks, eds., *Money Trade, and Power: The Evolution of Colonial South Carolina's Plantation Society* (Columbia: University of South Carolina Press, 2001), 324-325.

6. Her inventory and account, presented to the probate court on March 4, 1737, Suffolk County Probate Records, 33, 89-91.

7. According to Richard L. Bushman, coaches symbolized "genteel delicacy" and made coarse eighteenth-century city streets suitable for women. Elite men and women "traveled above the pavements, encased in decorated boxes that both advertised their position in society and formed a genteel space immediately about them." He argues that city streets provided a "genteel stage where performance was required." Katherine Winthrop and her friends clearly understood this cultural milieu and willingly acted their part. See Richard L. Bushman, *Refinement of America: Persons, Houses, Cities* (New York: Vintage Books, 1993), 168-169, 369.

8. Edmund Morgan, *The Puritan Family*, 58-59, argues that a widow was a much sought-after marriage partner because of the thirds she received from her deceased husband's estate, but he also suggests that, because Madam Winthrop's estate gave her "a choice of several suitors" and she ultimately "proved a better bargainer" than Sewall, the marriage did not take place. To counteract the negative portrayal of Katherine Winthrop in Sewell's diary, R. C. Winthrop wrote a pamphlet entitled *A Difference of Opinion Concerning the Reasons Why Katharine Winthrop Refused to Marry Chief Justice Sewell* (Boston: Privately Printed, 1885, copy at American Antiquarian Society, Worcester, Massachusetts). He particularly wanted to prove that Madam Winthrop was not mercenary.

9. According to Winslow, "the bargain she finally accepted with some compromise was harder than those he had attempted to drive with . . . Madam Winthrop"; Winslow, *Samuel Sewall of Boston*, 179.

10. Will of Katherine Winthrop, proved August 10, 1725, Suffolk County Wills, v. 24, 166-169.

11. Catherine Kerrison, *Claiming the Pen: Women and Intellectual Life in the Early American South* (Ithaca, NY: Cornell University Press, 2006), 146-149, analyzes courtship and the leverage of older wealthy widows in the South "when suitors came to call."

12. Both this letter and the following letter are dated July 29, 1728; Amory Family Papers, Massachusetts Historical Society, N279, Reel 1.

13. Suffolk County Probate Records, 26, 334-335; 28, 317-319.

14. Robert B. Shoemaker, *Gender in English Society, 1650-1850* (London: Addison Wesley Longman, 1998), 21-22. Kevin J. Hayes, *A Colonial Woman's Bookshelf* (Knoxville: University of Tennessee Press, 1996), 44, claims that it was read "throughout the colonies. Several copies were imported into New England during the 1680s, and Boston bookseller Michael Perry had it in stock in 1700." In addition, there were twenty-seven copies of it in various South Carolina library inventories.

15. Julia Cherry Spruill, *Women's Life and Work in the Southern Colonies* (1938, reprinted New York: Norton, 1972), 208.

16. David Hall suggests that the number of books listed in an estate or even the number of estates that listed books was smaller than the number of people who owned books at any one time because books "get used up or discarded" before the inventory gets taken: Hall, *Worlds of Wonder, Days of Judgment: Popular Religious Belief in Early New England* (New York: Knopf, 1989), 249.

17. Will of William Norris, proved January 27, 1749, Maryland Wills, Book 26, 32-33.

18. Will of Rebecca Evans, proved December 11, 1736, Maryland Wills, Book 21, 754-755; inventories of Sarah Weaver, presented January 20, 1737, South Carolina WPA Misc. Wills, 68, 122-131; Anna Palsgrave, taken March 26, 1669, Suffolk Co., 7, 106-108; and Mary Ring, proved with her will October 28, 1633; Plymouth Colony Wills, 1, 55-59. According to Kevin J. Hayes, *The Ladies Library* was advertised for sale from Massachusetts to South Carolina; Hayes, *A Colonial Woman's Bookshelf*, 65. See also Thomas Foxcroft, *The Character of Anna, the Prophetess, Consider'd and Apply'd in a Sermon Preach'd after the Funeral of Dame Bridget Usher [Being a Widow of Great Age]* (Boston, 1723), 13; and Charles E. Hambrick-Stowe, *The Practice of Piety: Purtian Devotional Dispciplines in Seventeenth-Century New England* (Chapel Hill: University of North Carolina Press, 1982), 136-140.

19. Spruill, *Women's Life and Work in the Southern Colonies*, 208, 213, 217-218.

20. Mary Sumner Benson, *Women in Eighteenth-Century America: A Study of Opinion and Social Usage* (New York: Columbia University Press, 1935), 105.

21. This copy of the third edition of Mather's *Ornaments for the Daughters of Zion* is at the American Antiquarian Society, Worcester, Massachusetts. Laurel Thatcher Ulrich, "Hannah Barnard's Cupboard: Female Property and Identity in Eighteenth-Century New England," in Ronald Hoffman, Mechal Sobel, and Fredrika J. Teute; eds., *Through a Glass Darkly: Reflections on Personal Identity in Early America* (Chapel Hill: University of North Carolina Press, 1997), 240, 266, 269, 271. She convincingly argues that "ironically, the force of patriarchy might have encouraged certain women to develop a more complex and in some ways autonomous sense of self than their brothers or sons. Never able to step into a ready-made identity, they learned to mediate" such roles, 263. See also Hayes, *A Colonial Woman's Bookshelf*, 7-11, for a discussion of books inscribed by colonial women.

22. Kenneth Silverman, ed., *Selected Letters of Cotton Mather* (Baton Rouge: Louisiana State University Press, 1971), 253; and MHS, *Diary of Samuel Sewall*, 177, 182.

23. February 13, 1724 and March 28, 1724, Worthington Chauncy Ford, ed., *Diary of Cotton Mather*, 2 vols. (New York: Frederick Ungar, n.d.), v. II, 697, 700; and Thomas James Holmes, *Cotton Mather: A Bibliography*, 3 vols. (Cambridge, MA: Harvard University Press, 1940), 1180.

24. Hall, Worlds of Wonder, 45.

25. Malmsheimer, "New England Funeral Sermons," 48. This discussion of sermons focuses on New England because sermons from South Carolina have not survived, and the popular sermons of Archbishop John Tilllotson, "whose works appear in nearly every southern colony," do not deal directly with issues of widowhood; Richard Beale Davis, *Intellectual Life in the Colonial South, 1585-1763*, 3 vols. (Knoxville: The University of Tennessee Press, 1978), v. II, 714, 755.

26. Foxcroft, *The Character of Anna*, 13; and Hambrick-Stowe, *Practice of Piety*, 136-140.

27. With the advent of professional theater companies and indoor playhouses in the late sixteenth century in Britain, plays became a more widely available commercialized form of leisure. A great variety of people joined the earlier wealthy, leisured male patrons. The shift in the class and gender of theatrical audiences created anxiety among the male elite. They worried about the theater's effect on audiences in general and on women more specifically. As in other areas of conduct literature, sixteenth-century English commentators expressed conflicting opinions about women's presence. Some argued that such public gatherings threatened women's morals, while others argued, more important, that women belonged in the audience because the plays instructed them about the world and their place in it. See Kathleen McLuskie, *Renaissance Dramatists*, ch. 4, "What Should Chaste Ears do at a Play?" (Atlantic Highlands, NJ: Humanities Press International, 1989), 87-99; Michael Hattaway, "Drama and Society," in A. R. Braunmuller and Michael Hattaway, eds., *The Cambridge Companion to English Renaissance Drama* (Cambridge: Cambridge University Press, 1990), 91-126; and Lee Bliss, "Pastiche, Burlesque, Tragicomedy," in ibid., 237-261.

28. According to Richard Beale Davis, Charleston "had a play or plays as early as 1703, though its first dramatic season was in 1735," and they were "almost always those popular in the mother country at the time." While smaller-town planters in Maryland rarely saw plays, "the larger planters staged and produced plays in the great halls of their mansions." In addition, "there were reading of plays . . . around manor house fireplaces." See Davis, *Intellectual Life in the Colonial South*, v. III, 1192, 1280, 1297, 1302.

29. Hall, *Worlds of Wonder*, 242.

30. Anne M. Haselkorn and Betty S. Travitsky, *The Renaissance Englishwoman in Print* (Amherst: University of Massachusetts Press, 1990), 10.

31. David Underdown, *Revel, Riot, and Rebellion: Popular Politics and Culture in England, 1603-1660* (Oxford: Clarendon Press, 1985), 28, 37-39; Virginia Walcott Beauchamp, Elizabeth H. Hageman, and Margaret Mikesell, eds., *The Instruction of a Christen Woman by Juan Luis Vives* (Urbana: University of Illinois Press, 2001), "The Work: Its Contexts, Content, and Translation," http://www.press.uillinois.edu/epub/books/vives/work.html (accessed May 21, 2005).

32. Linda Woodbridge, *Women and the English Renaissance: Literature and*

the Nature of Womankind, 1540-1620 (Urbana: University of Illinois Press, 1986), 13; and Katherine Henderson and Barbara F. McManus, *Half Humankind: Contexts and Texts of the Controversy About Women in England, 1540-1640* (Urbana: University of Illinois Press, 1985), 75. See also Margaret W. Ferguson, Maureen Quilligan, and Nancy J. Vickers, eds., *Rewriting the Renaissance: The Discourses of Sexual Difference in Early Modern Europe* (Chicago: The University of Chicago Press, 1986); Elaine V. Beilin, *Redeeming Eve: Women Writers of the English Renaissance* (Princeton: Princeton University Press, 1987); Haselkorn and Travitsky, *The Renaissance Englishwoman in Print*; and Kirby Farrell, Elizabeth H. Hageman, and Arthur F. Kinney, eds., *Women in the Renaissance: Selections From English Literary Renaissance* (Amherst: University of Massachusetts Press, 1990). Michael Zuckerman, "The Fabrication of Identity in Early America," *William and Mary Quarterly*, 3rd Series 34, no. 2 (April 1977), 189. In explaining the ideological shift between the Middle Ages and the early modern era, Zuckerman argues that the former "had admitted oppositions, but the 'distinctive feature of medieval thought' was that it absorbed 'contrasts which later were to be presented as irreconcilable antitheses.' . . . [T]he rage for categorization and compartmentalization that shaped the new bourgeois culture of the seventeenth century made distinctions central that had scarcely been salient for medieval folk, embedded as they were in a more intricate and multifarious web of human relations," 185, 188. In her study on the significance of speech in early New England, Jane Kamensky finds the same chronological burgeoning in England of an "intense anxiety about disorder and instability," especially as writers demonstrated a "virtual obsession with 'scolding' women." See Jane Kamensky, *Governing the Tongue: The Politics of Speech in Early New England* (New York: Oxford University Press, 1997), 20-22.

33. This triptych of ideal role models appears in both formal (advice books) and informal (plays and poems) literature throughout the Renaissance. See Linda Woodbridge's discussion of this paradigm in *Women and the English Renaissance*, 84, 93, and 233. The quote is from [Richard Allestree], *The Ladies Calling in Two Parts. By the Author of the Whole Duty of Man, the Causes of the Decay of Christian Pety, and the Gentlemans Calling* (Oxford, 1673), 2.

34. The poem appears in *The Witch*, but the passage is from Robert Trager Levine, *A Critical Edition of Thomas Middleton's "The Widow"* (Salzburg, Austria: Institut fur Englissche Sprache Und Literatur, 1975), liii, n. 10.

35. Samuel Rowlands, *Tis Merrie When Gossips Meet* (Sold by G. Loftus, 1602). Linda Woodbridge argues that, although this is a satirical look at the three phases of women's lives, "the widow also transcends stereotype" because the usual lechery is absent; that is, the widow is not painted as an "evil temptress, seducing virtuous women away from hearth and home." Nor does she "harp" on the joys of liberty as most such dialogues do. Woodbridge also argues that "there is at least a hint that her brash self-confidence conceals essential loneliness," *Women and the*

English Renaissance, 227-228. I agree with her first argument but disagree with the second. I do not think we need to see widows as pitiful because they have no one to go home to, nor do I think that was the point of the widow's advice. See, for example, Robert Copland's satirical *The Seven Sorrowes that Women Have When Theyr Husbandes be Deade* (W. Copland, 1568[?]), n.p. His widow's response to remarriage is:

Me think I lede a merely mery life
Whiche I should not yf that I were a wyfe
To bed I go and ryse whan I wyll
All that I do is reason and skyll
I commaunde other but none commandeth me
And eke I stande at myne owne liberte

36. Elaine Hobby, *The Virtue of Necessity: English Women's Writing, 1649-1688* (Ann Arbor: University of Michigan Press, 1988), 107.

37. Juan Luis Vives, *A Very Fruitfull and Pleasant Booke Called The Instruction of a Christian Woman* (written in Latin in 1523 and translated into English and published by Richard Hyrde in about 1540), 368.

38. T.E., *The Lawes Resolutions of Womens Rights; Or, The Lawes Provision for Woemen. A Methodicall Collection of such Statutes and Customes, with the Cases, Opinions, Arguments and points of Learning in the Law, as doe properly concerne Women* (London, 1632), 331-332.

39. Thomas Heywood, *Gunaikeion: Or Nine Bookes of Various History Concerninge Women; Inscribed by ye Names of ye Nine Muses* (London, 1624), 127, 281-282. *Gunaikeion* was a compilation of tales of brave queens, learned ladies, chaste damsels, Amazons, and witches culled from other books. Many advice books referred to the "turtle" or turtle dove, a bird noted for its devotion to its mate, to symbolize the good woman who did not remarry. See, for example, Joshuah Sylvester, *Monodia: An Elegy, in Commeroration of the Vertuous Life, and godly deth of the right worshipfull and most religious Lady, Dame Hellen Branch Widow . . . , 1594*, in Alexander B. Grosart, ed., *The Complete Works of Joshuah Sylvester* (London, 1880), 47. According to the *Aberdeen Bestiary*, "it is believed that the female dove will not take a second mate if her first mate dies. Parallels are drawn to virtuous widows remaining chaste and single, thus a single turtle dove is a symbol of chastity (and possibly purity), and a pair of turtle doves has some symbolism of love"; Aberdeen University, Aberdeen University Library MS 24, http://www.abdn.ac.uk/bestiary/translat/32r.hti (accessed May 16, 2005).

40. Hobby, *Virtue of Necessity*, 72-74. The full title of her autobiography is *Satan his Methods and Malice Baffled. A Narrative of God's Gracious Dealings* (London, 1683).

41. Vives, *Very Fruitfull and Pleasant Booke*, 364; T.E., *Lawes Resolutions*, 231.

42. Draft of a letter written August 28, 1729 (the intended recipient is unknown), Amory Papers, Massachusetts Historical Society, Boston, v. 1, n.p.

43. Increase Mather's preface to Cotton Mather's *Marah Spoken To*, i, 24. See also Cotton Mather's *The Widow of Nain*, 10-11.

44. T.E., *Lawes Resolutions*, 232.

45. This discussion of Thomas Elyot's *The Defence of Good Women* is taken from Woodbridge, *Women and the English Renaissance*, 20; and Constance Jordan, "Feminism and the Humanists: The Case of Sir Thomas Elyot's *Defence of Good Women*," in Ferguson, Quilligan, and Vickers, eds., *Rewriting the Renaissance*, 242-258. Similarly, the sixteenth-century Catholic humanist Juan Luis Vives, *A Very Fruitfull and Pleasant Booke*, 368, speculated that some widows were probably glad that their husbands were dead "as who were rid of yoke & bondage they rejoise yt they be out of dominion & bondage & have recovered their liberty."

46. John Taylor, *A Juniper Lecture, With the description of all sorts of women, good and bad: From the modest to the maddest, from the most Civil to the most Rampant, their praise and dispraise compendiously related. The Second Impression, with many new Additions* (London, 1639), reprinted in Woodbridge, Half Humankind, 300. Even the author of *The Lawes Resolutions* conceded the point by asking his female readers, "why mourne youse, you that be widowes Consider how long you have been in subjection under the predominance of parents, of your husbands, now you be free in libertie, and free at your owne law," 232. For a cross-cultural perspective, see Ann Marie Plane, *Colonial Intimacies: Indian Marriage in Early New England* (Ithaca, NY: Cornell University Press, 2000), 110; using the words of Experience Mayhew, she describes an eighteenth-century Indian woman "who chose not to remarry, . . . 'saying that if she married again, she might thereby bring such Troubles upon her self, as living a single Life she might be free from.'"

47. [Allestree], *The Ladies Calling in Two Parts*, 75, 79-81.

48. *South Carolina Gazette*, November 21, 1743. A similar reference to slavery came from an anonymous author who argued that the remarrying widow was like "a gally-slave, who, in the madness of joy for his liberty, runneth himself again into bondage," *The Whole Duty of Woman, By a Lady. Written at the Desire of a Noble LORD* (London, 1753), 85.

49. Vives, *Very Fruitfull and Pleasant Booke*, 368.

50. Here Swetnam is likely making a play on words and is, in fact, suggesting that widows will give up neither their self-control nor their estates. Joseph Swetnam [pseud. Thomas Tel-troth], *The Arraignment of Lewde, Idle, Froward, and Unconstant Women. Or the Vanitie of them, choose you whether. With a Commendacion of wife, vertuous and honest Women. Pleasant for married Men, profitable for young Men and hurtfull to none* (London: Printed by Edward Ailde for Thomas Arches, 1615), 59-60. This book was reprinted ten times between 1615 and 1634; see Underdown, *Revel, Riot, and Rebellion*, 38, and Angeline Gorneau, *The Whole Duty of a Woman: Female Writers in Seventeenth-Century England* (New York: Dial Press, 1985), 62.

51. Vives, *Very Fruitfull and Pleasant Booke,* 382; and Heywood, *Gunaikeion,* 127.

52. Vives, *Very Fruitfull and Pleasant Booke,* 383. These same sentiments were echoed in Thomas Fuller, *The Holy State* (Cambridge, 1642), 26 (this work describes the holy state as existing in the family and in public life and gives rules of conduct and model "characters" for the various professions and profane biographies. It was perhaps the most popular of all his writings); and T.E., *Lawes Resolutions,* 232.

53. Thomas Pritchard, *The Schoole of Honest and Vertuous Life: Profitable and necessary for all estates and degrees, to be trayned in: . . . Also a Laudable and learned Discourse . . . sent written as Jewell unto a worthy Gentlewoman, in the time of her widowhood . . .* (London, 1579), 60.

54. Patricia Meyer Spacks, ed., *Selections From* The Female Spectator *by Eliza Haywood* (Oxford: Oxford University Press, 1999), 256. According to Hayes, *The Female Spectator,* the first magazine by and for women, was "one of the most important books which could be found" among books read by women; Hayes, *The Colonial Woman's Bookshelf,* 69.

55. For sermons that mention Anna, see Benjamin Colman, *The Duty and Honour of Aged Women. A Funeral Sermon Occasion'd by the Decease of Mrs. Abigail Foster* (Boston, 1711), 15; Foxcroft, *The Character of Anna, the Prophetess*; Cotton Mather, *Ornaments for the Daughters of Zion; Cotton Mather, Tabitha Rediviva: An Essay to Describe and Commend the Good Works of a Vertuous Woman* (Boston, 1713), 47; and *The Notebook of John Saffin, 1665-1708,* "Elegy to the Religious Matron Mrs. Sarah Leveritt," American Antiquarian Society, Worcester, Massachusetts, typescript copied from the original manuscript in the possession of the Rhode Island Historical Society, 65. In his *Ornaments,* Mather explicitly elides the character of the "widow indeed" and Anna.

56. Cotton Mather, *Ecclesia Monilia: The Peculiar Treasure of the Almighty King Opened and the Jewels that are made up in it, Exposed. [The Funeral Sermon of] Mrs. Elizabeth Cotton, and Certain Instruments and Memorials of Piety, Written by that Valuable & Honourable Gentlewoman* (Boston, 1726), 37-38. The important shift in emphasis and its consequences are noted by Peter Brown in his study of permanent sexual renunciation and its relationship to the structure and meaning of society. He argues that "the fides [faith] that Romans occasionally expected a woman to show even to her dead husband, by refusing to remarry, was transformed into a perpetual loyalty to Christ, which good Christian widows were expected to show for the rest of their lives." Peter Brown, *The Body and Society: Men, Women, and Sexual Renunciation in Early Christianity* (New York: Columbia University Press, 1988), 147-149.

57. Quote taken from Henderson and McManus, *Half Humankind,* 75.

58. Ford, *The Diary of Cotton Mather,* v. 1, 1681-1709, 457. For a more extensive discussion of male remarriage see Lisa Wilson, *Ye Heart of a Man: The Domestic*

Life of Men in Colonial New England (New Haven: Yale University Press, 1999), 143-170.

59. For evidence of the threat wealthy unmarried widows could present to the community, see Karlsen, *The Devil in the Shape of a Woman.*

60. Pritchard, *Schoole of Honest and Vertuous Life,* 53.

61. Cotton Mather, *Ornaments for the Daughters of Zion,* Section IV.

62. Helen Spratt to Alicia Ross, January 15, 1725, Key Family Papers, MS 650, Manuscript Division, Maryland Historical Society Library, Baltimore, Maryland. For further information about the economic aspects of widow remarriage, see Alain Bideau, "A Demographic and Social Analysis of Widowhood and Remarriage: The Example of the Castellany of Thoissey-en-Dombes, 1670-1840," *Journal of Family History* 5 (Spring 1980), 34; Bridget Hill, *Women, Work and Sexual Politics in Eighteenth-Century England* (Oxford: Basil Blackwell, 1989), 241; Miranda Chaytor and Jane Lewis, Introduction, to Alice Clark, *Working Life of Women in the Seventeenth Century* (London: Routledge, 1919; repr. London: Routledge, 1982), xxxvi; Vivien Brodsky, "Widows in Late Elizabethan London: Remarriage, Economic Opportunity and Family Orientations," in Lloyd Bonfield, Richard M. Smith, and Keith Wrightson, eds., *The World We Have Gained: Histories of Population and Social Structure* (Oxford: Basil Blackwell, 1986), 132; B. A. Holderness, "Widows in Pre-Industrial Society: An Essay Upon Their Economic Functions," in Richard M. Smith, ed., *Land, Kinship, and Life-Cycle* (Cambridge: Cambridge University Press, 1985), 428; and Susan D. Amussen, "Governors and Governed: Class and Gender Relations in English Villages, 1590-1725" (Ph.D. diss., Brown University, 1982), 261.

63. Allestree, *The Ladies Calling,* 73; Vives, *Very Fruitfull and Pleasant Booke,* 401; and Fuller, *Holy State,* 26.

64. John Dunton, *Letters Written From New-England, A.D. 1686 by John Dunton. In Which are Described His Voyages by Sea, His Travels on Land, and the Characters of His Friends and Acquaintances, Notes and Appendix by W. H. Whitmore* (Boston: Published for the Prince Society, 1867), 108; and Vives, *Very Fruitfull and Pleasant Booke,* 404. See also the sayings of Fuller in which he argues that the widow "will not morgage her first husbands pawns, thereby to purchase the good will of a second," in Holy State, 26; and [Allestree], *The Ladies Calling,* who worries that the widow would defraud her own children of their estates, 73.

65. Spacks, *Selections from* The Female Spectator, 221-224.

66. McLuskie, *Renaissance Dramatists,* 90.

67. Hattaway, "Drama and Society," 106, 122.

68. W. S., *The Puritan: or, the Widow of Watling Street,* in William Kozlenko, ed., *Disputed Plays of William Shakespeare* (New York: Hawthorn Books, 1974, originally published 1607), 224-261; George Chapman, *The Widdowes Teares: A Comedie* (London: Printed for John Browne, 1612); Thomas Middleton, *The*

Widdow, A Comedie As it was Acted at the Private House in Black-Fryers (London: Humphrey Mosely, 1652); William R. Hersey, *A Critical Old-Spelling Edition of Aphra Behn's* The City Heiress (New York: Garland, 1987); and Aphra Behn, *The Widow Ranter or The History of Bacon in Virginia. A Tragi-Comedy, Acted by their Majesties Servants* (London, 1690). For recent analysis of such plays, see Jennifer Panek, "'My Naked Weapon': Male Anxiety and the Violent Courtship of the Jacobean Stage Widow," *Comparative Drama* 34, no. 3 (Fall 2000), 321-344; Karen R. Bloom, "My Worldly Goods Do Thee Endow"; Economic Conservatism, Widowhood, and the Mid- and Late-Eighteenth-Century Novel," *Intertexts* 7, no. 1 (Spring 2003), 27-48; and Elizabeth Hanson, "There's Meat and Money Too: Rich Widows and Allegories of Wealth in Jacobean City Comedy," *English Literary History* 72, no.1 (2005), 209-238.

69. Kozlenko, ed., *Widow of Watling Street*, 232.

70. Chapman, *Widdowes Teares*, n.p.

71. Susan Centlivre, *The Gamester: A Comedy, As it is Acted at the New-Theatre in Lincolns-Inn-Fields, by her Majesty's Servants in The Plays of Susanna Centlivre*, ed. Richard C. Frushell (New York: Garland, 1982). According to Davis, her plays were especially popular in the South; Davis, *Intellectual Life in the Colonial South*, v. III, 1296.

72. Kozlenko, ed., *Widow of Watling Street*. For a similar pattern, see William Congreve's *The Way of the World* (1700), in which he satirizes widows in portraying Lady Wishfort [wish-for-it] as a pathetic, lusty woman who flatters herself that young men want her. She is ultimately duped by a rake who uses her to get to her niece, and she almost marries a disguised servant. According to Mirabell, the rake in question: "An old woman's appetite is depraved like that of a girl. 'Tis the green sickness of a second childhood; and like the faint offer of a latter spring, serves but to usher in the fall, and withers in an affected bloom." Kathleen M. Lynch, ed., *William Congreve's* The Way of the World (Lincoln: University of Nebraska Press, 1965). My deep thanks to Patsy Fowler of Gonzaga University for bringing this to my attention and for engaging in a discussion of eighteenth-century widowhood in English literature.

73. Chapman, *Widdowes Teares*, B2.

74. Middleton, *The Widdow*, 15-19.

75. Swetnam, *Arraignment of Lewde, Idle, Froward and Unconstant Women*, 60.

76. Daniel Defoe, *Roxana, the Fortunate Mistress* (New York: Bibliophilist Society, 1931), 144-145.

77. Kozlenko, ed., *Widow of Watling Street*, 232.

78. Jennifer Panek argues that, in fact, this focus on the uncontrolled sexuality of widows compensates for deep-seated male anxiety about marrying a more experienced, wealthier, and, often, older woman. It "bolster[ed] the masculinity that the widow threatened in other facets of the relationships, and by reducing the

powerful widow to a mere woman, laughably at the mercy of her feminine appetite." See "'My Naked Weapon,'" 322. She has a full-length treatment of this subject in *Widows and Suitors in Early Modern English Comedy* (Cambridge: Cambridge University Press, 2004).

79. Kozlenko, ed., *Widow of Watling Street*, 235. In Chapman's *Widdowes Teares*, n.p., a widow's suitor and his friend carry on a similar conversation. A suitor claims that the widow disingenuously "spun out many a tedious lecture . . . against concupiscence," to which his friend replied, "these angry heats that break out at the lips of these strait-laced ladies are but as symptoms of a lustful fever that boils within them." To win over the licentious widow, Tharsalio bribed Arsace into telling her that Tharsalio had been known to make "nine in a night . . . mad with his love." Presumably, tales of his sexual prowess would sway the widow Eudora, who was embroiled in a lustful fever, to marry him.

80. Hersey, *Aphra Behn's* City Heiress, 168, 264.

81. Susannah Centlivre, *The Dramatic Works of the Celebrated Mrs. Centlivre, with a New Account of her Life*. Complete in Three Volumes. (New York: AMS Press, 1968. Reprinted from the London, 1872, edition), v. I, 208-209.

82. Defoe, *Roxana*, 146-151.

83. Kozlenko, ed., *Widow of Watling Street*, 260-261.

84. Middleton, *The Widdow*, 7.

85. This analysis was aided in large part by my reading and understanding of Mary Poovey's *Uneven Developments: The Ideological Work of Gender in Mid-Victorian England*, especially ch. 3, "Covered But Not Bound: Caroline Norton and the 1857 Matrimonial Causes Act" (Chicago: University of Chicago Press, 1988), 75–80.

86. Chapman, *Widdowes Teares*, n.p.

87. Hersey, *Aphra Behn's* City Heiress, 245.

88. Mary Ann O'Donnell, "Tory Wit and Unconventional Woman: Aphra Behn," in Katherine M. Wilson and Frank J. Warnke, eds., *Women Writers of the Seventeenth Century* (Athens: University of Georgia Press, 1989), 343-345.

89. Allyn B. Forbes, ed., *Winthrop Papers* (Boston: Massachusetts Historical Society, 1929-1947), v. II, 169-170. I want to thank Mary Beth Norton for this reference.

90. Amussen, "Governors and Governed," 224; Holderness, "Widows in Pre-Industrial Society," 431; Hill, *Women, Work, and Sexual Politics*, 240; and Philip Ariés, "Remarriage in France Under the *Ancien Régime* During the Seventeenth and Eighteenth Centuries: Differences Between Theory and Practice," in J. Dupâquier, E. Hélin, P. Laslett, M. Liv-Bacci, and S. Sogner, eds., *Marriage and Remarriage in Populations of the Past* (London: Academic Press, 1981), 48.

91. Ariés, "Remarriage in France Under the Ancien Régime, 48; Holderness, "Widows in Pre-Industrial Society," 431; Judith Bennett, *Women in the Medieval English Countryside: Gender and Household in Brigstock Before the Plague* (New

York: Oxford University Press, 1987), 146; and Barbara J. Todd, "The Remarrying Widow: A Stereotype Reconsidered," in Mary Prior, ed., *Women in English Society, 1500-1800* (London: Methuen Press, 1985), 60 and 65. Todd argues that the declining remarriage rates for Abington widows from a high of 50 percent from 1540 to 1599 to a low of just over 23 percent for the period 1660 to 1720 was due not only to the fact that older widows tended to remarry less than did younger widows but also to an increase in the number of women widowed at an older age. For a continuing debate on this issue, see Jeremy Boulton, "London Widowhood Revisited: The Decline of Female Remarriage in the Seventeenth and Early Eighteenth Centuries," *Continuity and Change* 5, no. 3 (1990), 325-355, and Barbara J. Todd, "Demographic Determinism and Female Agency: The Remarrying Widow Reconsidered . . . Again," *Continuity and Change* 9, no. 3 (1994), 421–450.

92. Susan Grigg, "Toward a Theory of Remarriage: A Case Study of Newburyport at the Beginning of the Nineteenth Century," *Journal of Interdisciplinary History* 8, no. 2 (1977), 185 and 193.

93. Faragher, "Old Women and Old Men," 18; and Grigg, "Toward a Theory of Remarriage," 200.

94. John Demos, *A Little Commonwealth: Family Life in Plymouth Colony* (Oxford: Oxford University Press, 1970), 67; John Demos, "Old Age in Early New England," 238; Faragher, "Old Women and Old Men," 18. Daniel Scott Smith, "Inheritance and the Social History of Early American Women," in Ronald Hoffman and Peter J. Albert, eds., *Women in the Age of the American Revolution* (Charlottesville: University Press of Virginia, 1989), 55, also discovered fifty to be the age after which widows did not remarry and found that women without children—that is, women still in their childbearing years—were likely to remarry, 55. Karen Andrésen found that widows who did not remarry were an average of nearly fifty years old and had raised six children. See Andrésen, "Marah Revisited: The Widow in Early New Hampshire," an unpublished paper given at the 1981 Berkshire Conference of Women's History, 7-9.

95. Keyssar, "Widowhood in Eighteenth-Century Massachusetts," 90; Gloria L. Main, "Widows in Rural Massachusetts on the Eve of the American Revolution," in Ronald Hoffman and Peter J. Albert, *Women in the Age of the American Revolution* (Charlottesville: University Press of Virginia, 1989), 69; Jones, *Village and Seaport Migration and Society*, 79, found that there were seven widows for every one widower; Wells, *The Population of the British Colonies*, 96; Toby L. Ditz, *Property and Kinship: Inheritance in Early Connecticut, 1750-1820* (Princeton: Princeton University Press, 1986), 178; Faragher, "Old Women and Old Men," 19.

96. Todd, "Demographic Determinism and Female Agency," makes a similar argument about widows in eighteenth-century England.

97. Speth, "More Than Her 'Thirds,' 27-28; Morgan, *American Slavery, American Freedom*, 166; Lorena Seebach Walsh, "Charles County, Maryland, 1658-1705: A Study of Chesapeake Social and Political Structure" (Ph.D. diss., Michigan State

University, 1977), 67; Carr and Walsh, "The Planter's Wife," 560; Main, *Tobacco Colony*, 92; Darrett B. Rutman and Anita H. Rutman, *A Place in Time: Explicatus* (New York: Norton, 1984), 66-69; Gampel, "The Planter's Wife Revisited," 25. For more on the high remarriage rate in seventeenth-century South Carolina, see Lorri Glover, *All Our Relations: Blood Ties and Emotional Bonds Among the Early South Carolina Gentry* (Baltimore: Johns Hopkins University Press, 2000), 9.

98. Russell Menard, *Economy and Society in Early Colonial Maryland* (New York: Garland, 1985), 53; John E. Crowley, "Family Relations and Inheritance in Early South Carolina," *Social History* 17, no. 33 (1984), 43; Carr and Walsh, "The Planter's Wife," 567; Rutman and Rutman, *A Place in Time: Explicatus*, 66. See Anzilotti, *In the Affairs of the World*, 3-8, 53, 97-99, 109, 140, for an extensive discussion of the effects of skewed demographics in South Carolina; like Barbara Todd, she argues that historians put too much emphasis on such demographics and not enough emphasis on women's choice to remain unmarried when explaining women's power in colonial South Carolina; Kierner, *Beyond the Household*, 4, 11; Glover, *All Our Relations*, 7.

99. Charles Carlton, "The Widow's Tale: Male Myths and Female Reality in 16th and 17th Century England," *Albion* 10, no. 2 (Summer 1978), 128-129, argues that the discrepancy between the stereotypical widow and her counterpart in reality was so great because widowhood "combines two of the most fundamental tensions within the male psyche—the contemplation of their woman's sexuality . . . and their own death"; in creating tales about widows, men were able to resolve the "problem of the widow" by parodying their fears, guilt, and ambivalence toward widows.

100. Letters from Rebecca Holmes Amory, Boston, to Isaac Holmes, Charleston, South Carolina, December 2, 1738, and January 29, 1739, Amory Family Papers, Massachusetts Historical Society, N279, Reel 1.

101. Cotton Mather, *The Widow of Nain*, 10.

102. Letter dated August 28, 1728, Amory Family Papers, Massachusetts Historical Society, v. I, 1698-1784.

CHAPTER 2

1. Anne King Gregorie, ed., *Records of the Court of Chancery of South Carolina, 1671-1779* (Washington, DC: American Historical Association, 1950), Case Papers, December 28, 1704, 82-87.

2. Pruden, "Family, Community, Economy," 70, argues that men's wills were legal obligations that restricted women's control of real and personal property, that they made women recipients of men's governance and not agents of family authority. In eschewing willmaking, women like Rebecca Amory may have eschewed their motherly governance in favor of their exerting their own authority.

3. The laws themselves have been thoroughly described and analyzed by Julius

Goebels, George Haskins, David Konig, Robert Morris, and Marylynn Salmon. Throughout this discussion I will use the terms "the law" and "laws" in very distinct ways. I will use "the law" to mean the broad collection of rules and regulations that establish, maintain, and modify the social behavior of the members of a community. By "laws," I mean the specific acts making up the broad collection.

4. George Haskins, *Law and Authority in Early Massachusetts: A Study in Tradition and Design* (New York: Archon, 1968), 2, 6; Konig, *Law and Society*, 37; Marylynn Salmon, *Women and the Law of Property in Early America* (Chapel Hill: University of North Carolina Press, 1986), xi-xii.

5. See, for example, Dayton, *Women Before the Bar*.

6. Between 1650 and 1680 Maryland widows made up 56.7 percent of all female civil plaintiffs and 49.5 percent of all female civil defendants. New England widows also made up "a large proportion of the female litigants." Widows made up 64 percent of all women's appearances in civil cases between 1710 and 1729 and 41 percent of civil cases between 1730 and 1749; see Dayton, "Women Before the Bar," 39, 56. I am grateful for Professor Norton's willingness to share her findings with me.

7. Christine de Pizan, *A Medieval Woman's Mirror of Honor: The Treasury of the City of Ladies*, Charity Cannon Willard, trans., and Madeleine Pelner Cosman, ed. (New York: Bard Hall Press, 1989), 120.

8. Ibid., 199.

9. William Hand Browne et al., eds., *Archives of Maryland: Proceedings and Acts of the General Assembly of Maryland*, 72 vols. (Baltimore, 1883-1972), hereafter cited as *MD Archives*, LIII, 424-425. On widows turning to the "local legal fraternity" in Virginia, see Snyder, *Brabbling Women*, 117-119, 127-130. She argues that, because widows were "theoretically the most independent of women householders," they found "themselves to be the most vulnerable to conflict." When push came to shove, women relied of the service of empowered men.

10. Fuller, *Holy State*, 25; and Vives, *Very Fruitfull and Pleasant Booke*, 393-399. The two-sentence poem appears at the close of the widow Ann Marcomb's petition to the Maryland Provincial Court, June 5, 1667, seeking relief from the "meane estate" in which she was forced to live after her husband's death, *MD Archives*, LVII, 207.

11. Although the word "patriarchy," especially its narrow definition as the legal power of a father over his wife, children, and other dependents, would have been appropriate, I have explicitly avoided using it. Patriarchy encompasses meanings that are often too all-encompassing, too overarching, and too inflexible to be useful in this context, and the very use of the word itself tends to hides women's agency and women's power over and against a patriarchal system.

12. For a more in-depth and systematic discussion of these issues in specifically legal anthropological terms, see June Starr and Jane F. Collier, eds., *History*

and Power in the Study of Law: New Directions in Legal Anthropology (Ithaca, NY: Cornell University Press, 1989).

13. *MD Archives*, LVII, Provincial Court, June 5, 1667, 207.

14. T.E., *The Lawes Resolutions*, 6.

15. William Blackstone, *Commentaries on the Laws of England* (Oxford: Clarenden Press, 1765-1769), v. I, 442.

16. In the language of the day, they would have been called executrix or administratrix. For a more detailed discussion of *feme sole* and *feme covert* status, see Marylynn Salmon, "Equality or Submersion? *Feme Covert* Status in Early Pennsylvania," in Carol Ruth Berkin and Mary Beth Norton, eds., *Women of America: A History* (Boston: Houghton Mifflin, 1979), 93–111; Marylynn Salmon, "Women and Property in South Carolina, The Evidence From Marriage Settlements, 1730 to 1830," *William and Mary Quarterly*, 3rd series 39, no. 4 (October 1982), 655–657; and Salmon, *Women and the Law of Property*. In the American colonies under study here, a third of all male testators named their wives alone as executors, and another 16 percent named their wives as co-executors. The courts named widows as administrators alone more than 40 percent of the time and named widows as co-administrators 5 percent of the time.

17. T.E., *Lawes Resolutions*, 233; Petition of Priscilla Raynsford, Suffolk County Probate Records, New Series 4, May 14, 1700, 406-408.

18. Maria L. Cioni, "The Elizabethan Chancery and Women's Rights," in Delloyd J. Guth and John W. Mckenna, eds., *Tudor Rule and Revolution: Essays for G. R. Elton from His American Friends* (Cambridge: Cambridge University Press, 1974), 179-180.

19. T.E., *Lawes Resolutions*, 98-99, 106. For a clear explanation of the complex issue of dower and jointure, see Eileen Spring, *Law, Land, and Family: Aristocratic Inheritance in England, 1300-1800* (Chapel Hill: University of North Carolina Press, 1993), ch. 2, "The Widow," 38-65.

20. Cioni, "The Elizabeth Chancery," 174-176. According to Susan Staves, The Dower Act of 1833 settled the tug of war between widows and their husbands' heirs by declaring that dower could be restricted or even barred by declaration in the husband's will and that, by bequeathing her any land in which she had dower rights, the husband barred her from dower rights in the remaining land. See Susan Staves, *Married Women's Separate Property in England, 1660-1833* (Cambridge, MA: Harvard University Press, 1990).

21. Ralph Houlbrooke, *The English Family, 1450-1700* (London: Longman, 1984), 43, 210.

22. Shammas et al., *Inheritance in America*, 26-27; Houlbrooke, *The English Family*, 210; Henry Horwitz, "Testamentary Practice, Family Strategies, and the Last Phases of the Custom of London, 1660-1725," *Law and History Review* 2, no. 2 (Fall 1984), 223; and Cioni, "The Elizabethan Chancery," 169.

23. Spring, *Law, Land, and Family*, 63.

24. Widows' rights under testamentary law were not always clear. Initially, bequests of land from husband to wife were illegal. In order to circumvent the prohibition, landholders created a use, which was an indirect method of bequeathing. To prevent even this method of bequest, the crown instituted the Statute of Uses in 1535. In part, this statute specified that a woman could elect either dower *or* a postnuptial jointure, but not both. In 1540, the Statute of Wills allowed bequests of real property, but, because a wife was not legally a descendant of her husband and because husband and wife were accounted one person in law, bequests from husband to wife were generally void unless made in the form of a jointure. Initially, the bequest of land through jointure did not bar dower rights but became a "benevolence to be enjoyed in addition to dower." In 1560, Bushe's Case complicated the issue even further when it found that lands a husband bequeathed in recompense for dower barred his widow from taking her dower rights in any other property. See J. H. Baker, *An Introduction to English History*, 2nd ed. (London: Butterworths, 1979), 217 and 229; and Staves, *Married Women's Separate Property*, 104-113. For an examination of this issue in the colonial context, see Salmon, "Women and Property in South Carolina," 655-685.

25. George L. Haskins, "Reception of the Common Law in Seventeenth-Century Massachusetts: A Case Study," in George Athan Billias, ed., *Law and Authority in Colonial America* (Barre, MA: Barre, 1964), 18-19, 24; Haskins, *Law and Authority in Early Massachusetts*, 6; Konig, *Law and Society*, 37; and Salmon, *Women and the Law of Property*, 4-5.

26. Gregorie, *Records of the Court of Chancery*, Journal of the Grand Council, 61.

27. Robert M. Weir, *Colonial South Carolina: A History* (Millwood, NY: KTO Press, 1983), 173-174, claims that John Yeamans was the first Englishman to "import slaves in any number." It may be that his wife learned how to fight for her rights from her husband, whom Weir characterized as "ruthless and tough, . . .and] out to make a pound at all costs." Anzilotti, *In the Affairs of the World*, 53, argues that "in South Carolina, slavery was institutionalized from the earliest years of colonization [and] . . . patriarchy was modified to provide for a sufficient population of white masters to effectively control a rapidly growing body of slaves. White women were called upon to step into the breach. These female members of the white minority became essential partners in establishing white authority in the colony."

28. The quote is from Jack P. Greene's "Early South Carolina and the Psychology of British Colonization," in Greene, *Imperatives, Behaviors, and Identities: Essays in Early American Cultural History* (Charlottesville: University Press of Virginia, 1992), 107. For an excellent description of the legal and political discord in South Carolina prior to 1729, see M. Eugene Sirmans, *Colonial South Carolina: A Political History, 1663-1763* (Chapel Hill: University of North Carolina Press, 1966).

29. Salmon, *Women and the Law of Property*, 160; Crowley, "Family Relations and Inheritance," 56.

30. Crowley, "Family Relations and Inheritance," 52; M. Eugene Sirmans, "The Legal Status of the Slave in South Carolina, 1670-1740," *Journal of Southern History* 27, no. 4 (November 1962), 464, 466-467, 471. Sirmans traces in detail the historical debate about when South Carolina officially classified slaves as personal property.

31. Agreement between Sophia Hume and Alexander Hume, July 21, 1743, South Carolina WPA Miscellaneous Wills, 69a, 33-37.

32. Gregorie, *Records of the Court of Chancery*, Case Papers, 252-254.

33. Ibid., June 7, 1717, 204-208.

34. Anzilotti, *In the Affairs of the World*, 16; Crowley, "Family and Inheritance," 43; and Weir, *Colonial South Carolina*, 206-207.

35. Joseph H. Smith, "The Foundations of Law in Maryland, 1634-1715," in George Billias, ed., *Law and Authority in Colonial America* (Barre, MA: Barre, 1964), 95, 98; Thomas Bacon, ed., *The Laws of Maryland at Large, with Proper Indexes* (Annapolis: 1765); and William Kilty, ed., *The Laws of Maryland*, 2 vols. (Annapolis: Printed by Frederick Green, 1799).

36. Rose Scotcher's petition, *MD Archives*, XLI, 320; and Ruth Knowles's petition, *MD Archives*, LIV, 223-224. For similar requests see also the petitions of Susan Porter, *MD Archives*, X, 8; and Rebecca Manners, *MD Archives*, X, 108-109.

37. *MD Archives*, X, 228; *MD Archives*, LVII, 215-216.

38. Salmon, *Women and the Law of Property*, 5; *MD Archives*, 2, Assembly Proceedings, October 1671, 325-327.

39. Smith, "The Foundations of Law in Maryland, 1634-1715," 95-96, discusses the uncertainty created by the temporary laws that were continually passed, repealed, and revived.

40. *MD Archives*, VII, 195-201; Bacon, *The Laws of Maryland*.

41. *MD Archives*, XXXVIII, 41-43; ibid., XXXII, 542-544.

42. Ibid., XIII, 215-217.

43. Ibid., XXVI, 235-249.

44. Ibid., XXX, 344-345.

45. Ibid., XXXVI, 487.

46. MD Will Book, 21, Henry Moore's will, proved February 2, 1736, 509-511; MD Inventory Book, 21, Henry Moore's inventory, taken April 9, 1736, 341-343; MD Will Book, 23, Henry Neale's will, proved March 8, 1743, 34-35; MD Inventory Book, Henry Neale's inventory, presented June 12, 1743, 450-454; MD Will Book, 23, John Howard's will, proved March 22, 1743, 35-37; and MD Inventory Book, John Howard's inventory, taken April 26, 1743, 441-443.

47. For a similar New England case, see Phoebe Brintnall, who chose her thirds over a room in one of her husband's houses, her best bed and furniture,

?£30 annually, and transportation to meetings. Suffolk County Probate Records, 29, will proved October 29, 1731, 266-271.

48. Statement of James Tilghman, May 1, 1777, Galloway-Maxcy-Markoe Family Papers, Correspondence Book 1, Library of Congress Manuscripts Division. I want to thank Mary Beth Norton for telling me about the existence of this material.

49. James Galloway to Samuel Galloway, November 21, 1776, Galloway-Maxcy-Markoe MSS.

50. John Galloway to Samuel Galloway, January 15, 1777, Galloway-Maxcy-Markoe MSS.

51. Salmon, *Women and the Law of Property*, 6-9, 183-184. The quotation appears on p. 8.

52. This quotation is taken from George Haskins, "Reception of the Common Law in Seventeenth-Century Massachusetts: A Case Study," in George Athan Billias, ed., *Law and Authority in Colonial America* (Barre, MA: Barre, 1964), 20.

53. *The Book of the General Laws and Libertyes Concerning the Inhabitants of the Massachuets Collected out of the Records of the General Court for the Several Years Wherein They were Made and Established* (Cambridge, MA, 1648), 17.

54. *Essex County Probate Records*, II, April 5, 1673, 299-300.

55. Sarah Andrews, for example, was denied her rights in land her husband sold to Simon Bradstreet and Mr. Price, in George F. Dow, ed., *Essex County Quarterly Court Records*, 8 vols. (Salem: Essex Institute, 1911-1921) (hereafter *ECQCR*), v. III, March 1663, 46-47, 56.

56. Petition of Martha Ely, Northampton County Court at Springfield, September 1683, Forbes Library.

57. One of Eunice's neighbors, Ellin Stone, claimed to have "talked with Eunice Porter about the sale and she said nothing about her thirds." Roger Hascall, attorney of Eunice Porter v. Osman Trask, November 27, 1660, *ECQCR*, II, 251-252.

58. Susanna Rogers, late wife of Robert Rogers, deceased, administratrix of his estate vs. Mr. Philip Nelson, *ECQCR*, III, September 27, 1664, 186-189.

59. Suffolk County Probate Records, New Series 19, 265-266.

60. Mather, *The Widow of Nain*, 14.

61. Hampshire County Probate Records, I, 233.

62. Koehler, *A Search for Power*, 207.

63. The full petition, dated May 7, 1662, can be found in the Massachusetts Historical Society's Photostat Collection.

64. Essex County Wills, v. 325, Thomas Brown's will, proved July 4, 1743, 283-284. See also Essex County Wills, 328, Samuel Poor's will, proved October 10, 1748, 170-172.

65. Hampshire County Probate Records, William Partrigg's will, proved April 30, 1669, 103-104.

66. Suffolk County Probate Records, 16, his will, proved August 20, 1709, 606-608.

67. Nathaniel B. Shurtleff, ed., *Records of the Governor and Company of the Massachusetts Bay in New England*, Vol. 1 (Boston: William White, 1853), 281.

68. There are several versions of Frances Quilter's petition to the court, as well as testimony from several witnesses to the questionable will, taken June 2 and 3, 1679, Massachusetts Historical Society, Photostat Collection.

69. In Suffolk County, Massachusetts, just over 19 percent of testate men left estates valued at more than £500. Thus, 80 percent of Suffolk county testators left estates much smaller than Quilter's. This, indeed, was a large estate and one worth fighting for.

70. *Essex County Court Records*, VII, 255-256.

71. *The [1642] Book of the General Lawes and Libertyes*, 53-54.

72. Shurtleff, *Records of the Governor and Company*, 281; *The [1660] Book of the General Laws and Libertyes*, 81; and *[The 1692] Acts and Laws*, 6-8.

73. *Records of the Suffolk County Court*, I, 428, 544, 546.

74. *Essex County Probate Records*, I, Robert Tamsen's inventory, presented November 15, 1669, 227-229; and *Essex County Probate Records*, II, 174-77.

75. *Records of the Suffolk County Court*, I, 93, 95, 373-375.

76. *Essex County Probate Records*, II, 158-160; and *ECQCR*, IV, 27, 306-309.

77. *[The 1692] Acts and Laws*, 6-8; and *Acts and Laws, of His Majesties Province of the Massachusetts-Bay, in New-England* (Boston: By Bartholonew Green and John Allen, 1699), 5.

78. *Records of the Suffolk County Court*, II, 675.

79. *Records of the Suffolk County Court*, II, 845.

80. *Suffolk County Probate Records*, New Series 5, Petition of Mary Veazey dated September 11, 1700, and the Executors' response date October 22, 1700, 29-36. For example, in 1662, courts in Essex County gave Eliza Stevens £167, her son John £74, and each of her remaining children £37 each; in 1674, they granted Triphany (or Tryphena) Geare her husband's entire estate for her lifetime (on her death, *they* would divide the estate between her two daughters); and, in 1711, they awarded Anne Stickney, along with her eldest son, a double portion of her husband's real property, and the two remaining sons received one portion. See *Essex County Probate Records*, I, 377; ibid., II, 324; *ECQCR*, V, 311, and Essex County Microfilm Probate Records, 234-235, 310.

81. *Records of the Suffolk County Court*, II, 1064, 1096-1097.

CHAPTER 3

1. *MD Archives*, XLIX, 291-294, 319-21, 352-53; LVII, xxxix, 50-54, 335-338.

2. Salmon, "Equality or Submersion," 92-111; Salmon, "Women and Property," 655-685; and Salmon, *Women and the Law of Property*, 81-140.

3. Ostensibly, marriage settlements kept the widow's share of her dead husband's estate from being used to pay his debts and ensured that it would be used to provide her with support; clearly, they did not always succeed. Salmon, *Women and the Law of Property*, 93, 143; and Gampel, "The Planter's Wife Revisited," 33.

4. The quotation is from John J. Waters, "Patrimony, Succession, and Social Stability: Guilford, Connecticut in the Eighteenth Century," *Perspectives in American History* 10 (1976), 132, but other historians have used similar, if not the exact, terms in discussing male bequeathing patterns. See James W. Deen Jr., "Patterns of Testation: Four Tidewater Counties in Colonial Virginia," *The American Journal of Legal History*, 16 (1972), 158 and 170; Ditz, *Property and Kinship*, 42; Keyssar, "Widowhood in Eighteenth-Century Massachusetts," 104, 109, and 117; Kulikoff, *Tobacco and Slaves*, 47-51; Gloria L. Main, "Probate Records as a Source for Early American History," *William and Mary Quarterly*, 3rd series, 33 (1975), 91; David Narrett, "English Social Customs in a New World Setting: Patterns of Inheritance and Family Life in Colonial Suffolk County, New York," unpublished paper presented at the Conference on British Studies, October, 31, 1981, 13; Darrett B. Rutman and Anita H. Rutman, "'Now-Wives and Sons-in-Law': Parental Death in a Seventeenth-Century Virginia County," in Thad W. Tate and David L. Ammerman, eds., *The Chesapeake in the Seventeenth Century: Essays on Anglo-American Society* (Chapel Hill: University of North Carolina Press, 1979), 164; Shammas, "Early American Women and Control Over Capital"; Shammas et al., *Inheritance in America*, 209; Daniel Scott Smith, "Underregistration and Bias in Probate Records: An Analysis of Data From Eighteenth-Century Hingham, Massachusetts," *William and Mary Quarterly*, 3rd series, vol. 32, no. 1 (January 1975), 105; James K. Somerville, "The Salem (Mass.) Woman in the Home, 1660-1770," *Eighteenth-Century Life* 1 (1974), 11-12; Walsh, "Charles County, Maryland, 1658-1705," 143-144; and John J. Waters, "The Traditional World of the New England Peasants: A View From Seventeenth-Century Barnstable," *New England Historical Genealogical Society* (January 1976), 12, n. 30, 15.

5. According to Joan M. Jensen, by the midnineteenth century, throughout the Northeast and the Midwest, as a rule families divided their estates equally among all of their children—male and female: Jenson, *Loosening the Bonds: Mid-Atlantic Farm Women, 1750-1850* (New Haven: Yale University Press, 1987), 25-26; see also Suzanne Lebsock, *The Free Women of Petersburg: Status and Culture in a Southern Town, 1784-1860* (New York: Norton, 1984), ch. 5, "Women Alone: Property and Personalism," specifically, 77-79, 136-138; and Mary P. Ryan, *Cradle of the Middle Class: The Family in Oneida County, New York, 1790-1865*, 3rd ed. (New York: Cambridge University Press, 1981).

6. *Acts and Laws*, 1692, 2-3 and 6-8.

7. *Acts and Laws* [of Massachusetts Bay Colony], *Passed . . . Twenty-Ninth of May* (Boston, 1700), 185.

8. Margaret George, *Women in the First Capitalist Society: Experience in*

Seventeenth-Century England (Urbana: University of Illinois Press, 1988), 1-5; Bennett, *Women in the Medieval English Countryside*, 144. Changes in gender roles did not occur suddenly in the sixteenth century. That Bennett finds many of the same divisions and gender boundaries in the medieval period that I do suggests a gradual evolution. It was with the shift to capitalism, however, that such roles became more clearly defined and certainly more clearly articulated. Zuckerman reviews this transformation (and the vast literature addressing it) in the colonial American context in "The Fabrication of Identity in Early America," 185-192.

9. Susan Amussen, *An Ordered Society: Gender and Class in Early Modern England* (Oxford: Basil Blackwell, 1988), 1-34. See also Susan Cahn, *Industry of Devotion: The Transformation of Women's Work in England, 1500-1600* (New York: Columbia University Press, 1987), 1-8; and Bonnie S. Anderson and Judith P. Zinsser, *A History of Their Own: Women in Europe From Prehistory to the Present*, 2 vols. (New York: Harper & Row, 1988), v. I, 392-394.

10. Juan Luis Vives, *The Office and Duty of an Husband*, 1529 trans., Thomas Paynell (London, [1555?]), in Joan Larsen Klein, *Daughters, Wives, and Widows: Writings by Men About Women and Marriage in England, 1500-1640* (Urbana: University of Illinois Press, 1992), 32.

11. Thomas Tusser, *The Points of Housewifery, United to the Comfort of Husbandry* (London, 1580) (collated with 1573 and 1577), in Joan Larsen Klein, *Daughters, Wives, and Widows: Writings by Men About Women and Marriage in England, 1500-1640* (Urbana: University of Illinois Press, 1992), 211. Klein claims that "it is hard to find another work in English (apart from the Bible, The Book of Common Prayer and the Homilies) that had a more distinguished publishing history"; it appeared in print well into the nineteenth century, 206-208. See Lisa Wilson, *Ye Heart of a Man: The Domestic Life of Men in Colonial New England* (New Haven: Yale University Press, 1999), chs. 3 and 4, for a similar discussion of the interdependence of colonial husbands and wives.

12. Bennett, *Women in the Medieval Countryside*, 7.

13. Tusser, *The Points of Housewifery*, 211.

14. This practice continued throughout the colonial period in America. Church, tax, and court records identified widows not by their occupations (if they had any) but by their marital status. See Waters, "Patrimony, Succession, and Social Stability," 140, for a similar discussion.

15. Leonard Hoar, *The Sting of Death and Death Unstung . . . Preached on the occasion of the Death of the truely nobel and virtuous Lady Mildmay* (Boston, 1680), unpaginated.

16. Fuller, *Holy State*, 24; Mather, *Ornaments for the Daughters of Zion*, 99; and Dunton, *Letters Written From New-England*, 106.

17. Mather, *Marah Spoken To*, iii.

18. [Richard Steele], ed., *The Ladies Library Written by a Lady*, 3 vols., 4th

ed. [London, 1732], 234; Fuller, *Holy State*, 24; Vives, *Very Fruitfull and Pleasant Booke*, 364.

19. W.C., *Widowes Joy*, 9.

20. Cotton Mather, *Virtue in its Verdure: A Christian Exhibited as a Green Olivetree, in the House of God; with a Character of the Virtuous Mrs. Abigail Brown Who Expired Feb. 18. 1725.6* (Boston, 1725), i; and Charles Chauncy, *Man's Life Considered under the Similitude of a Vapour, that appeareth for a little Time, and then vanisheth away. A Sermon on the Death of that Honorable & Vertuous Gentlewoman Mrs. Sarah Byfield, the amiable Consort of the Honorable Nathanael Byfield, Esq.* (Boston, 1731), 38; Wilson, *Ye Heart of a Man*, 143-154.

21. See Vives, *Very Fruitfull and Pleasant Booke*, 364, 372; Dunton, *Letters Written From New England*, 106; Fuller, *Holy State*, 24; W.C., *Widowes Joy*, 9.

22. Heywood, *Gunaikeion*, 137; [Allestree], *The Ladies Calling*, 68-69; and *The Whole Duty of Woman. By a Lady. Written at the Desire of a Nobel LORD* (London, 1753), 85.

23. Cotton Mather, *Monica Americana: A Funeral Sermon, Occasioned by the Death of Mrs. Sarah Leverett [or Female Piety Exemplified in a Funeral Sermon on the Death . . .]* (Boston, 1705), 26.

24. Foxcroft, *Character of Anna*, 9.

25. T.E., *The Lawes Resolutions*, 231. See also Vives, *A Very Fruitfull and Pleasant Booke*, 364; Fuller, *The Holy State*, 24; and W.C., *The Widowes Joy or Christ His Comfortable Salvation to a Comfortless Widow* (London, 1622), 8.

26. Mather, *Marah Spoken To*, iii.

27. Dunton, *Letters Written From New-England*, 106. Note that the words Dunton used throughout his lengthy discussion of the widow Brick exactly copied those found in the various English advice books.

28. Ulrich, *Good Wives*, 35-50; Synder, *Brabbling Women*, 119-120; see especially Jane Kamensky's excellent analysis of "loquacious" wives in *Governing the Tongue*, 21, 40, 77-78, 80, 86-86, 89-90, 92. Ch. 3, "Misgovernment of Woman's Tongue," looks at the cases of Anne Hutchinson and Ann Hibbens in this context and helped inform this brief discussion.

29. Mather, *Ornaments for the Daughters of Zion*, 100-101. Norton, *Founding Mothers and Fathers*, 138, argues that "no one asked whether a woman could unproblematically assume the role of household head, or considered whether the gendered definition of power was so deeply embedded in her society that she might encounter difficult not experienced by her male contemporaries." Norton's work focuses on political theorists, and I focus on prescriptive literature authors, whom I would call "social theorists." The two sets of writers had different perspectives and brought different sensibilities to their work.

30. Quotation taken from Cooper, *A Sermon Concerning the Laying the Deaths of Others to Heart . . . Occasion'd by the lamented Death of that Ingenious and Religious Gentleman John Gore of Harvard College in Cambridge, N.E. Who*

died of the Small-Pox, Nov. 7. 1720. In the 38th Year of his Age (Boston, 1720), 2. For similar references see Increase Mather, *A Faithful Man, Described and Rewarded. Some Observable & Serviceable Passages in the Life and Death of Mr. Michael Wigglesworth, Late Pastor of Maldon; Who Rested from His Labours, on the Lords-Day, June 10th. 1705. In the Seventy Fourth Year of his Age* (Boston, 1705), 25; Samuel Danforth, *An Elegy in Memory of the Worshipful Major Thomas Leonard Esq., of Taunton in New-England; Who departed this Life on the 14th Day of November, 1713. In the 73d. Year of his Age*, nd, np; Benjamin Colman, *The Hope of the Righteous in their Death. A Sermon Preached on the Lord's Day after the Funeral of William Harris, Esq., Who departed this Life, September 22. 1721. In the Fifty-Fifth Year of his Age* (Boston, 1721), 24; *Jeremiah Wise, A Funeral Sermon Preached upon the Death of the Honourable Charles Frost, Esq; One of His Majesty's Council for the Province of the Massachusetts-Bay in N.E. Who Departed this Life Decem. 17. 1724. In the 47th Year of his Age* (Boston, 1725), 30-31; and *Charles Chauncy, Nathanael's Character Displayed. A Sermon Preach'd The Lord's Day after the Funeral of the Honourable Nathanael Byfield, Esq., . . . Who died at his House in Boston, on the 6th of June, 1733 In the 80th Year of his Age* (Boston, 1733), 28.

31. [Allestree], *The Ladies Calling*, 70. Dunton's *Letters Written From New-England*, 108, claims that the widow Brick of Boston, "the Flower of Boston," said those exact words to him in describing her responsibility to her children. Her thought exactly echoes that stated in Allestree's *The Ladies Calling*. While I doubt that the widow Brick actually said the words as they appeared in the text, it is clear that both Dunton and Brick were familiar with the book, and Dunton may have even had it in front of him as he wrote his letters home.

32. Vives, *Very Fruitfull and Pleasant Booke*, 388, is quoting from 1 Timothy 5:4. The King James Version reads: "if any widow have children or nephews, let them learn first to shew piety at home, and to requite their parents for that is good and acceptable before God." At least one widow had *Calvin on Timothy 1 and 2* listed in the inventory of her estate. See will of Ann Atwood, proved December 3, 1654, Plymouth Colony Wills, 1, 204-209.

33. See, for example, Mather, *Nepenthes Evangelicum. A Brief Essay upon a Soul at Ease; In What Piety will bring both Parents and children to. A Sermon Occasion'd by the Death of a Religious Matron, Mrs. Mary Rock. Boston, 1713*, 43; Mather, *Ecclesia Monilia*, 42; and Prince, *Be Followers of Them, who . . . inherit the Promises*, 22.

34. Saffin, *Note Book*, 65. Jeannine Hensley, ed., *The Works of Anne Bradstreet* (Cambridge, MA: Belknap Press of Harvard University Press, 1967), 195-198.

35. Cotton Mather, *Ecclesia Monilia*, 24.

36. Suffolk County Probate Records, 22, 557-559; 25, 455; 26, 48-49; and NS9, 522-523. The exact relationship between Hannah Sharpe of Boston and Mary Sharpe of Jamaica is unclear.

37. Kamensky, *Governing the Tongue*, 12.

38. Ditz, *Property and Kinship*, 40-42, finds that, in Connecticut, between 30 and 60 percent of the adult male population left wills and that women rarely made up more than 25 percent of those leaving wills; Main, "Probate Records as a Source for Early American History," 91, argues that 33 to 50 percent of the adult male population left wills; Smith, "Underregistration and Bias in Probate Records," 104, estimates that 36 percent of men and only 6 percent of women left wills; and Waters, "The Traditional World of the New England Peasants," 12, n. 30, calculates that 40 percent of adult males wrote wills.

39. See, for example, Mather, *Nepenthes Evangelicum*, 29-30, 43; Mather, *Ecclesia Monilia*, 42; and Prince, *Be Followers of Them, who . . . inherit the Promises*, 22; *The Whole Duty of Man*, 288; and Fuller, *Holy State*.

40. The rates for male testators in Massachusetts, Maryland, and South Carolina were 46.6, 51.4, and 32.9 percent, respectively. Interestingly, when testacy rates are broken down by urban and rural areas, the figures do not differ a great deal from those for the general population, but the rates were slightly higher for widows in urban areas. Fifty-four percent of all urban widows whose estates went through probate died leaving wills (the figure is 47.3 percent for male testators), while 52.3 percent of all rural widows were testate (50.9 for men). For an analysis of male testacy, see Crowley, "Family Relations and Inheritance," 41; and Linda Auwers, "Fathers, Sons, and Wealth in Colonial Windsor, Connecticut," *Journal of Family History* 3 (Summer 1978), 143-144.

41. Lebsock, *The Free Women of Petersburg*, 133, explicitly claims that higher rate (more than 50 percent) of widow testacy than male testacy (34.5 percent) in nineteenth-century Virginia demonstrates that women were unhappier with intestacy laws than were men.

42. Will of Joanna Newman, Suffolk County Wills, Book 6, 341, proved February 24, 1680. See also the wills of Elizabeth Hearsey, Suffolk County Wills, Book 7, 161-163; Elizabeth Mercer, Suffolk County Wills, Book 20, 383-385; and Elizabeth Roger, Maryland Wills, Book 20, 674-675. Lisa Wilson Waciega makes a similar claim in "Widowhood and Womanhood in Early America: The Experience of Women in Philadelphia and Chester Counties, 1750-1850" (Ph.D. diss., Temple University, 1986), 233.

43. According to 2 Kings 20:1, the Lord commanded Hezekiah to "set your house in order; for thou shalt die." The exhortation to provide for one's own family comes from 1 Timothy 5:8. Many colonial sermons proclaimed the virtue of doing as Hezekiah was commanded. See, for example, sermons 132, 133, 134, and 136 in Parsons Family Papers, Box 1, Folder 2, American Antiquarian Society.

44. Wills of Mary Ward, Suffolk County Wills, Book 6, 7-8, and Margaret Haugh, Suffolk County Wills, Book 21, 569-571, proved December 7, 1719. For other widows who used their wills to keep peace in the family see Elizabeth Carr, Essex County Wills, 303, 33-34; Mary Lindall, Essex County Wills, 319, 307-310;

Catherine LaNoble, South Carolina Wills, 1671-1727, 243-244; Sarah Mather, Suffolk County Wills, Book 6, 153-154; and Elizabeth Minor, Suffolk County Wills, Book 6, 441.

45. Mather, *The Widow of Nain*, 10-11. See also W.C., *The Widowes*, 10, in which the author claims that the widow who was the subject of his sermon "tooke it as a pledge of Gods great favor unto her that hee had given her a sonne to be a stay and a comfort unto her in her widowhood."

46. Wills of Daniel Harris, proved January 8, 1734, Suffolk County Wills, 30, 76-78, and Thomas Day, proved August 27, 1739, Hampshire County Wills, VI, 59-60. See also wills of Jeremiah Meachen, proved November 18, 1695, Essex County Wills, 305, 94-96; will of William Brown, proved June 18, 1745, Suffolk County Wills, 37, 547-551; Nathaniel Gill, proved April 30, 1734, Suffolk County Wills, 30, 240-243; Ralph Hemenway, proved July 11, 1678, Suffolk County Wills, 6, 239; James Pennyman, proved January 31, 1665, Suffolk County Wills, 1, 439-440; John Smith, proved July 25, 1678, Suffolk County Wills, 6, 246-248; John Cook, proved November 19, 1716, Essex County Wills, v.311, 454-455; Thomas Witham, proved June 12, 1737, Essex County Wills, 322, 81-85. Thomas Day's will, proved August 27, 1739, Hampshire County Wills, VI, 59-60, required one of his brothers to take care of his widowed mother.

47. Will of John Clark, proved June 5, 1727, Suffolk County Wills, 25, 355-358.

48. Jacob Franklin to Samuel Galloway, October 18, 1754, Correspondence Book 1, Galloway-Maxcy-Markoe MSS, Library of Congress Manuscript Division, Washington, DC.

49. Wills of Mary Barker, proved September 30, 1684, Essex County Wills, 304, 87-88; Hannah Beadle, proved July 25, 1736, Essex County Wills, 320, 326-327, and 322, 178; and Experience Miller, MHS Photostat Collection, September 19, 1747. See also the wills of Mercy Kimball, proved February 1708, Essex County Probate Records, 309, 283-284; Hephzibah Marsh, proved March 25, 1684, Hampshire County Wills, 1, 234b-235; and Sarah Bragg, proved March 2, 1714, Suffolk County Wills, 18, 253-254. For an example of a man acting similarly, John Abbey Sr.'s "living will," written August 3, 1683, Essex County Wills, 307, 451. All of these wills provide compelling evidence that the contents of wills were public knowledge before the testator died.

50. Will of Sarah Button, proved December 13, 1731, Suffolk County Wills, 29, 318-320.

51. Will of Sarah Pemberton, proved July 11, 1709, Suffolk County Wills, 16, 594-595. For other examples of widows rewarding those who cared for them see wills of Elizabeth Mercer, proved April 14, 1718, Suffolk County Wills, 20, 383-385; Sarah Attwood, proved May 1, 1739, Essex County Wills, 324, 99-101; Exercise Miles, proved August 14, 1704, Essex County Wills, 308, 262-263; Sarah Merrit, proved March 2, 1740, Essex County Wills, 324, 241; Mary Sparks, proved July 27, 1712, Essex County Wills, 310, 453; Elizabeth Bacon, proved March 6, 1679,

Hampshire County Wills, I, 202a-202b; Clemens Judd, proved December 31, 1699, Hampshire County Wills, III, 26-27; Mary Root, proved February 7, 1710, Hampshire County Wills, III, 108 & 226-229; Elizabeth Fernside, proved June 29, 1704, Suffolk County Wills, 15, 304-306; Ann Hibbins, proved July 2, 1656, Suffolk County Wills, 1, 274-276; and Anis Morse, proved March 3, 1693, Suffolk County Wills, 13, 126-127.

52. Will of Sarah Burnham, proved June 30, 1746, Essex County Wills, 327, 28-30.

53. Will of Mary Root, proved February 7, 1710, Hampshire County Wills, III, 108 and 226-229.

54. The March 20, 1727, will, spoken "not long before her death," and accompanying papers of Mary Fisher, Suffolk County Wills, New Series Book 14, 28-29.

55. The mean values of widows' estates were 41 percent of men's estates in Massachusetts and South Carolina and 62 percent of men's estates in Maryland. I've analyzed wealth only for the period 1720–1750 because there were no widows' inventories in South Carolina and very few widows' inventories in Maryland for the years before 1720, making any comparative analysis of wealth in all three colonies before 1720 meaningless, if not impossible.

56. A comparison of the mean values of estates that included only personal property reveals a gap between widow wealth in the three colonies. This procedure equalized the values of estates in Massachusetts with the other two colonies, which did not include real estate in the inventory. The mean value of estates of Massachusetts widows was £226; of Maryland widows, £1,048; and of South Carolina widows, £1,343.

57. Waters, "The Traditional World of New England Peasants," 139; Deen, "Patterns of Testation," 159.

58. Regardless of colony or rural or urban economy, male testators never bequeathed real property to their daughters that approached equality with that bequeathed to their brothers. The findings dispute the model of frontier equality, particularly when theory is explored through the prism of gender with a particular focus on the gender of the testators. Carr, "Inheritance in the Colonial Chesapeake," 179; Deen, "Patterns of Testation"; Gampel, "The Planter's Wife Revisited, 28-29; and Main, "Widows in Rural Massachusetts," 69, 75.

59. Main, *Tobacco Colony*, ch. 4, "Housing," discusses the lack of importance people in Maryland attached to their houses. She claims they focused more on the critical work of planting, growing. and reaping their crops.

60. Anzilotti, *In the Affairs of the World*, 2-3; Glover, *All Our Relations*, x. For the antebellum period, Kirsten Wood argues, like Anzilotti, that slaveholding widows did not challenge the gender order. However, similar to my argument here, she claims that widows, "by doing work normatively assigned to both genders," also "confounded the contemporary presumption that women and men were fundamentally different sorts of beings, intellectually, morally, and physically." Like

men, they made important decisions, dispensed charity, and suppressed slave resistance; slaveholding widows assumed a privileged position "over mere white manhood." See Kirsten Wood, *Masterful Women: Slaveholding Widows From the American Revolution Through the Civil War* (Chapel Hill: University of North Carolina Press, 2004), 6, 59, 82, 194.

61. See Lane, "Economic Power Among Eighteenth-Century Women of the Carolina Lowcountry," 337-338, for a similar argument.

62. The term is Toby Ditz's, *Property and Kinship*, 54.

63. Butler, *Becoming America*, 55.

64. Kierner, *Beyond the Household*, 6-13; Anzilotti, *In the Affairs of the World*, 2-5, 54.

65. Henrietta Fisher's Deed of Sale dated May 7, 1748, South Carolina WPA Misc. Wills, v. 75b, 542.

66. Kierner, *Beyond the Household*, 15-16; Pruden, "Family, Community, Economy," 244-245.

67. Walter Johnson, *Soul by Soul: Life Inside the Antebellum Slave Market* (Cambridge, MA: Harvard University Press, 1999), 89-102; quotations appear on 89 and 92; Phyllis Whitman Hunter, *Purchasing Identity in the Atlantic World: Massachusetts Merchants, 1670-1780* (Ithaca, NY: Cornell University Press, 2001), 89.

68. *Essex County Probate Records*, 303, 33-34, and *ECQCR*, v. VIII, 295.

69. *ECQCR*, VIII, 354-355, 424-430.

70. Marcia Pointon, "Women and Their Jewels," in Jennie Batchelor and Cora Kaplan, eds., *Women and Material Culture, 1660-1830* (New York: Palgrave Macmillan, 2007), 12-13, 17, 23. Pointon points out that jewelry was also critical to "sociable masculinity" but that this masculinity was not "tied in with a relationship to jewels in the way femininity was," 11. See also Hannah Greig, "Leading the Fashion: The Material Culture of London's *Beau Monde*," in John Styles and Amanda Vickery, eds., *Gender, Taste, and Material Culture in Britain and North America, 1700-1830* (New Haven: Yale University Press, 2006), 303-307; and Linda Levy Peck, *Consuming Splendor* (Cambridge: Cambridge University Press, 2005), 63.

71. Susan Staves, "'Books without which I cannot write': How Did Eighteenth-Century Women Writers Get the Books They Read?" in Jennie Batchelor and Cora Kaplan, eds., *Women and Material Culture, 1660-1830* (New York: Palgrave Macmillan, 2007), 193, 203-207. Claire Walsh, in discussing shopping as a gendered activity, claims that men acquired "objects of male material culture, such as globes, guns, books, and scientific instruments." Those books might include merchants' manuals that were concomitantly how-to guides and prescriptive instructions on how to behave. See Walsh, "Shops, Shopping, and the Art of Decision Making in Eighteenth-Century England," in John Styles and Amanda Vickery, eds., *Gender, Taste, and Material Culture in Britain and North America, 1700-1830* (New Haven: Yale University Press, 2006), 163; Daniel Rabuzzi, "Eighteenth-

Century Commercial Mentalities as Reflected and Projected in Business Handbooks," *Eighteenth-Century Studies* 29 (1995-96), 170.

72. Paul G. E. Clemens, "The Consumer Culture of the Middle Atlantic, 1760-1820," *William and Mary Quarterly* 62 (2005), 577-580, 616-617; Carole Shammas, "Changes in English and Anglo-American Consumption from 1550 to 1800," in John Brewer and Roy Porter, eds., *Consumption and the World of Goods* (London: Routledge, 1993), 198; David Blanke, *Sowing the American Dream: How Consumer Culture Took Root in the Rural Midwest* (Athens: Ohio University Press, 2000), analyzes rural consumption patterns for the late nineteenth century.

73. Will of Sarah Morse, proved February 11, 1718, *Essex County Probate Records*, 31, 2178-2180.

74. Gloria L. Main, "The Distribution of Consumer Goods in Colonial New England: A Subregional Approach," in Peter Benes and Jane Benes, eds., *Early American Probate Inventories* (Boston: Boston University Press, 1989), 153-168.

75. T. H. Breen, *The Marketplace of Revolution: How Consumer Politics Shaped American Independence* (Oxford: Oxford University Press, 2004), 64; Kierner, *Beyond the Household*, 36. See also Neil McKendrick, John Brewer, and J. H. Plumb, *The Birth of a Consumer Society: The Commercialization of Eighteenth-Century England* (Bloomington: Indiana University Press 1982); Carole Shammas, *The Preindustrial Consumer in England and America* (Oxford: Oxford University Press, 1990); Bushman, *The Refinement of America*; Brewer and Porter, *Consumption and the World of Goods* (of the twenty-five essays in this collection, see especially Amanda Vickery, "Women and the World of Goods: A Lancashire Consumer and Her Possessions, 1751-81"); Cary Carson, Ronald Hoffman, and Peter J. Albert, eds., *Of Consuming Interests: The Style of Life in the Eighteenth Century* (Charlottesville: University Press of Virginia, 1994); Hunter, *Purchasing Identity*; Kierner, *Beyond the Household*, 1, 36, 39-40.

76. Ulrich, "Hannah Barnard's Cupboard," 241, 252, 261, 269, 271, 273.

77. Will of Sarah Howard, proved May 20, 1735, Maryland Wills, Book 21, 344-345.

78. Will of Johannah Davis, proved August 21, 1679, Suffolk County Wills, 6, 308-311.

79. The details of this case are found in *Essex County Probate Records*, I, 144-5; *Essex County Probate Records*, II, 115-120; *ECQCR*, I, 113; *ECQCR*, III, 321, 352, 371-373, 456, 458.

80. The following paragraphs are based on these sources: Will of Mary Ward, proved July 21, 1667, Suffolk County Wills, 6, 7-8; Petition of Mary Ward, May 18, 1667, Massachusetts Historical Society Photostat Collection; *Records of the Suffolk County Court*, 1671-1680, II, July 29, 1679, 1029-1037.

81. Will and accompanying papers of Mary Fisher, Suffolk County Wills, New Series Book 14, 28-29.

82. Will of Anthony deBourdeaux, proved February 19, 1726, South Carolina

Wills, 1671-1727, 234-235; Browne, *Proceedings and Acts of the General Assembly of Maryland, October 1678-November 1683*, 197; Kilty, *The Laws of Maryland*, 1, Act passed May 22, 1695, n.p.; *The Book of the General Lawes and Libertyes, 1660*, 80-81; *Acts and Laws . . .f the Massachusetts-Bay, 1692*, 43-44. Lisa Wilson Waciega discusses the "burden" of executorship at great length in "Widowhood and Womanhood in Early America: The Experience of Women in Philadelphia and Chester Counties, 1750-1850" (Ph.D. diss., Temple University, 1986), 100-104.

83. Jensen, *Loosening the Bonds*, 24; Lebsock, *The Free Women of Petersburg*, 120, 125.

84. Administration of Esther Houchin's estate granted November 27, 1693, to Nathaniel Green [her son-in-law] and Samuel Wheelwright on November 27, 1693, Suffolk County Wills, 13, 302-303; Saffin's testimony presented March 8, 1694, Massachusetts Historical Society Bound Collection.

85. Wills of Mary Baker, proved July 8, 1713, Suffolk County Wills, 18, 120-121, and Sarah Bragg, proved March 2, 1714, Suffolk County Wills, 18, 253-254. For additional widows who noted they had not received their lawful share of their husband's estate, see wills of Sarah Rouse, proved October 2, 1705, Suffolk County Wills, 16, 53-55, and Elizabeth Tyley, proved April 1, 1723, Suffolk County Wills, New Series 11, 308-310.

86. Petitions and testimony about Frances Quilter's complaint, Massachusetts Historical Society Photostat Collection, 1679.

87. Jones, *Village and Seaport Migration and Society*, 96-98; David Konig, *Law and Society in Puritan Massachusetts: Essex County, 1628-1692* (Chapel Hill: University of North Carolina Press, 1979), 38 and 44; and Kulikoff, *Tobacco and Slaves*, 48 and 52.

88. Carr and Walsh, "The Planter's Wife," 567, and Carr, "Inheritance in the Colonial Chesapeake," 171.

89. Kulikoff, *Tobacco and Slaves*, 85, and Menard, *Economy and Society*, 320.

90. The term "domestic patriarchy" is Allan Kulikoff's, but Kulikoff and Greven both argue for similar circumstances; Kulikoff, *Tobacco and Slaves*, 7, and 51-52 and Philip Greven Jr., *Four Generations: Population, Land, and Family in Colonial Andover, Massachusetts* (Ithaca, NY: Cornell University Press, 1970). See also Jack P. Greene, *Pursuits of Happiness: The Social Development of Early Modern British Colonies and the Formation of American Culture* (Chapel Hill: University of North Carolina Press, 1988), 95.

91. Mary Beth Norton, "Reflections on Women in the Age of the American Revolution," in Hoffman and Albert, eds., *Women in the Age of the American Revolution*, 486-487.

92. Wills of Elizabeth Hardy, proved December 1, 1654, *Essex County Court Records*, I, 200-201; Elizabeth Walker, proved February 20, 1714, Suffolk County Wills, 18, 250-252; Martha Clark proved, June 9, 1738, Suffolk County Wills, 33, 514-517; and Susanna Condy, proved November 4, 1747, Suffolk County Wills, 40, 258-262.

93. Lebsock, *Free Women of Petersburg*, 112, 142-43.

94. Will of William Flint, proved June 26, 1672, and petition of Alice Flint, presented February 10, 1696, *Essex County Court Records*, II, 363-71.

95. Will of Elizabeth Phelps, proved December 30, 1712, Hampshire County Wills, II, 77-78; Hampshire County Wills, II, 65-66; and MD Wills, Book 20, 674-67. For similar motives, see also wills of Sarah Hobart, Suffolk County Wills, 27, 388-390; Mary Caldwell, proved September 27, 1748, Essex County Wills, 328, 167-169; and Sarah Raymond, proved May 7, 1747, Essex County Wills, 327, 254-6; see also the nuncupative will of Elizabeth Coombs attested to on June 12, 1722, Suffolk County Wills, New Series 12, 352-354.

CHAPTER 4

1. *ECQCR*, II, 443-446. There is a growing body of scholarship on gossip in early America; see, for example, Robert Blair St. George, "Heated Speech and Literacy in Seventeenth-Century New England," in David G. Allen and David D. Hall, eds., *Seventeenth-Century New England* (Boston: University of Virginia Press for the Colonial Society of Massachusetts, 1985); Mary Beth Norton, "Gender and Defamation in Seventeenth-Century Maryland," *William and Mary Quarterly* (1987), 3-39; Norton, *Founding Mothers & Fathers*, 253-277; Kamensky, *Governing the Tongue*; and Snyder, *Brabbling Women*.

2. *ECQCR*, III, 16. According to Norton in *Founding Mothers and Fathers*, 243, "early colonists were a contentious lot, quick to anger and prone to physical violence or verbal abuse of others."

3. For a discussion of "the force of community," that is, the rules and regulations regarding proper behavior and the intolerance of conflict within the colonial neighborhood, see Helena M. Wall, *Fierce Communion: Family and Community in Early America* (Cambridge, MA: Harvard University Press, 1990), 13-29. Norton, *Founding Mothers and Fathers*, 217, 219-222, states that "men who refused to join such an evolving consensus were viewed as presenting dangerous threats to social, and they faced constant pressure until they surrendered to the general will." Contrary to Wall, she argues that Maryland and Virginia did not impose consensus.

4. *South Carolina Gazette*, January 10, 1736; for a similar ad, see *South Carolina Gazette*, August 23, 1735. Jeanne Boydston, *Home & Work: Household, Wages, and Ideology of Labor in the Early Republic* (New York: Oxford University Press, 1994), 13-14; Wall, *Fierce Communion*, 13-15, 30, 126-128; Norton, *Founding Mothers and Fathers*, 248-249; Dena Goodman, "Public Sphere and Private Life: Toward a Synthesis of Current Historiographical Approaches to the Old Regime," *History and Theory* 31 (1992), 5. For a discussion of the ambiguity of widows speaking out publicly in Virginia, see Snyder, *Brabbling Women*, 117-139; and Norton, *Founding Mothers and Fathers*, 164.

5. The supporting quotation is from Norton, *Founding Mothers and Fathers*, 156.

6. The phrase "small politics" is Mary Beth Norton's. She argues for two separate communities—of men *and* of women. Men belonged to the world of politics and business, for they were legally the heads of households and the components of the polity; women belonged to the world of reproduction, sexuality, and childbirth. Of course, widows, especially elite widows, complicated this division: Norton, *Founding Mothers and Fathers*, 10, 139-149, 203, 242. See Laurel Thatcher Ulrich, "'Daughters of Liberty': Religious Women in Revolutionary New England," in Ronald Hoffman and Peter J. Albert, eds., *Women in the Age of the American Revolution* (Charlottesville: University Press of Virginia, 1989), 212; Linda K. Kerber, "The Paradox of Women's Citizenship in the Early Republic: The Case of Martin vs. Massachusetts, 1805," *American Historical Review* 97 (1992), 354-355.

7. Perry Miller, *Errand Into the Wilderness* (Cambridge, MA: Belknap Press of Harvard University Press, 1981), 145; John Winthrop, "A Modell of Christian Charity [1630]," in David A. Hollinger and Charles Capper, eds., *The American Intellectual Tradition*, Vol. 1, *1630-1865* (New York: Oxford University Press, 1993), 12, 15.

8. Craig Calhoun, "Introduction: Habermas and the Public Sphere," in Craig Calhoun, ed., *Habermas and the Public Sphere* (Cambridge, MA: MIT Press, 1991), 8-9.

9. The material in this paragraph draws heavily upon Goodman's "Public Sphere and Private Life." She analyzes Habermas's *The Structural Transformation of the Public Sphere: An Inquiry Into a Category of Bourgeois Society*, Roger Chartier's *A History of Private Life*, and Joan Landes's *Women and the Public Sphere in the Age of the French Revolution* to clear up what she sees as "a misunderstanding of the relationship between these two spheres of activity." This article was instrumental in helping me think through Habermas's theoretical arguments and historians' use of his theories; see especially 1, 5-6, 14, 16-19. I thank my good colleague Karin Breuer for pointing this article out to me.

10. Cooper, *A Sermon Concerning the Laying the Deaths of Others to Heart*, 2. For similar references see Mather, *A Faithful Man, Described and Rewarded*, 25; Danforth, *An Elegy in Memory of the Worshipful Major Thomas Leonard*, np; Colman, *The Hope of the Righteous in their Death*, 24; Jeremiah Wise, *A Funeral Sermon Preached upon the Death of the Honourable Charles Frost*, 30-31; and Chauncy, *Nathanael's Character Displayed*, 28.

11. Stoddard, *Gods Frown in the Death of Usefull Men, Shewed in a Sermon Preached at the Funeral of the Honourable Col. John Pynchon, Esq, Who Deceased January the 17th. 1702.3* (Boston, 1703), 8, 9, 10, 22. For further discussion of men's public service to the town and the community see Increase Mather, *A Discourse Concerning the Death of the Righteous. Occasioned by the Death of the Honourable*

John Foster . . . And of his Pious Consort, Mrs. Abigail Foster who departed soon after him . . . (Boston, 1711), 25; Samuel Danforth, *An Elegy in Memory of the Worshipful Major Thomas Leonard,* np; Joseph Baxter, *A Discourse on the Great Priviledge and Happiness of Dying in Faith. . . . upon the Death of John Watts, Esq . . .* (Boston, 1718), 30; and Cotton Mather, Detur Digniori. *The Righteous Man Described & Asserted as the Excellent Man . . . In a Sermon, upon the Death of the Reverend Mr. Joseph Gerrish, . . .* (Boston, 1720), 28.

12. Wise, *A Funeral Sermon Preached upon the Death of the Honourable Charles Frost,* 10.

13. Chauncy, *Nathanael's Character Displayed,* 28.

14. Mather, *Good Man Making a Good End,* 33; Wise, *A Funeral Sermon Preached upon the Death of the Honourable Charles Frost,* 29; and Chauncy, *Nathanael's Character Displayed,* iii, 5, 7. Many ministers described men as useful, including Stoddard, *Gods Frown in the Death of Usefull Men,* 7; Danforth, *Elegy in Memory of the Worshipful Major Thomas Leonard*; Colman, *The Hope of the Righteous in the Death,* 24.

15. Carr and Walsh, "The Planter's Wife," 559; Lois Green Carr, "The Development of the Maryland Orphans' Court, 1654-1715," in Aubrey Land, Lois Green Carr, and Edward Papenfuse, eds., *Law, Society and Politics in Early Maryland* (Baltimore: Johns Hopkins University Press, 1977), 41-61.

16. For a more general discussion of gender in early American communities, see Norton, *Founding Mothers & Fathers,* 203-239. Boydston, *Home & Work,* 9, argues that, by association, wives of such men came in for ministerial praise—not for their usefulness but for the emotional support they provided their husbands; this differed from "earlier formulations that praised wives as 'fellow labourers.'"

17. Sylvester, *Monodia,* 47; Fuller, *Holy State,* 25; and Pritchard, *The Schoole of Honest and Vertuous Life,* 73. David S. Shields found a similar association between unchaperoned women in public and "illicit" rendezvous. He also claims, "What seizes attention in the complaints about female incursions into public spaces is the insistence that they were organized and deliberate." David S. Shields, *Civil Tongues: Polite Letters in British America* (Chapel Hill: University of North Carolina Press, 1997) 109-110.

18. Colman, *Duty and Honour of Aged Women,* 23, 24.

19. Colman, *Duty and Honour of Aged Women,* 5, 7, 10, 12, 15. For similar praise of an older widow, see Thomas Prince, *Precious in the Sight of the Lord is the Death of his Saints: A Sermon upon the Death of Mrs. Elizabeth Oliver, Relict of the Honourable Daniel Oliver, Esq.* (Boston, 1735), 23.

20. *The Widowes Lamentation for the Absence of Their Deare Children, and Suitors. And for Divers of their Deaths in These Fatall Civill Warres. Presented in the Names and Behalfes of the Rich and Wealthy Widowes Throughout the Whole Kingdome* (London, 1643), 5-6. According to the Oxford English Dictionary,

mumping meant "assuming a demure sanctimonious or miserable aspect of countenance."

21. Hobby, *Virtue of Necessity*, 18; and Patricia Higgins, "The Reactions of Women with Special Reference to Women Petitioners," in Brian Manning, ed., *Politics, Religion, and the English Civil War* (New York: St. Martin's Press, 1973), 210.

22. A. G. Roeber, "Authority, Law, and Custom: The Rituals of Court Day in Tidewater Virginia, 1720-1750," in Robert Blair St. George, ed., *Material Life in America, 1600-1860*, 419-21. Cornelia Dayton also talks about the drama of the courthouse; Dayton, *Women Before the Bar*, 17; Peter Bardaglio called it "a form of moral theater"; Bardaglio, *Reconstructing the Household: Families, Sex, and the Law in the Nineteenth-Century South* (Chapel Hill: University of North Carolina Press, 1995), 17. Like Roeber, he argues that southern courts helped to "establish boundaries" and set "limits that confirmed social norms."

23. Dayton, *Women Before the Bar*, 16; Roeber, "Authority, Law, and Custom," 422-424, 426-427.

24. Dayton argues that they also "found fewer barriers to coming to court over civil matters" since the early courts tended relax English common law rules. This would change dramatically in the late eighteenth century, *Women Before the Bar*, 20, 30, 37. See also Roeber, "Authority, Law, and Custom," 422, and Martha J. McNamara, *From Tavern to Courthouse: Architecture and Ritual in American Law, 1658-1860* (Baltimore: Johns Hopkins University Press, 2004), 1-53.

25. Edmund S. Morgan, *Inventing the People: The Rise of Popular Sovereignty in England and America* (New York: Norton, 11988), 230; see also his more extensive analysis of petitions on 224-230.

26. Jay Fliegelman, *Declaring Independence: Jefferson, Natural Language, and the Culture of Performance* (Palo Alto, CA: Stanford University Press, 1993), 130, 159, 195. Fliegelman's analysis of public and private virtue focuses on the post-revolutionary period. His contrast between a public man ("publicus" defined as magistrate) and a public woman ("publica" defined as prostitute) resonates with the late seventeenth and early eighteenth centuries' identification of a widow in public as a sexually suspect woman.

27. There has been no systematic analysis of gender differences in the petitions of women and men, but a study of English petitions suggests, as does my reading of selected colonial American petitions, that women stood in a peculiar relationship to those in authority. Higgins, "The Reactions of Women," 180 and 210-213, and Hobby, *The Necessity of Virtue*, 17-18; Dayton, *Women Before the Bar*, 20.

28. The information on petitions in this paragraph draws from Marcia Schmidt Blaine, "The Power of Petitions: Women and the New Hampshire Provincial Government, 1695-1770," *International Review of Social History* 46 (2001), Suppl. 9; Ruth Bogin, "Petitioning and the New Moral Economy of Post-Revolutionary

America," *William and Mary Quarterly* 45 (1988), 391-425; Richard L. Bushman, *King and People in Provincial Massachusetts* (Chapel Hill: University of North Carolina Press, published for the Institute of Early American History and Culture, 1985), 46-54; Crane, *Ebb Tide in New England*, 141-143, 151; and Stephen A. Higginson, "A Short History of the Right to Petition Government for the Redress of Grievances," *Yale Law Journal* 96 (1986), 142-155. Bardaglio, *Reconstructing the Household*, 17-18, asserts that judges took "a distinctly masculine stance," thereby "institutionalizing masculine values." But, of course, he did not look specifically at petitions by widows and how they challenged those values.

29. Catherine Prichard to Daniel Dulany, June 6, 1751, Dulany Papers, Maryland Historical Society, Baltimore (hereafter MdHS).

30. Lemuel Shaw Papers, Massachusetts Historical Society, Microfilm Reel 1, Folder 3 (1759-1774).

31. May 7, 1662, petition of Alice Thomas to the Massachusetts General Court, Photostat Collection, Massachusetts Historical Society, Boston.

32. Suffolk County Probate Records, New Series 2, petition dated January 29, 1684, 401. Anna Perry had previously been married to Thomas Sheffield, a seaman. On May 12, 1679, Charles Perry gave her power of attorney, and on October 13, 1679, Joseph Holmes bought a house and land of Charles Perry. It appears that she was claiming her dower rights in this property, but she never explicitly makes that argument in her petition.

33. Wayside Inn Collection, 1662-1879, Massachusetts Historical Society, Boston. Silence Allen, John Beaudre, Elisha Odin, William Griggs, and David Collison (Colson) signed the petition.

34. Martha Cogan's petition to the Massachusetts General Court, May 20, 1658, Photostat Collection, Massachusetts Historical Society.

35. Suffolk County Probate Records, 3, 216-218.

36. *MD Archives*, X, 108, X, 75, LIV, 212; Catherine Prichard to Daniel Dulany, June 6, 1751, Dulany Papers, MS 1265, Box 2, (hereafter MdHS); Rebecca Heath to Walter Dulany, January 27, 1747, Dulany Papers, MS 1265, Box 2, MdHS. 37. Gary B. Nash, "Poverty and Poor Relief in Pre-Revolutionary Philadelphia," *William and Mary Quarterly* 33 (1976), 5; Gary B. Nash, "Poverty and Politics in Early American History," in Billy G. Smith, ed., *Down and Out in Early America* (University Park: Pennsylvania State University Press, 2004), 3-5, 15; Matthew Mulcahy, "The 'Great Fire' of 1740 and the Politics of Disaster Relief in Colonial Charleston," *South Carolina Magazine*, 99 (1998): 138, 146; Wall, *Fierce Communion*, 14. See also Crane, *Ebb Tide in New England*, 116-119; Wulf, *Not All Wives*, 153-79; Laurel Thatcher Ulrich, "Sheep in Parlor, Wheels on the Common: Pastoralism and Poverty in Eighteenth-century Boston," Billy G. Smith, ed., in *Down and Out in Early America* (University Park: Pennsylvania State University Press, 2004), 183-184; and Tim Lockley, "Rural Poor Relief in Colonial South Carolina," *Historical Journal* 48 (2005), 955-976. Kirsten Wood, "'The Strongest Ties That Bind

Poor Mortals Together': Slaveholding Widows and the Construction of Family in the Southeast, 1790-1860," in Janet L. Coryell, Thomas H. Appleton Jr., Anastasia Sims, and Sandra Gioia Treadway, eds., *Negotiating Boundaries of Southern Womanhood: Dealing with the Powers that Be* (Columbia: University of Missouri Press, 2000), 137, argues that widows were not necessarily vulnerable in this situation; "instead of constructing themselves as hapless supplicants for charity, widows integrated their requests for assistance into the matrix of familial exchange."

38. *South Carolina Gazette*, May 21, 1737. It is worth noting that Isaac Holmes undertook this event; his sister Rebecca Holmes Amory probably made him acutely aware of the economic issues widows faced.

39. Cotton Mather, Manuscript sermon dated December 28, 1710, Mather Family Papers, Octovo Volume 77, American Antiquarian Society, Worcester, Massachusetts; Mather, *Marah Spoken To*, 35; Foxcroft, *The Character of Anna*, 55.

40. Mather, *Marah Spoken To*, 3.

41. Ibid., 25. According to Puritan theology, this would suggest that such widows deserved this succor. Between 1700 and 1750, when Massachusetts faced tremendous poverty, "Ministers sought to uncover divinely appointed instrumentalities or formulas through which God would provision his creatures": J. Richard Olivas, "'God Helps Them Who Help Themselves': Religious Explanations of Poverty in Colonial Massachusetts, 1630-1776," in Billy G. Smith, ed., *Down and Out in Early America* (University Park: Pennsylvania State University Press, 2004), 272; see generally 270-277.

42. Mather, *Marah Spoken To*, iii; Ford, *Diary of Cotton Mather*, II, June 23, 1711, 82; January, 1712, 148; April, 1713, 200; March, 1718, 523; May, 1718, 534; and December, 1718, 573.

43. Mather, *Ornaments for the Daughters of Zion*, 100; Dunton, *Letters Written From New England*, 110; [Allestree], *The Ladies Calling*, 76; and Colman, *Duty and Honour of Aged Women*, 26.

44. Foxcroft, *Character of Anna*, 47; Saffin, Note Book 65; Mather, *Monica Americana*, 26; and Mather, *Ecclesia Monilia*, 24.

45. See also Saffin, Note Book, 65; Colman, *Duty and Honour of Aged Women*, 26; Jabez Fitch, *A Discourse on Serious Piety, Being a Funeral Sermon Preach'd Upon the Death of Mrs. Mary Martyn, Who Departed this Life at Portsmouth in the Province of New-Hampshire*, January 26th[, 1725] (Boston, 1725), 18; and Mather, *Ecclesia Monilia*, 24.

46. Widows played key roles in the community as charitable neighbors and as economic operators in that same community; in fact, the two roles sometimes overlapped. But bequests to female nonkin were not necessarily charity and more likely helped support a vibrant economic place for women.

47. [Allestree], *The Ladies Calling*, 76-79.

48. Increase Mather, *A Discourse Concerning the Death of . . . Abigail Foster*, 24.

49. *South Carolina Gazette*, August 26, 1732.

50. Will of Hannah Boulton, proved November 8, 1742, Essex County Microfilm, V. 325, 230-232.

51. Among French Protestants, many of whom lived in South Carolina, it was traditional to leave legacies to the poor and to the church. Although it was impossible for me to determine with any certainty which widows were Huguenots, it seems clear that they greatly influenced the rate of charitable giving in South Carolina. Jon Butler argues that such bequests declined in South Carolina after 1720, the period for which I have the most information, which may explain why the rates were not higher. Jon Butler, *The Huguenots in America: A Refugee People in New World Society* (Cambridge, MA: Harvard University Press, 1983), 121, 140.

52. See wills of Elizabeth Cushing, proved February 26, 1690, Suffolk County Wills, 11, 125-126; Elizabeth Gerrish, Essex County Microfilm, 321, 216-217, and 320, 200-201; and Mary Combassye, proved June 13, 1733, South Carolina WPA Wills, v. 3, 1732-1737, 51-52.

53. Crane, *Ebb Tide in New England:* 123-4; Kierner, *Beyond the Household*, 3. For the ways that the institutionalization of women's benevolence in the early republic moved women's duties from a notion of charity as individual service to a collective public identity and thus created an explicit source of power (albeit ambiguously so) for women, see Boylan, *The Origins of Women's Activism*.54. [Allestree], *The Ladies Calling*, 76-79. For other references to a widow's role as mother to the community, see Sylvester, *Monodia*, 47.

55. Dunton, *Letters Written From New-England*, 110; [Allestree], *Ladies Calling*, 76; and Colman, *Duty and Honour of Aged Women*, 26.

56. Fuller, *Holy State*, 33-34.

57. Wulf, *Not All Wives*, 155. For a fuller exploration of the male "provider" role see Wilson, *Ye Heart of a Man*, 99-114.

58. Massachusetts Historical Society Photostat Collection, 1662.

59. *Suffolk County Wills*, 15, 78-80; *Suffolk County Wills*, 6, 221-224; *Suffolk County Wills*, 38, 125-127; and *South Carolina Wills*, 1671-1727, 292-294. Kirsten Wood, "Slaveholding Widows in the Old Southwest," finds a similar pattern of widows supporting other widows, although her focus is more on kin rather than nonkin and on the postrevolutionary era, 148-149. For an analysis of changing structure of female networks between 1700 and 1775, see Joan Gunderson, "Kith and Kin: Women's Networks in Colonial Virginia," in Catherine Clinton and Michelle Gillespie, *The Devil's Lane: Sex and Race in the Early South* (New York: Oxford University Press, 1997), 90-108.

60. Wulf, *Not All Wives*, 107; Kierner, *Beyond the Household*, 38.

61. Deed dated June 16, 1732, Amory Family Papers, 1698-1894, Unbound Vol. 1, Massachusetts Historical Society.

62. Sarah Middlecot, Ann Coppin, Mary Mico, Marcy Bant (she had half a pew at Dr. Colman's meeting house and half a pew at Mr. Welsted's), and Mary

Watson. Suffolk Country Wills, Book 27, 33-35 and 176-177; Suffolk County Wills, Book 29, 206-207, Suffolk County Wills, Book 33, 89-91; Suffolk County Wills, Book 32, 41-43; and Suffolk County Wills. Book 37, 69-71, respectively. The Boston merchant Thomas Banister bequeathed his "pew in the new Meeting House in Brattle Street for her Life"; Suffolk County Wills, 16, 606-608.

63. Robert J. Dinkin, "Seating the Meeting House in Early Massachusetts," *New England Quarterly* 43 (1970), 453, 455-457, 460, 462. He explains that in the seventeenth century, meetinghouses were "divided by gender," that is, men sat on one side and women on the other. That did not put women in a subordinate position, however, because "women, especially married women or widows, had as prominent seats as did men." See also Richard Archer, *Fissures in the Rock: New England in the Seventeenth Century* (Hanover, NH: University Press of New Hampshire, 2001), 59-66.

64. South Carolina WPA Wills, 5 (1740-1747), 344-349; *Suffolk County Probate Records*, 16, 606-608.

65. This and the following discussions of memory draw upon Valerie Grim, "History Shared Through Memory: The Establishment and Implementation of Education in the Brooks Farm Community, 1920-1957," *Oral History Review* 23 (1996), 2, 4, 5, 6, 9; David Glassberg, "Public History and the Study of Memory," *Public Historian*, 18 (1996): 9-11. See also Wulf Kansteiner, "Finding Meaning in Memory: A Methodological Critique of Collective Memory Studies, *History and Theory* 41 (2002), 179-197, and Alon Confino, "Collective Memory and Cultural History: Problems of Method," *American Historical Review* 102 (1997), 1386-1403.

66. I use the passive voice here because the records did and it is impossible to determine whether Mrs. Thatcher or the seating committee "gave" the pew to Wharton and Sheafe.

67. Wendy Katz, "Portraits and the Production for the Civil Self in Seventeenth-Century Boston," *Winterthur Portfolio* 39 (2005), 125.

68. Evidence from the three married women, Mrs. Simkins, Mrs. Cook, and Mrs. Kilby, supported the testimony of the three widows.

69. Salem Town Records, microfilm edition, 150, 285, 300.

70. Eliot, *The Blessings Bestow'd upon Them That Fear God*, 24.

71. For further discussion of these points, see Carole Pateman, *The Sexual Contract* (Stanford: Stanford University Press, 1988), and Susan Muller Okin, *Women in Western Political Thought* (Princeton: Princeton University Press, 1979).

72. John Frederick Martin, *Profits in the Wilderness: Entrepreneurship and the Founding of New England Towns in the Seventeenth Century* (Chapel Hill: University of North Carolina Press, 1991), 172; Defoe, *Roxana*, 149.

73. Salem Town Records, 1636, microfilm edition, 14-15, 19.

74. Salem Town Records, microfilm edition, January 21, 1640, 95.

75. Salem Town Records, February 3, 1718, 204; February 3, 1725, 249; February

2, 1730, 104; March 6, 1737, 147; February 9, 1743, 337; March 3, 1745, 423; February 9, 1747, 470; and February 17, 1748, 524.

76. Salem Town Records, July 2, 1722, 190; December 2, 1723, 343; and November 22, 1711, 60. Boydston, *Home & Work*, 6-7, analyzes a similar public recognition of women's contribution to the community. In this case, the Massachusetts Court of Elections paid Richard Sherman and his wife separately paid for their services to the court and community, thereby publicly recognizing the economic value of both. However, "neither the nature of the claims or the values awarded were identical." Richard based his claim for reimbursement on his right in the ownership of property (one of the hallmarks of citizenship), and his wife based her claim on the work she performed. Therefore, because the court reimbursed Richard at a higher rate, his masculine property rights had a greater value than her feminine direct labor. If this argument is correct, it suggests another example of widows' unique position in the community, for they assumed rights as property owners.

77. Michael B. Katz, *In the Shadow of the Poorhouse: A Social History of Welfare in America* (New York: Basic Books, Inc., 1986), 13-15.

78. Salem Town Records.

CHAPTER 5

1. Wills of Benedicta Netmaker, Suffolk County Wills, 36, 165-167, and Magdalen Wroe, Suffolk County Wills, 36, 160-161. Proving a will means presenting it in court and testifying to its veracity. It is impossible to determine when each widow died, but executors generally proved a will as soon as possible after the death of the will maker.

2. *Boston Gazette*, April 28, 1735, November 3, 1735, October 4, 1737, May 9, 1737; April 6, 1741. See also her one advertisement in *Boston News-Letter*, November 10, 1737.

3. *Boston Gazette*, November 13, 1738, November 26, 1739, January 19, 1741.

4. Boydston, *Home & Work*, 18, 23, 24, 26-29.

5. There has much excellent work analyzing early American women's economic roles recently; see, for example, Gloria L. Main, "Gender, Work and Wages in Colonial New England," *William and Mary Quarterly* 51 (1994): 39-66; Crane, *Ebb Tide in New England*; Patricia Cleary, *Elizabeth Murray: A Woman's Pursuit of Independence in Eighteenth-Century America* (Amherst: University of Massachusetts Press, 2000); Wulf, *Not All Wives*; Sturtz, *Within Her Power*; Anzilotti, *In the Affairs of the World*; and Marla R. Miller, *The Needle's Eye: Women and Work in the Age of Revolution* (Amherst: University of Massachusetts Press, 2006). See also *Early American Studies*, "Special Forum: Women's Economies in North America Before 1820," vol. 4 (2006).

6. For the high value placed on women's domestic economic roles in the

seventeenth and eighteenth *centuries, see Boydston, Home & Work, 1-29; Kierner, Beyond* the Household, 9-35; and Amanda Vickery, *The Gentleman's Daughter: Women's Lives in Georgian England* (New Haven: Yale University Press, 2003), 127-160.

7. Daniel Defoe, *The Complete English Tradesman* (London, 1839, originally published 1726), Project Gutenberg E-Book.

8. *The Dramatic Works of the Celebrated Mrs. Centlivre*, 204-205, 207, 249-251. I discussed the sexual licentiousness of Centlivre's widows in an earlier chapter, but the line between work and sexuality cannot be clearly drawn.

9. Will of Ann Pollard, Suffolk County Wills, Book 24, 328-331. See also the wills of Elizabeth Bowdoin, Suffolk County Wills, Book 21, 801-803; Joanna Bulkley, Suffolk County Wills, Book 19, 296-298; Johanna Carthew, Suffolk County Wills, Book 18, 291-293; Sarah Dolbear, Suffolk County Wills, Book 37, 377-380; Susanna Newell, Suffolk County Wills, Book 21, 751-752; Sarah Oliver, Suffolk County Wills, Book 21, 184-185; Sarah Pemberton, Suffolk County Wills, Book 16, 594-595; Sarah Vincent, Suffolk County Wills, Book 26, 183-186; Mary Wilson, Suffolk County Wills, New Series Book 5, 302-303; Ruth Allin, Hampshire County Wills, v. VII, 41-42 and 131-132; and Alicia Ward, South Carolina Wills, 1731-1733, 375-376.

10. *Boston News-Letter*, January 18, 1720. Thomas Amory Account Book, 1720-1728, Massachusetts Historical Society: August 2, 1722, October 10, 1722, April 23, 1734, May 2, 1723, June 12, 1723, October 17, 1723, November 9, 1723, and July 27, 1724. My student, Jason Gunning, transcribed the Amory account book for me, and we had several interesting discussions about Sarah Cross and the implications of remarriage for widows' economic independence. Analyzes of shopkeeping women include Cleary, *Elizabeth Inman*; Cleary, "'She Will be in the Shop,'" 181-202; Elizabeth Mancke, "At the Counter of the General Store: Women and the Economy in Eighteenth-Century Horton, Nova Scotia," in Margaret Conrad, *Intimate Relations: Family and Community in Planter Nova Scotia* (Fredericton, NB: Acadiensis Press, 1995), 167-181; Aileen Button Agnew, "Silent Partners: The Economic Life of Women on the Frontier of Colonial New York," (Ph.D. diss., University of New Hampshire, 1998); Serena Zabin, "Women's Trading Networks and Dangerous Economies in Eighteenth-Century New York City," *Early American Studies: An Interdisciplinary Journal* 4 (2006), 291-321; Marla R. Miller, "The Last Mantua Maker: Craft Tradition and Commercial Change in Boston, 1760-1845," *Early American Studies: An Interdisciplinary Journal* 4 (2006), 372-424. Laurel Thatcher Ulrich, "Vertuous Women Found: New England Ministerial Literature, 1668-1735," *American Quarterly* 28 (1976), 20. The phrase is now the title of a new book by Ulrich, *Well-Behaved Women Seldom Make History* (New York: Knopf, 2007).

11. Petition dated July 7, 1696, Massachusetts Historical Society, Photostat Collection. A recent study of eighteenth-century newspaper advertisements placed

by women shows that nearly 6 percent of all advertisements were for innkeepers and tavernkeepers. Dexter, *Colonial Women of Affairs*, ch. 1; Schultz and Lantz, "Occupational Pursuits of Free Women in Early America," 98. Widows frequently transformed their domestic skills of providing food and drink for their family into an ability to ensure their family's economic survival.

12. May 7, 1662, petition of Alice Thomas to the Massachusetts General Court, Photostat Collection, Massachusetts Historical Society, Boston. This and the following paragraphs draw from Samuel E. Morison, ed., *Records of the Suffolk County Court, 1671-1680*, 2 vols., Collections of the Colonial Society of Massachusetts (Boston: Published by the Society, 1933), v. 1, 82-84, 92, 126, 158, 159, 266, 339, and v. 2, 721, 1071; John Hull, "Memoir and Diaries of John Hull," *Archaelogia Americana, Transactions and Collections of the American Antiquarian Society* 3 (1857), 232; John A. Noble, ed., *Records of the Court of Assistants of the Colony of the Massachusetts Bay, 1630-1692*, 3 vols. (Boston, 1901-1908), v. III, 225-227; Koehler, *A Search for Power*, 118, 207-220; and Suffolk County Probate Records, 11, 354-357.

13. Sharon V. Salinger, *Taverns and Drinking in Early America* (Baltimore: Johns Hopkins University Press, 2002), 168, 170, 207. For a discussion of the licensing of lower-sort widows as tavern owners, see Joanne Lloyd, "Beneath the City on the Hill: 'Alley Society' and Interracial Community in Boston, 1700-1850" (Ph.D. diss., Boston College, 2007). Gayle K. Brunelle, "Policing the Monopolizing Women of Early Modern Nantes," *Journal of Women's History* 19 (2007), 10-35, addresses this issue for sixteenth- and seventeenth-century French women. She argues, 30, that this attempt to control women "permanently gendered independent female labor as poor, or at least low in capital and social esteem, and thus subordinate to the work of better-capitalized, wealthier male retailers and wholesalers."

14. *Records of the Suffolk County Court*, II, 781. Taverns and their keepers raised suspicion among the leaders of the community. Everyone living in New England towns was required to have the approval of the community members or law enforcement officials to do so. Newcomers or "strangers" were required to meet with the selectmen upon their arrival in town to apply for admission to residency. The scrutiny "strangers" underwent, as well as their possible rejection if they did not meet local economic and moral qualifications, often meant that they skirted the law either simply by failing to register or by being hidden by local tavernors. Widows were thus vulnerable to charges of harboring such "strangers." See David H. Flaherty, *Privacy in Colonial New England* (Charlottesville: University Press of Virginia, 1967), 105-106 and 170-174.

15. The details of Elizabeth George's case are drawn from *Records of the Suffolk County Court* II, 701, 917, 942, 957, 1015, 1160.

16. Hampshire County Probate Records, I, 258a; Suffolk County Court Records, I, 442; *MD Archives*, LVII, 616, LX, 439; and Suffolk County Probate Records, v. 3, New Series 129, October 30, 1683. See also the case of the widow Elizabeth Russell, who was whipped for fornication, Suffolk County Court Records, II, 942.

17. Bushman, *Refinement of America*, 161-164. He discusses the way male tavern owners transformed potentially disreputable establishments into the site of polite respectability by the quality of food they served, the service they provided, and the elaborate decoration of their rooms. Salinger argues that taverns operated by widows "tended to be of less quality" and that "women proprietors engaged their clientele differently than did their male counterparts," Salinger, *Taverns and Drinking*, 180.

18. This was a nearly universal phrase used in colonial American wills. This phrase, however, embodied more than mere form; it signified the testators' public proclamation of their relationships with family, kin, neighbors, and community. Indeed, as one historian claimed, will making was the "ultimate public act." Stephen Coppel, "Wills and the Community in Grantham," in Philip Riden, ed., *Probate Records and the Local Community* (Gloucester: Alan Sutton, 1985), 80. Dayton, *Women Before the Bar*, also found that "Only a handful of New Haven County widows ran taverns," 94.

19. *South Carolina Gazette*, November 27, 1740, and February 22, 1748. The widow Sarah Lloyd also advertised her tavern as a place "where Gentlemen . . . may depend on being accommodated with the best of Liquor and Entertainment," *South Carolina Gazette*, October 17, 1748.

20. *Boston Gazette*, January 1, 1728, and January 12, 1730. Similarly, the *South Carolina Gazette* ran the following advertisement on November 27, 1749: "On Friday Evening next, at the Court-Room at Mrs. Blythe's, several DRAMATICK ENTERTAINMENTS will be performed." See also the widow Thompson's advertisement seeking to rent the Swan Tavern, *Boston Gazette*, June 6, 1726, and again on June 13, June 20, and June 27. *South Carolina Gazette*, July 1, 1732, September 29, 1732, and October 28, 1732. Kirsten Wood, "See You at the Tavern: Women's Participation in Associational, Political, and Musical Gatherings at Early Republican Taverns" (paper presented annual meeting for the Society for Historians of the Early American Republic, Philadelphia, July 21-24, 2005), similarly explores taverns operated by widows as civic and politics sites and of widows as agents of activities that made their inns quasi public institutions.

21. Amussen, *An Ordered Society*, 91-93; Amussen, "Governors and Governed," 176-182; Brodsky, "Widows in Late Elizabethan London," 52; Nesta Evans, "Inheritance, Women, Religion and Education in Early Modern Society as Revealed by Wills," in Philip Riden, ed., *Probate Records and the Local Community* (Gloucester: Alan Sutton, 1985), 67; and Joel Rosenthal, "Aristocratic Widows in Fifteenth-Century England," in Barbara Harris and Jo Ann McNamara, eds., *Women and the Structure of Society: Selected Research from the Fifth Berkshire Conference on the History of Women* (Durham, NC: Duke University Press, 1984), 46. Richard Wall, "Women Alone in English Society," *Annales de démographie historique* 16, no. 314 (1981) estimates that approximately 60 percent of widows had either married children or no living children at all. For the contrasting argument that

widows "shared with their men many of the same attitudes about their society and the proper roles of men and women" and thus bequeathed in much the same way that men did, see Main, "Widows in Rural Massachusetts," 89.

22. Wills of Rachel Bigg, Suffolk County Wills, Book 1, 89-91, and Rebecca Flavel, South Carolina WPA Wills, v. 5, 1740-1747, 344-349. See also the wills of Mary Atherton, fifteen heirs, Suffolk County Wills, Book 7, 245-246; Mary Norton, twenty-six heirs, Suffolk County Wills, Book 6, 221-223; Sarah Simms, seventeen heirs, Suffolk County Wills, Book 6, 147-148; Susannah White, thirteen heirs, Suffolk County Wills, Book 11, 66-68; Anne Lynes, fourteen heirs, Maryland Wills, Book 13, 325-327; Mary Barnard, twenty-two heirs, Hampshire County Wills, I, 48-51; Sarah Allen, eleven heirs, South Carolina WPA Wills, Vol. 6, 125-126; and Mary Stewart, fourteen heirs, South Carolina WPA Wills, Vol. 6, 423-426.

23. Jean Butenhoff Lee, "Land and Labor: Parental Bequest Practices in Charles County, Maryland," in Lois Green Carr, Philip D. Morgan, and Jean B. Russo, eds., *Colonial Chesapeake Society* (Chapel Hill: University of North Carolina Press, 1988), 307-310. See also Shammas et al., *Inheritance in America.*

24. *Boston News-Letter*, February 25, 1731; *Boston Gazette*, April 21, 1729; *Boston Gazette*, September 19, 1749.

25. Coclanis, *Shadow of a Dream*, Tables 3.2 and 3.3, 88-89. Between 1720 and 1750, slaves made up about 50 percent of the total probated wealth.

26. Magdalen Evans's Deed of Sale dated December 30, 1745, South Carolina WPA Misc. Wills, v. 75a, 158-159; Henrietta Fisher's Deed of Sale dated May 7, 1748, South Carolina WPA Misc. Wills, v. 75b, 542; Mary Lesur's Deeds of Sale dated April 17, 1744, South Carolina WPA Misc. Wills, v. 69a, 359, and April 10, 1745, South Carolina WPA Misc. Wills, v. 69b, 373; and Elizabeth Hawkins's Deed of Sale dated August 15, 1749, South Carolina WPA Misc. Wills, v. 78a, 105-107.

27. For two excellent analyses on the development and growth of communities in colonial Maryland, see Lorena S. Walsh, "Community Networks in the Early Chesapeake," in Lois Green Carr, Philip D. Morgan, and Jean B. Russo, eds., *Colonial Chesapeake Society* (Chapel Hill: University of North Carolina Press, 1988), 200-241; and Michael Graham, "Meetinghouse and Chapel: Religion and Community in Seventeenth Century Maryland," in Lois Green Carr, Philip D. Morgan, and Jean B. Russo, eds., *Colonial Chesapeake Society* (Chapel Hill: University of North Carolina Press, 1988), 242-275.

28. Crane, *Ebb Tide in New England*, 159.

29. *South Carolina Gazette*, June 8, 1748.

30. The median plantation size was between two hundred and nine hundred acres, and the average land sale was five hundred acres: David B. Ryden and Russell R. Menard, "South Carolina's Colonial Land Market: An Analysis of Rural Property Sales, 1720–1775," *Social Science History* 29 (2005), 604-606, 616.

31. *South Carolina Gazette*, October 19, 1734; February 15, 1735; April 11, 1743, and July 23, 1744. Like Elizabeth Hill, Sarah Woodward rented out six hundred

acres, *South Carolina Gazette*, February 10, 1746. Sarah Lloyd employed a wide variety of economic strategies; in addition to selling land, town lots, a house, and slaves, as well as renting rooms and taking in boarders, she rented out a wharf and ran a bakeshop; see also *South Carolina Gazette*, October 17, 1748.

32. *Boston Gazette*, March 7, 1749; *Boston News-Letter*, May 5, 1714.

33. *Boston Gazette*, January 18, 1725 and July 18, 1749.

34. The material for this and the two following paragraph was drawn from Trevor Burnard, *Creole Gentlemen: The Maryland Elite, 1691-1776* (New York: Routledge, 2002), 61-99 (according to him, young men were more likely to have outstanding debts in their inventories than were older men, who likely had had the opportunity to pay off their debts before they died); Paul Clemens, "Economy and Society on Maryland's Eastern Shore, 1689-1733," in Aubrey C. Land, Lois Green Carr, and Edward C. Papenfuse, eds., *Law, Society, and Politics in Early Maryland* (Baltimore: Johns Hopkins University Press, 1977), 157; Cathy Matson, *Merchants & Empire: Trading in Colonial New York* (Baltimore: Johns Hopkins University Press, 1998), 113, 160-161; Elizabeth M. Pruden, "Investing Widows: Autonomy in a Nascent Capitalist Society," in Jack P. Green, Rosemary Brana-Shute, and Randy J. Sparks, eds., *Money Trade, and Power: The Evolution of Colonial South Carolina's Plantation Society* (Columbia: University of South Carolina Press, 2001), 344-345; Gloria Main, *Peoples of a Spacious Land: Families and Cultures in Colonial New England* (Cambridge, MA: Harvard University Press, 2001), 178-180 (she argues that mortgages become common in the Boston area well before the end of the seventeenth century and that their use spread to other parts of the region in the eighteenth century); Konig, *Law and Society*, 82-84; Main, *Tobacco Colony*, 70-71; Shields, *Civil Tongues*, 296; Dayton, *Women Before the Bar*, 70, 77-79; Rosen, *Courts and Commerce*, 50-51, 54. She claims, "The mutually supportive and tolerant economic relationships normally attributed to a communal society do not lead to lawsuits."

35. Rosen, *Courts and Commerce*, 50; Maryland Archives, XLI, 65-66.

36. *South Carolina Gazette*, March 26, 1744. She was not alone; the widows Sarah Ward, Charlotte Gourian, Mary Saureau, Lydia Viart (who "designed to leave this Province"), and Ann Drayton similarly threatened lawsuits; *South Carolina Gazette*, January 13, 1733, January 20, 1733; April 14, 1733; March 2, 1734; February 15, 1735; and April 10, 1736. *Boston Gazette*, February 15, 1731. While widows in Massachusetts tended not to place such advertisements in the paper, according to Dayton, *Women Before the Bar*, 94, "Nearly 90 percent of litigating widows had extended small amounts of credit by notes. Thus some widows, whether they were running a family enterprise or augmenting their income through cautious lending, displayed considerable facility with written credit instruments. The number of widows appearing county court to sue or be sued over their own debts increased about sevenfold between the 1710s and 1750s. . . . Well propertied widows . . . were an important source of both consumer and commercial loans and

therefore, it must be acknowledged, played a modest but significant part in the capitalization and commercial development of the countryside."

37. Wulf, *Not All Wives*, 148; there were 20 shillings in a pound, thus Herredge's creditors got back about 50 percent of the original debt; *Suffolk County Probate Records*, 17, 191, and 202. No such declarations of insolvency appeared in the other countries in Massachusetts, in Maryland, or in South Carolina. This reflects not the lack of insolvency in those areas but rather the peculiar nature of early American recordkeeping.

38. Main, *Peoples of a Spacious Land*, 178-180. She qualified her optimistic view of widowed creditors by pointing out that mortgages were complicated forms of credit that could be used only by those widows who had gained the necessary skills from their husbands or who had the initiative to learn them upon their husbands' deaths—that is, elite women with access to an education. Those widows who failed to acquire these skills became even more dependent on male relatives, especially in the increasingly commercialized world of the eighteenth-century seaboard. Mary Greenhill, *Suffolk County Probate Records*, New Series 13, 8-11. Of course, that lack also hid the extent of the female debt network. Pruden, "Investing Widows," 344-362, discusses widows and their mortgage practice in Charleston, South Carolina. She agrees with Main about the freedom and independence mortgages provided for widows. She found that 21 percent of widows were involved in some degree in the mortgage and bond market of South Carolina. Unlike Main, however, she does not see mortgages as an instrument only of elite women; "77 percent . . . were not of the elite and wealthy population but, nonetheless, found a way to extend their legacies by a means other than buying land or slaves." For a discussion of women's participation in the debt network in another colony at a slightly later time, see Kristi Rutz-Robbins, "'Divers Debts': Women's Participation in the Local Economy, Albemarle, North Carolina, 1663-1729," *Early American Studies* 4 (2006), 425-441; and Ellen Hartigan-O'Connor, "'She Said she did not Know Money': Urban Women and Atlantic Market in the Revolutionary Era," *Early American Studies* 4 2006), 322-352.

39. Will of Mary Baker, Suffolk County Wills, Book 18, 120-121.

40. *Boston Gazette*, March 14, 1720, *Boston News-Letter*, March 14, 1715, and *South Carolina Gazette*, January 25, 1739. Between 1720 and 1750, no fewer than twenty-nine, thirteen, and twenty-six similar ads appeared in the three newspapers, respectively. For a discussion of women's immediate immersion in the colonial debt network, see Dayton, *Women Before the Bar*, 76, 91-92, 97 (she found that 93 percent of women's lawsuits were with fellow town residents; only 40 percent of men's were); Crane, *Ebb Tide in New England*, 158-159; Rosen, *Courts and Commerce*, 50-51; Konig, *Law and Society*, 82-84; and Main, *Tobacco Colony*, 70-71.

41. Suffolk County Will Book, 37, 377-380, and 26, 146-148. Burnard, *Creole Gentlemen*, 77, found that two-thirds of elite male debtors owed money to more than ten creditors and a third owed money to more than twenty creditors; of

those who were owed money, more than half had more than fifty debtors. Unlike widows, these male debtors created a vast debt network; similar to the female debt network among widows, however, it was a network based on gender.

42. Inventory of Margaret Wilson taken in 1747, South Carolina WPA Misc. Wills, v. 7, 352; inventory of Sarah Harley taken February 6, 1744, South Carolina WPA Misc. Wills, v. 71, 368; and inventory of Mary Sumner taken March 19, 1750, South Carolina WPA Misc. Wills, v. 77b, 454. See also the inventory of Mary Allen taken July 9, 1750, South Carolina WPA Misc. Wills, 77b, 522. She left an estate valued at £721, and, of that, £680 (94 percent) was debts due to her.

43. Inventory of Sarah Allen taken March 14, South Carolina WPA Misc. Wills, 77a, 120-122.

44. Suffolk County Wills, 13, 226-227; New Series 10, 290-293; 26, 360-365; New Series 13, 8-10; New Series 18, 215-216.

45. Amory Family Papers, Massachusetts Historical Society, Genealogy of Ana Amory, Vol. 154, 180-181.

46. Amory Family Papers, Massachusetts Historical Society, N279, Reel 1, October 1729; June 12, 1736; December 16, 1738; and August 1739.

47. *Boston Gazette*, July 8, 1728; she ran this same ad again on July 15, July 22, and July 29; *Boston Gazette*, February 24, 1729; she ran this ad again on March 3 and March 10.

48. For a similar Boston/Charleston connection see the "Letters from the Schenckingh Smiths of South Carolina to the Boyston Smiths of Massachusetts," *South Carolina Historical and Genalogical Magazine* 35, no. 1 (January 1934), 1-12.

49. Letter dated October 4, 1716, Amory Family Papers, Massachusetts Historical Society, N279, Reel 1.

50. Oxford English Dictionary.

51. Toby L. Ditz, "Formative Ventures Formative Ventures: Eighteenth-Century Commercial Letters and the Articulation of Experience," presents a brief but important analysis of John Hill's *Young Secretary's Guide* in which he teaches merchants how to write letters that explicitly connect the personal and the commercial, in Rebecca Earle, ed., *Epistolary Selves: Letters and Letter-Writers, 1600-1945* (Aldershot: Ashgate, 1999), 6.

52. Letter dated April 5, 1720, Amory Family Papers, Massachusetts Historical Society, N279, Reel 1.

53. Oxford English Dictionary.

54. Anzilotti, *In the Affairs of the World*, 4-8; Glover argues that we must understand the importance of "horizontal" ties between siblings and kin—that they exerted a profound influence over one another and that they created a sense of belonging and identity within the family group. She also argues that "this determination to use kin to secure status and power" meant that the elite in South Carolina had a lot in common with merchant families in Boston." Glover, *All Our Relations*, ix-x, xiv.

55. Ditz convincingly argues that such "extended face to face conversations to a global network, a collective association that redefined and expanded public life"; Ditz, "Formative Ventures," 61, 70-72.

56. Letter from Isaac Holmes to Rebecca Amory, April 11, 1730, Amory Family Papers, Massachusetts Historical Society, N279, Reel 1.

57. South Carolina Department of Archives and History, Conveyance Book C, 171-81 and 182-4.

58. Letter from Elizabeth Holmes of Charleston, South Carolina, to Rebecca Holmes Amory in Boston, October 17, 1730, Amory Family Papers, Massachusetts Historical Society, N279, Reel 1.

59. Letter from Isaac Holmes from Charleston, South Carolina, to Rebecca Holmes Amory in Boston, February 21, 1731, Amory Family Papers, Massachusetts Historical Society, N279, Reel 1.

60. Letter from Elizabeth Holmes from Charleston, South Carolina, to Rebecca Holmes Amory in Boston, March 1, 1732, Amory Family Papers, Massachusetts Historical Society, N279, Reel 1. As I've "translated" it, the letter reads: "Hoping it will find you and yours well, as blessed be God we are at present. Am glad to hear Frankie behaves himself better than he did [earlier]. Hope God will enable him to see his folly and to mend. He wrote me he was going to apprentis [and] hope business will divert him from folly."

61. Letter from Isaac Holmes from Charleston, South Carolina, to Rebecca Holmes Amory in Boston, October 21, 1732, Amory Family Papers, Massachusetts Historical Society, N279, Reel 1; Oxford English Dictionary.

62. Glover, *All Our Relations*, 60-61; see also Anzilotti, *In the Affairs of the World*, 37-38, for a similar argument

63. *Boston Gazette*, September 29, 1735.

64. "Rebecca Amory's Receipt Book," Amory Family Papers, 1698-1894, Massachusetts Historical Society. It was bound in green leather with a dainty gold clasp; unfortunately, it details only the money she expended. Dayton, *Women Before the Bar*, found that "only a few widows kept their own account books," 94.

65. *Boston News-Letter*, May 21, 1730. For a fuller discussion of female support networks, see Patricia Cleary, *Elizabeth Murray*, 72-74, 73, 92-93, 97, 210, and 220-222. According to Cleary, "She Will be in the Shop," 188, women's shops attracted women customers, so, while there is little evidence of a strong female network in Amory's receipt book, it is likely that she created such a network within the shop itself. See also Richard Bushman, "Shopping and Advertising in Colonial America," in Cary Carson, Ronald Hoffman, and Peter J. Albert, eds., *Of Consuming Interests: The Style of Life in the Eighteenth Century* (Charlottesville: University of Virginia Press, 1994), 247.

66. *Boston Gazette*, March 6, 1738; *Boston News-Letter*, April 4, 1740; *Boston Gazette*, April 14, 1740.

67. *Boston Gazette*, September 27, 1748;*Boston Gazette*, May 2, 1749.

CONCLUSION

1. Dunton, *Letters Written From New-England*, 98.

2. Jeremiah Bumstead Diaries (interleaved and annotated Almanacs), American Antiquarian Society, Worcester, Massachusetts. Jeremiah Bumstead, 1678-1747, was a middling artisan and an enthusiastic member of the Old South Church in Boston.

3. Jensen, *Loosening the Bonds*, 25-26; Lebsock, *The Free Women of Petersburg*, ch. 5, "Women Alone: Property and Personalism," specifically, 77-79, 136-138; Wood, *Masterful Women*, 1, 82,102.

Bibliography

PRIMARY SOURCES

UNPUBLISHED MATERIALS

Aberdeen University, *The Aberdeen Bestiary*, Aberdeen University Library MS 24, http://www.abdn.ac.uk/bestiary/translat/32r.hti.

American Antiquarian Society, Worcester, Massachusetts
  John Saffin Note-Book
  Mather Family Papers
  Parson Family Papers
  Jeremiah Bumstead Diaries

Forbes Library, Northampton, Massachusetts
  Northampton County Court Records on microfilm

Library of Congress Manuscript Division
  Galloway-Maxcy-Markoe Family Papers

Maryland Historical Society, Baltimore, Maryland
  Dulany Family Papers
  Key Family Papers

Massachusetts Historical Society, Boston, Massachusetts
  Photostat Collection
  Amory Family Papers

Essex County Probate Records on Microfilm, Genealogical Library, Society of the Church of Jesus Christ of Latter-Day Saints

Hampshire County Probate Records on Microfilm, Genealogical Library, Society of the Church of Jesus Christ of Latter-Day Saints

Maryland Probate Records on Microfilm, Hall of Records, Maryland State Archives

Plimoth Plantation, Plymouth Colony Wills (transcripts), Plymouth, Massachusetts

Suffolk County Probate Records on Microfilm, Genealogical Library, Society of the Church of Jesus Christ of Latter-Day Saints

South Carolina Probate Records on Microfilm, Genealogical Library, Society of the Church of Jesus Christ of Latter-Day Saints

PUBLISHED MATERIALS

Acts and Laws, of His Majesties Province of the Massachusetts-Bay, in New-England. Boston: By Bartholonew Green and John Allen, 1699.

Acts and Laws, Passed by the Great and General Court or Assembly of Their Majesties, Province of the Massachusets-Bay, in New-England. Boston: By Benjamin Harris, 1692

The Acts and Resolves, Public and Private of the Province of the Massachusetts Bay. Vol. 1, 1692-1714. Boston: Wright & Potter, 1869.

[Allestree, Richard.] *The Ladies Calling in Two Parts. By the Author of the Whole Duty of Man, the Causes of the Decay of Christian Piety, and the Gentlemans Calling*. Oxford, 1673.

Bacon, Thomas, ed. *The Laws of Maryland at Large, with Proper Indexes*. Annapolis: 1765.

Baxter, Joseph. *A Discourse on the Great Priviledge and Happiness of Dying in Faith. Deliver'd at George-Town on Arowsick, upon the Death of John Watts, Esq; Who departed this Life Nov. 26th. 1717*. Boston, 1718.

Beauchamp, Virginia Walcott, Elizabeth H. Hageman, and Margaret Mikesell, eds. *The Instruction of a Christen Woman by Juan Luis Vives* (Urbana: University of Illinois Press, 2001), "The Work: Its Contexts, Content, and Translation," http://www.press.uillinois.edu/epub/books/vives/work.html.

Behn, Aphra. *The Widow Ranter or The History of Bacon in Virginia. A Tragi-Comedy, Acted by their Majesties Servants*. London, 1690.

Blackstone, William. *Commentaries on the Laws of England*. Oxford: Clarendon Press, 1765–1769.

The Book of the General Laws and Libertyes Concerning the Inhabitants of the Massachusetts Collected out of the Records of the General Court for the Several Years Wherein They were Made and Established. Cambridge, 1648.

The Book of the General Lawes and Libertyes . . . Now Revised by the same Court. Cambridge, 1660.

Browne, William Hand, ed. *Archives of Maryland: Proceedings and Acts of the General Assembly of Maryland*. 72 vols. Baltimore, 1883-1972.

[Centlivre, Susanna.] *The Dramatic Works of the Celebrated Mrs. Centlivre, with a New Account of her Life. Complete in Three Volumes*. Vol. 1. New York: AMS Press, 1968. Reprinted from the London, 1872 edition.

[Centlivre, Susanna.] "The Gamester: A Comedy, As it is Acted at the New-Theatre in Lincolns-Inn-Fields, by her Majesty's Servants." In *The Plays of Susanna Centlivre*, ed. Richard C. Frushell New York: Garland, 1982.

Chapman, George. *The Widdowes Teares: A Comedie*. London: Printed for John Browne, 1612.

Chauncy, Charles. *Man's Life Considered under the Similitude of a Vapour, that appeareth for a little Time, and then vanisheth away. A Sermon on the Death of that Honorable & Vertuous Gentlewoman Mrs. Sarah Byfield, the amiable Consort of the Honorable Nathanael Byfield, Esq.* Boston, 1731.

Chauncy, Charles. *Nathanael's Character Displayed. A Sermon Preach'd The Lord's Day after the Funeral of the Honourable Nathanael Byfield, Esq., . . . Who died at his House in Boston, on the 6th of June, 1733 In the 80th Year of his Age.* Boston, 1733.

Colman, Benjamin. *The Duty and Honour of Aged Women. A Funeral Sermon Occasion'd by the Decease of Mrs. Abigail Foster.* Boston, 1711.

Colman, Benjamin. *The Hope of the Righteous in their Death. A Sermon Preached on the Lord's Day after the Funeral of William Harris, Esq., Who departed this Life, September 22. 1721. In the Fifty-Fifth Year of his Age.* Boston, 1721.

Cooper, Thomas, ed. The *Statutes at Large of South Carolina.* Vol. 1. Columbia: A. S. Johnston, 1836.

Cooper, William. *A Sermon Concerning the Laying of the Deaths of Others to Heart. Occasion'd by the lamented Death of that Ingenious and Religious Gentleman John Gore of Harvard College in Cambridge, N.E. Who died of the Small-Pox, Nov. 7. 1720. In the 38th Year of his Age.* Boston, 1720.

Copland, Robert. *The Seven Sorrowes that Women Have When Theyr Husbandes be Deade.* *W. Copland, 1568[?].

Cushing, John D. *The Earliest Printed Laws of South Carolina, 1692-1734.* Vol. 1. Wilmington, DE: Michael Glazier, 1978.

Danforth, Samuel. *An Elegy in Memory of the Worshipful Major Thomas Leonard Esq., of Taunton in New-England; Who departed this Life on the 14th Day of November, 1713.* In the 73d. Year of his Age.

Defoe, Daniel. *The Complete English Tradesman.* London, 1839, originally published 1726.

Defoe, Daniel. *Roxana, the Fortunate Mistress.* New York: Bibliophilist Society, 1931.

de Pizan, Christine. *A Medievel Woman's Mirror of Honor: The Treasury of the City of Ladies.* Charity Cannon Willard, trans., and Madeleine Pelner Cosman, ed. New York: Bard Hall Press, 1989.

Dexter, Franklin B., and Zara J. Powers, eds. *New Haven Town Records, 1649-1769.* 3 vols. New Haven: New Haven Colony Historical Scoiety, 1917-1962.

Dow, George Francis, ed. *Records and Files of the Quarterly Coruts of Essex County.* 8 vols. Salem: Essex Institute, 1911-1921.

Dunton, John. *Letters Written From New-England, A.D. 1686 by John Dunton. In Which are Described His Voyages by Sea, His Travels on Land, and the Characters of His Friends and Acquaintances. Notes and Appendix by W. H. Whitmore.* Boston: Published for the Prince Society, 1867.

Elegy upon the much lamented Death of two desireable Brothers, the two eldest Sons of Capt. Joshua and Mrs. Comfort Weeks, of Greenland; Who departed this Life in February 1736, the youngest whose Name was Ichabod, died the 3d Day in 22d

Year of his Age, and the eldest whose Name was Joshua, deceased the 10th Day, in the 24th Year of his Age, leaving his honoured Parents and a desirable Widow with other near-Relations in mournful Tears. nd, np.

Eliot, Jared. *The Blessings Bestow'd on Them That Fear God, as was Shewed in a Sermon Occasion'd by the Death of the Truly Vertuous Mrs. Elizabeth Smithson.* New London, 1739.

Fitch, Jabez. *A Discourse on Serious Piety, Being a Funeral Sermon Preach'd Upon the Death of Mrs. Mary Martyn, Who Departed this Life at Portsmouth in the Province of New-Hampshire, January 26th[, 1725].* Boston, 1725.

Forbes, Allyn B., ed. *Winthrop Papers.* Boston: Massachusetts Historical Society, 1929-1947.

Ford, Worthington Chauncy, ed. *Diary of Cotton Mather.* 2 vols. New York: Frederick Ungar, n.d.

Foxcroft, Thomas. *The Character of Anna, the Prophetess, Consider'd and Apply'd in a Sermon Preach'd after the Funeral of Dame Bridget Usher [Being a Widow of Great Age].* Boston, 1723.

Fuller, Thomas. *The Holy State.* Cambridge, 1642.

Gregorie, Anne King, ed. *Records of the Court of Chancery of South Carolina, 1671-1779.* Washington, DC: American Historical Association, 1950.

Hersey, William R. *A Critical* Old-Spelling Edition of Aphra Behn's The City Heiress. New York: Garland, 1987.

Heywood, Thomas. *Gunaikeion: Or Nine Bookes of Various History Concerninge Women; Inscribed by ye Names of ye Nine Muses.* London, 1624.

Hoadly, Charles J., ed. *Records of the Colony and Plantation of New Haven, 1638-1649.* Hartford: Case, Tiffany, 1857.

Hoadly, Charles J., ed. *Records of the Colony or Jurisdiction of New Haven, 1653 to the Union.* Hartford: Case, Lockwood, 1858.

Hoar, Leonard. *The Sting of Death and Death Unstung Delivered in Two Sermons in which is shewed the Misery of the Death of those that dye in their Sins, & out of Christ, and the Blessedness of their that Dye in the Lord. Preached on the occasion of the Death of the truely nobel and virtuous Lady Mildmay.* Boston, 1680.

Hull, John. "The Memoir and Diaries of John Hull." *Archaelogia Americana,* Transactions and Collections of the American Antiquarian Society, 3 (1857).

[Kenrick, William.] *The Whole Duty of Woman. By a Lady. Written at the Desire of a Nobel LORD.* London, 1753.

Kent, James. *Commentaries on American Law.* New York: Halsted, 1830.

Kozlenko, William, ed. The Puritan: or, the Widow of Watling Street. In *Disputed Plays of William Shakespeare.* New York: Hawthorn Books, 1974.

"Letters from the Schenckingh Smiths of South Carolina to the Boyston Smiths of Massachusetts." *South Carolina Historical and Genalogical Magazine* 35 (January 1934): 1-12.

Levine, Robert Trager. *A Critical Edition of Thomas Middleton's "The Widow."* Salzburg, Austria: Institut fur Englissche Sprache Und Literatur, 1975.

Lynch, Kathleen M., ed. *William Congreve's* The Way of the World. Lincoln: University of Nebraska Press, 1965.

Mather, Cotton. *Detur Digniori. The Righteous Man Described & Asserted as the Excellent Man . . . In a Sermon, upon the Death of the Reverend Mr. Joseph Gerrish, . . . Who was Received, where the wary are at Rest, On the 6 d. XI m. 1719. In the Seventieth Year of His Age*. Boston, 1720.

Mather, Cotton. *Ecclesia Monilia: The Peculiar Treasure of the Almighty King Opened and the Jewels that are made up in it, Exposed. [The Funeral Sermon of] Mrs. Elizabeth Cotton, and Certain Instruments and Memorials of Piety, Written by that Valuable & Honourable Gentlewoman*. Boston, 1726.

Mather, Cotton. *A Good Man Making a Good End., The Life and Death of the Reverend Mr. John Baily, Comprised and Expressed in a Sermon, On the Day of his Funeral, Thursday, 16 d. 10. m. 1697*. Boston, 1698.

Mather, Cotton. *Marah Spoken To: A Brief Essay to do Good Unto the Widow*. Boston, 1718.

Mather, Cotton. *Monica Americana: A Funeral Sermon, Occasioned by the Death of Mrs. Sarah Leverett [or Female Piety Exemplified in a Funeral Sermon on the Death . . .]*. Boston, 1705.

Mather, Cotton. *Nepenthes Evangelicum. A Brief Essay upon a Soul at Ease; In What Piety will bring both Parents and children to. A Sermon Occasion'd by the Death of a Religious Matron, Mrs. Mary Rock*. Boston, 1713.

Mather, Cotton. *Ornaments for the Daughters of Zion or the Character and Happiness of a Vertuous Woman: in a Discourse which Directs the Female-Sex how to Express, the Fear of God, in every Age and State of their Life; and obtain both Temporal and Eternal Blessedness*. Boston, 1692.

Mather, Cotton. *Tabitha Rediviva: An Essay to Describe and Commend the Good Works of a Vertuous Woman*. Boston, 1713.

Mather, Cotton. *Virtue in its Verdure: A Christian Exhibited as a Green Olivetree, in the House of God; with a Character of the Virtuous Mrs. Abigail Brown Who Expired Feb. 18. 1725.6*. Boston, 1725.

Mather, Cotton. *The Widow of Nain: Remarks on the Illustrious Miracle Wrought by our Almighty Redeemer on the behalf of a Desolate Widow*. Boston, 1728.

Mather, Increase. *A Discourse Concerning the Death of the Righteous. Occasioned by the Death of the Honourable John Foster who dyed at Boston in New-England February 9, 1711 And of his Pious Consort, Mrs. Abigail Foster who departed soon after him, viz. on the 5th of March*. Boston, 1711.

Mather, Increase. *A Faithful Man, Described and Rewarded. Some Observable & Serviceable Passages in the Life and Death of Mr. Michael Wigglesworth, Late Pastor of Maldon; Who Rested from His Labours, on the Lords-Day, June 10th. 1705. In the Seventy Fourth Year of his Age*. Boston, 1705.

Middleton, Thomas. *The Widdow, A Comedie As it was Acted at the Private House in Black-Fryers*. London: Humphrey Mosely, 1652.

Morison, Samuel E., ed. "Records of the Suffolk County Court, 1671-1680." 2 vols. *Colonial Society of Massachusetts Publications*, 29-30. Boston: Published by the Society, 1933.

Noble, John B., ed. *Records of the Court of Assistants of the Colony of the Massachusetts Bay, 1630-1692*. 3 vols. Boston, 1901-1928.

Prince, Thomas. *Be Followers of Them, who through Faith and Patience inherit the Promises. A Sermon Occasion'd by the Decease of Mrs. Hannah Fayerweather, of Boston, on January 27th, 1755. Age 53*. Boston, 1755.

Prince, Thomas. *Precious in the Sight of the Lord is the Death of his Saints: A Sermon upon the Death of Mrs. Elizabeth Oliver, Relict of the Honourable Daniel Oliver, Esq. Boston, [1735]*.

Pritchard, Thomas. *The Schoole of Honest and Vertuous Life: Profitable and necessary for all estates and degrees, to be trayned in: but (cheefly) for the pettie Schoolers, the younger sorte of both kindes, bee they men or Women. Also a Laudable and learned Discourse, of the worthynesse of honorable Wedlocke, written the behalfe of all (aswell) Maydes as Wydowes, (generally) for their singuler instruction, to choose them vertuous andhonest Husbandes: But (most specially) sent written as Jewell unto a worthy Gentlewoman, in the time of her widowhood, to direct & guide her in the new election of her seconde husband*. London, 1579.

Rowlands, Samuel. *Tis Merrie When Gossips Meet*. Sold by G. Loftus, 1602.

Reeve, Tapping. *The Law of Baron and Femme, of Parent and Child, of Guardian and Ward, of Master and Servant, and of the Powers of Courts of Chancery*. New Haven: Printed by Oliver Steele, 1816.

Sewall, Samuel. *Diary of Samuel Sewall, 1714, 1730*. Fifth series, Vol. 7. Boston: Massachusetts Historical Society, 1882.

Shurtleff, Nathaniel B., ed. *Records of the Governor and Company of the Massachusetts Bay in New England*. Vol. 1. Boston: William White, 1853.

Shurtleff, William. *The Faith and Prayer of a Dying Malefactor: A Sermon Preach'd December 27,1739 On Occasion at the Execution of two Criminals, Namely, Sarah Simpson and Penelope Kenny, And in the Hearing of the Former*. Boston, 1740.

Silverman, Kenneth, ed. *Selected Letters of Cotton Mather*. Baton Rouge: Louisiana State University Press, 1971.

Spacks, Patricia Meyer, ed. *Selections from* The Female Spectator *by Eliza Haywood*. Oxford: Oxford University Press, 1999.

[Steele, Richard, ed.] *The Ladies Library Written by a Lady*. 3 vols. 4th ed. [London, 1732].

Stoddard, Solomon. *Gods Frown in the Death of Usefull Men, Shewed in a Sermon Preached at the Funeral of the Honourable Col. John Pynchon, Esq., Who Deceased January the 17th. 1702.3*. Boston, 1703.

Swetname, Joseph [pseud. Thomas Tel-troth]. *The Arraignment of Lewde, Idle, Froward, and Unconstant Women. Or the Vanitie of them, choose you whether. With a Commendacion of wife, vertuous and honest Women. Pleasant for married Men, profitable for young Men and hurtfull to none.* London: Printed by Edward Ailde for Thomas Arches, 1615.

Sylvester, Joshuah. "Monodia: An Elegy, in Commeroraion of the Vertuous Life, and goldly deth of the right worshipfull and most religious Lady, Dame Hellen Branch Widow . . . , 1594." In *The Complete Works of Joshuah Sylvester*, ed. Alexander B. Grosart. London, 1880.

Taylor, John. *A Juniper Lecture, With the description of all sorts of women, good and bad: From the modest to the maddest, from the most Civil to the most Rampant, their praise and dispraise compendiously related. The Second Impression, with many new Additions.* London, 1639.

T.E. *The Lawes Resolutions of Womens Rights; Or, The Lawes Provision for Woemen. A Methodicall Collection of such Statutes and Customes, with the Cases, Opinions, Arguments and points of Learning in the Law, as doe properly concerne Women. London, 1632.*

The Whole Duty of Man, laid down in a Plain and Familiar Way for the Use of All, but especially the Meanest Reader . . . Necessary for All Families. London, 1701.

The Whole Duty of Woman. By a Lady. Written at the Desire of a Nobel LORD. London, 1753.

Tusser, Thomas. *The Points of Housewifery, United to the Comfort of Husbandry.* London, 1580. Quoted in Joan Larsen Klein, *Daughters, Wives and Widows: Writings by Men About Women and Marriage in England, 1500-1640.* Urbana: University of Illinois Press, 1992, 211.

Vives, Juan Luis. *The Office and Duty of an Husband.* 1529. Trans., Thomas Paynell, London, (1555?). Quoted in Joan Larsen Klein, *Daughters, Wives, and Widows: Writings by Men About Women and Marriage in England, 1500-1640.* Urbana: University of Illinois Press, 1992.

Vives, Juan Luis. *A Very Fruitfull and Pleasant Booke Called the Instruction of a Christian Woman.* London, 1540.

[Ward, Edward.] *Female Policy Detected: Or the Arts of a Designing Woman Laid Open, Treating of Their Allurements, Inconstancy, Love, Revenge, Pride and Ingratitude.* First published, 1695; reprint, Boston, 1786.

W.C. *The Widowes Joy or Christ His Comfortable Salvation to a Comfortless Widow.* London, 1622.

The Widowes Lamentation for the Absence of Their Deare Children, and Suitors. And for Divers of their Deaths in These Fatall Civill Warres. Presented in the Names and Behalfes of the Rich and Wealthy Widowes Throughout the Whole Kingdome. London, 1643.

Wise, Jeremiah. *A Funeral Sermon Preached upon the Death of the Honourable Charles Frost, Esq; One of His Majesty's Council for the Province of the*

Massachusetts-Bay in N.E. Who Departed this Life Decem. 17. 1724. In the 47th Year of his Age. Boston, 1725.

SECONDARY SOURCES

Agnew, Aileen Button. "Silent Partners: The Economic Life of Women on the Frontier of Colonial New York." Ph.D. diss., University of New Hampshire, 1998.

Amussen, Susan. *An Ordered Society: Gender and Class in Early Modern England*. Oxford: Basil Blackwell, 1988.

Amussen, Susan D. "Governors and Governed: Class and Gender Relations in English Villages, 1590-1725." Ph.D. diss., Brown University, 1982.

Anderson, Bonnie S., and Judith P. Zinsser. *A History of Their Own: Women in Europe from Prehistory to the Present*. 2 vols. New York: Harper & Row, 1988

Anderson, Virginia DeJohn. *New England's Generation: The Great Migration and the Formation of Society and Culture in the Seventeenth Century*. Cambridge: Cambridge University Press, 1993.

Andrésen, Karen. "Marah Revisited: The Widow in Early New Hampshire." An unpublished paper given at the Berkshire Conference of Women's History, June 18, 1981.

Anzilotti, Cara. *In the Affairs of the World: Women, Patriarchy, and Power in Colonial South Carolina*. Westport, CT: Greenwood Press, 2002

Archer, Richard. *Fissures in the Rock: New England in the Seventeenth Century*. Hanover: University of New Hampshire, 2001.

Ariés, Philip. "Remarriage in France Under the *Ancien Régime* During the Seventeenth and Eighteenth Centuries: Differences Between Theory and Practice." In *Marriage and Remarriage in Populations of the Past*, ed. J. Dupâquier, E. Hélin, P. Laslett, M. Liv-Bacci, and S. Sogner, 5-48. London: Academic Press, 1981.

Auwers, Linda. "Fathers, Sons, and Wealth in Colonial Windsor, Connecticut." *Journal of Family History* 3, no. 2 (Summer 1978): 136-149.

Baker, J. H. *An Introduction to English History*, 2nd ed. London: Butterworths, 1979.

Bardaglio, Peter. *Reconstructing the Household: Families, Sex, and the Law in the Nineteenth-Century South*. Chapel Hill: University of North Carolina Press, 1995.

Beilin, Elaine V. *Redeeming Eve: Women Writers of the English Renaissance*. Princeton: Princeton University Press, 1987.

Bennett, Judith. *Women in the Medieval English Countryside: Gender and Household in Brigstock Before the Plague*. New York: Oxford University Press, 1987.

Benson, Mary Sumner. *Women in Eighteenth-Century America: A Study of Opinion and Social Usage*. New York: Columbia University Press, 1935.

Bideau, Alain. "A Demographic and Social Analysis of Widowhood and

Remarriage: The Example of the Castellany of Thoissey-en-Dombes, 1670-1840." *Journal of Family History*, 5, no. 1 (Spring 1980): 28-43.

Biemer, Linda Briggs. *Women and Property in Colonial New York: The Transition from Dutch to English Law, 1643-1727*. Ann Arbor: UMI Research Press, 1983.

Blaine, Marcia Schmidt. "The Power of Petitions: Women and the New Hampshire Provincial Government, 1695-1770." *International Review of Social History* 46 (2001) (Suppl. 9): 57-77.

Blanke, David. *Sowing the American Dream: How Consumer Culture Took Root in the Rural Midwest*. Athens: Ohio University Press, 2000.

Bliss, Lee. "Pastiche, Burlesque, Tragicomedy." In *The Cambridge Companion to English Renaissance Drama*, ed. A. R. Braunmuller and Michael Hattaway, 237-261. Cambridge: Cambridge University Press, 1990.

Bloom, Karen R. "My Worldly Goods Do Thee Endow; Economic Conservatism, Widowhood, and the Mid-and Late-Eighteenth-Century Novel." *Intertexts* 7 (2003): 27-48.

Bogin, Ruth. "Petitioning and the New Moral Economy of Post-Revolutionary America." *William and Mary Quarterly* 45 (1988): 391-425.

Boulton, Jeremy. "London Widowhood Revisited: The Decline of Female Remarriage in the Seventeenth and Early Eighteenth Centuries." *Continuity and Change* 5, no. 3 (1990): 325-355.

Boydston, Jeanne. *Home & Work: Household, Wages, and Ideology of Labor in the Early Republic*. New York: Oxford University Press, 1994.

Boylan, Anne M. *The Origins of Women's Activism: New York and Boston, 1797-1840*. Chapel Hill: University of North Carolina Press, 2002.

Breen, T. H. *The Marketplace of Revolution: How Consumer Politics Shaped American Independence*. Oxford: Oxford University Press, 2004.

Brewer, John, and Roy Porter, eds. *Consumption and the World of Goods*. London: Routledge, 1993.

Bridenbaugh, Carl. *Cities in the Wilderness: The First Century of Urban Life in America, 1625-1742*. Oxford: Oxford University Press, 1966.

Brodsky, Vivien. "Widows in Late Elizabethan London: Remarriage, Economic Opportunity and Family Orientations." In *The World We Have Gained: Histories of Population and Social Structure*, ed. Lloyd Bonfield, Richard M. Smith, and Keith Wrightson, 122-154. Oxford: Basil Blackwell, 1986.

Brown, Kathleen M. *Good Wives, Nasty Wenches, and Anxious Patriarchs: Gender, Race, and Power in Colonial Virginia*. Chapel Hill: Published for the Institute of Early American History and Culture by the University of North Carolina Press, 1996.

Brown, Peter. *The Body and Society: Men, Women, and Sexual Renunciation in Early Christianity*. New York: Columbia University Press, 1988.

Brunelle, Gayle K. "Policing the Monopolizing Women of Early Modern Nantes." *Journal of Women's History* 19 (2007): 10-35.

Burnard, Trevor. *Creole Gentlemen: The Maryland Elite, 1691-1776*. New York: Routledge, 2002.

Bushman, Richard L. *King and People in Provincial Massachusetts*. Chapel Hill: University of North Carolina Press. Published for the Institute of Early American History and Culture, 1985.

Bushman, Richard L. *The Refinement of America: Persons, Houses, Cities*. New York: Vintage Press, 1993.

Bushman, Richard L. "Shopping and Advertising in Colonial America." In *Of Consuming Interests: The Style of Life in the Eighteenth Century*, ed. Cary Carson, Ronald Hoffman, and Peter J. Albert. Charlottesville: University of Virginia Press, 1994.

Butler, Jon. *Becoming America: The Revolution Before 1776*. Cambridge, MA: Harvard University Press, 2000.

Butler, Jon. *The Huguenots in America: A Refugee People in New World Society*. Cambridge, MA: Harvard University Press, 1983.

Cahn, Susan. *Industry of Devotion: The Transformation of Women's Work in England, 1500-1600*. New York: Columbia University Press, 1987.

Calhoun, Craig, ed. *Habermas and the Public Sphere*. Cambridge, MA: MIT Press, 1991.

Carlton, Charles. "The Widow's Tale: Male Myths and Female Reality in 16th and 17th Century England." *Albion* 10, no. 2 (Summer 1978): 118-129.

Carr, Lois Green. "The Development of the Maryland Orphans' Court, 1654-1715." In *Law, Society and Politics in Early Maryland*, ed. Aubrey Land, Lois Green Carr and Edward Papenfuse, 41-61. Baltimore: Johns Hopkins University Press, 1977.

Carr, Lois Green. "Inheritance in the Colonial Chesapeake." In *Women in the Age of the American Revolution*, ed. Ronald Hoffman and Peter J. Albert, 155-208. Charlottesville: University Press of Virginia, 1989.

Carr, Lois Green, and Lorena S. Walsh. "The Planter's Wife: The Experience of White Women in Seventeenth-Century Maryland." *William and Mary Quarterly*, 3rd series, 34 (1977): 542-557.

Carr, Lois Green, Philip D. Morgan, and Jean B. Russo, eds. *Colonial Chesapeake Society*. Chapel Hill: University of North Carolina Press, 1988.

Carson, Cary, Ronald Hoffman, and Peter J. Albert, eds. *Of Consuming Interests: The Style of Life in the Eighteenth Century*. Charlottesville: University Press of Virginia, 1994.

Chaytor, Miranda. "Household and Kinship: Ryton in the Late Sixteenth and Early Seventeenth Centuries." *History Workshop Journal* 10 (Autumn 1980): 25-60.

Cioni, Maria L. "The Elizabethan Chancery and Women's Rights." In *Tudor Rule and Revolution: Essays for G. R. Elton from His American Friends*, ed. Delloyd J. Guth and John W. Mckenna, 159-182. Cambridge: Cambridge University Press, 1974.

Clark, Alice. *Working Life of Women in the Seventeenth Century*. With an introduction by Miranda Chaytor and Jane Lewis. London: Routledge, 1919; repr. London: Routledge, 1982.

Cleary, Patricia. *Elizabeth Murray: A Woman's Pursuit of Independence in Eighteenth-Century America*. Amherst: University of Massachusetts Press, 2000.

Cleary, Patricia. "'She Will be in the Shop': Women's Sphere of Trade in Eighteenth-Century Philadelphia and New York." *The Pennsylvania Magazine of History & Biography* 119 (1995): 181-202.

Clemens, Paul. "The Consumer Culture of the Middle Atlantic, 1760-1820." *William and Mary Quarterly*, 3rd series, 62 (2005): 577-620.

Clemens, Paul. "Economy and Society on Maryland's Eastern Shore, 1689-1733." In *Law, Society, and Politics in Early Maryland*, ed. Aubrey C. Land, Lois Green Carr, and Edward C. Papenfuse. Baltimore: Johns Hopkins University Press, 1977.

Coclanis, Peter A. *The Shadow of a Dream: Economic Life and Death in the South Carolina Low County, 1670-1920*. New York: Oxford University Press, 1989.

Confino, Alon. "Collective Memory and Cultural History: Problems of Method." *American Historical Review* 102 (1997): 1386-1403.

Conger, Vivian Bruce. "'Being Weak of Body but Firm of Mind and Memory': Widowhood in Colonial America, 1630-1750." Ph.D. diss., Cornell University, 1994.

Coppel, Stephen. "Wills and the Community in Grantham." In *Probate Records and the Local Community*, ed. Philip Riden, 71-90. Gloucester: Alan Sutton, 1985.

Crane, Elaine Forman. "Dependence in the Era of Independence: The Role of Women in a Republican Society." In *The American Revolution: Its Characters and Limits*, ed. Jack P. Greene, 253-275. New York: New York University Press, 1987.

Crane, Elaine Forman. *Ebb Tide in New England: Women, Seaports, and Social Change, 1630-1800*. Boston: Northeastern University Press, 1998.

Crowley, John E. "Family Relations and Inheritance in Early South Carolina." *Social History* 17, no. 33 (May 1984): 35-57.

Davidoff, Leonore, and Catherine Hall. *Family Fortunes: Men and Women of the English Middle Class, 1780-1850*. Chicago: University of Chicago Press, 1987.

Davis, Richard Beale. *Intellectual Life in the Colonial South, 1585-1763*. 3 vols. Knoxville: University of Tennessee Press, 1978.

Dayton, Cornelia Hughes. "Women Before the Bar: Gender, Law, and Society in Connecticut, 1710-1719." Ph.D. diss., Princeton University, 1986.

Dayton, Cornelia Hughes. *Women Before the Bar: Gender, Law, and Society in Connecticut, 1639-1789*. Chapel Hill: University of North Carolina Press, 1995.

Deen, James W., Jr. "Patterns of Testation: Four Tidewater Counties in Colonial Virginia." *American Journal of Legal History* 16 (1972): 154-176.

Demos, John Putnam. *Entertaining Satan: Witchcraft and the Culture of Early New England*. New York: Oxford University Press, 1982.

Demos, John Putnam. *A Little Commonwealth: Family Life in Plymouth Colony*. Oxford: Oxford University Press, 1970.

Demos, John Putnam. "Old Age in Early New England." In *The American Family in Socio-Historical Perspective*, ed. Michael Gordon, 220-256. New York: St. Martin's Press, 1978.

Dexter, Elisabeth Anthony. *Colonial Women of Affairs: A Study of Women in Business and the Professions in America Before 1776*. Boston: Houghton Mifflin, 1924.

Diefendorf, Barbara B. "Widowhood and Remarriage in Sixteenth-Century Paris." *Journal of Family History* 7, no. 4 (Winter 1982): 379-395.

Dierks, Konstantin. "Letter Writing, Stationery Supplies and Consumer Modernity in the Eighteenth-Century Atlantic World." *Early American Literature* 41 (2006): 473-494.

Dinkin, Robert J. "Seating the Meetinghouse in Early Massachusetts." *New England Quarterly* 43 (1970), 450–464.

Ditz, Toby L. "Formative Ventures: Eighteenth-Century Commercial Letters and the Articulation of Experience." In *Epistolary Selves: Letters and Letter-Writers. 1600-1945*, ed. Rebecca Earle, 59-78. Aldershot: Ashgate, 1999.

Ditz, Toby L. *Property and Kinship: Inheritance in Early Connecticut, 1750-1820*. Princeton: Princeton University Press, 1986.

Earle, Alice Morse. *Colonial Dames and Good Wives*. American Classics Edition. New York: Frederick Ungar, 1962.

Earle, Alice Morse. *Customs and Fashions in Old New England*. Rutland, VT: Charles E. Tuttle, 1973, originally published 1893.

Erickson, Amy Louise. *Women and Property in Early Modern England*. London: Routledge, 1995.

Evans, Nesta. "Inheritance, Women, Religion and Education in Early Modern Society as Revealed by Wills." In *Probate Records and the Local* Community, ed. Philip Riden. Gloucester: Alan Sutton, 1985.

Ezell, Margaret J. M. *The Patriarch's Wife: Literary Evidence and the History of the Family*. Chapel Hill: University of North Carolina Press, 1987.

Faragher, John. "Old Women and Old Men in Seventeenth-Century Wethersfield, Connecticut." *Women's Studies* 4 (1976): 11-31.

Farrell, Kirby, Elizabeth H. Hageman, and Arthur F. Kinney, eds. *Women in the Renaissance: Selections From English Literary Renaissance*. Amherst: University of Massachusetts Press, 1990.

Ferguson, Margaret W., Maureen Quilligan, and Nancy J. Vickers, eds. *Rewriting the Renaissance: The Discourses of Sexual Difference in Early Modern Europe*. Chicago: University of Chicago Press, 1986.

Flaherty, David H. *Privacy in Colonial New England.* Charlottesville: University Press of Virginia, 1967.

Fliegelman, Jay. *Declaring Independence: Jefferson, Natural Language, and the Culture of Performance.* Palo Alto, CA: Stanford University Press, 1993.

Gampel, Gwen Victor. "The Planter's Wife Revisited: Women, Equity Law, and the Chancery Court in Seventeenth-Century Maryland." In *Women and the Structure of Society: Selected Research from the Fifth Berkshire Conference on the History of Women*, ed. Barbara Harris and Jo Ann McNamara, 20-35. Durham, NC: Duke University Press, 1984.

George, Margaret. *Women in the First Capitalist Society: Experience in Seventeenth-Century England.* Urbana: University of Illinois Press, 1988.

Glassberg, David. "Public History and the Study of Memory." *Public Historian* 18 (1996), 7–23.

Glendon, Mary Ann. *Abortion and Divorce in Western Law.* Cambridge, MA: Harvard University Press, 1987.

Glover, Lorri. *All Our Relations: Blood Ties and Emotional Bonds Among the Early South Carolina Gentry.* Baltimore: Johns Hopkins University Press, 2000.

Goodman, Dena. "Public Sphere and Private Life: Toward a Synthesis of Current Historiographical Approaches to the Old Regime." *History and Theory* 31 (1992): 1-20.

Gorneau, Angeline. *The Whole Duty of a Woman: Female Writers in Seventeenth-Century England.* New York: Dial Press, 1985.

Graham, Michael. "Meetinghouse and Chapel: Religion and Community in Seventeenth-Century Maryland." In *Colonial Chesapeake Society,* ed. Lois Green Carr, Philip D. Morgan, and Jean B. Russo, 242-274. Chapel Hill: University of North Carolina Press, 1988.

Greene, Jack P. *Imperatives, Behaviors, and Identities: Essays in Early American Cultural History.* Charlottesville: University Press of Virginia, 1992.

Greene, Jack P. *Pursuits of Happiness: The Social Development of Early Modern British Colonies and the Formation of American Culture.* Chapel Hill: University of North Carolina Press, 1988.

Greig, Hannah. "Leading the Fashion: The Material Culture of London's *Beau Monde.*" In *Gender, Taste, and Material Culture in Britain and North America, 1700-1830*, ed. John Styles and Amanda Vickery, 293-313. New Haven: Yale University Press, 2006.

Greven, Philip, Jr. *Four Generations: Population, Land, and Family in Colonial Andover, Massachusetts.* Ithaca, NY: Cornell University Press, 1970.

Grigg, Susan. "Toward a Theory of Remarriage: A Case Study of Newburyport at the Beginning of the Nineteenth Century." *Journal of Interdisciplinary History* 8, no. 2 (1977): 183-220.

Grim, Valerie. "History Shared Through Memory: The Establishment and

Implementation of Education in the Brooks Farm Community, 1920-1957." *Oral HistoryReview*23(1996).

Gunderson, Joan. "Kith and Kin: Women's Networks in Colonial Virginia." In *The Devil's Lane: Sex and Race in the Early South*, edited by Catherine Clinton and Michelle Gillespie, 90-108. New York: Oxford University Press, 1997.

Hall, David D. *Worlds of Wonder, Days of Judgment: Popular Religious Belief in Early New England*. New York: Knopf, 1989.

Hambrick-Stowe, Charles E. *The Practice of Piety: Purtian Devotional Dispciplines in Seventeenth-Century New England*. Chapel Hill: University of North Carolina Press, 1982.

Hanson, Elizabeth. "There's Meat and Money Too: Rich Widows and Allegories of Wealth in Jacobean City Comedy." *English Literary History* 72 (2005): 209-238.

Hansson, Robert O., and Jacqueline H. Remondet. "Old Age and Widowhood: Issues in Personal Control and Independence." *Journal of Social Issues* 44, no. 3 (1988): 159-174.

Hartigan-O'Connor, Ellen. "'She Said she did not Know Money': Urban Women and Atlantic Market in the Revolutionary Era." *Early American Studies* 4: 322-352.

Haselkorn, Anne M., and Betty S. Travitsky. *The Renaissance Englishwoman in Print*. Amherst: University of Massachusetts Press, 1990.

Haskins, George. *Law and Authority in Early Massachusetts: A Study in Tradition and Design*. New York: Archon Books, 1968.

Haskins, George L. "Reception of the Common Law in Seventeenth-Century Massachusetts: A Case Study." In *Law and Authority in Colonial America*, ed. George Athan Billias, 17–31. Barre, MA: Barre, 1964.

Hattaway, Michael. "Drama and Society." In *The Cambridge Companion to English Renaissance Drama*, ed. A. R. Braunmuller and Michael Hattaway, 91-126. Cambridge: Cambridge University Press, 1990.

Hayes, Kevin J. *A Colonial Woman's Bookshelf*. Knoxville: University of Tennessee Press, 1996.

Henderson, Katherine, and Barbara F. McManus. *Half Humankind: Contexts and Texts of the Controversy About Women in England, 1540-1640*. Urbana: University of Illinois Press, 1985.

Hensley, Jeannine, ed. *The Works of Anne Bradstreet*. Cambridge, MA: Belknap Press of Harvard University Press, 1967.

Heyrman, Christine Leigh. *Commerce and Culture: The Maritime Communities of Colonial Massachusetts, 1690-1750*. New York: Norton, 1984.

Higgins, Patricia. "The Reactions of Women with Special Reference to Women Petitioners." In *Politics, Religion, and the English Civil War*, ed. Brian Manning, 178-222. New York: St. Martin's Press, 1973.

Higginson, Stephen A. "A Short History of the Right to Petition Government for the Redress of Grievances." *Yale Law Journal* 96 (1986): 142-166.

Hill, Bridget. *Women, Work, and Sexual Politics in Eighteenth-Century England.* Oxford: Basil Blackwell, 1989.

Hirsch, Arthur H. *The Huguenots of Colonial South Carolina.* Columbia: University of South Carolina Press, Reprint ed., 1999.

Hobby, Elaine. *The Virtue of Necessity: English Women's Writing, 1649-1688.* Ann Arbor: University of Michigan Press, 1988.

Holderness, B. A. "Widows in Pre-Industrial Society: An Essay Upon Their Economic Functions." In *Land, Kinship, and Life-Cycle,* ed. Richard M. Smith, 423-442. Cambridge: Cambridge University Press, 1985.

Hollinger, David A., and Charles Capper, eds. *The American Intellectual Tradition,* Vol. 1, *1630-1865.* New York: Oxford University Press, 1993.

Holmes, Thomas James. *Cotton Mather: A Bibliography.* 3 vols. Cambridge, MA: Harvard University Press, 1940.

Horwitz, Henry. "Testamentary Practice, Family Strategies, and the Last Phases of the Custom of London, 1660-1725." *Law and History Review* 2, no. 2 (Fall 1984): 223-239.

Houlbrooke, Ralph. *The English Family, 1450-1700.* London: Longman, 1984.

Hunt, Margaret R. *The Middling Sort: Commerce, Gender, and the Family in England, 1680-1780.* Berkeley: University of California Press, 1996.

Hunter, Phyllis Whitman. *Purchasing Identity in the Atlantic World: Massachusetts Merchants, 1670-1780.* Ithaca, NY: Cornell University Press, 2001.

Hyman, Herbert H. *Of Time and Widowhood: Nationwide Studies of Enduring Effects.* Durham, NC: Duke University Press, 1983.

Isaac, Rhys. "Stories and Constructions of Identity: Folk Tellings and Diary Inscriptions in Revolutionary Virginia." In *Through a Glass Darkly: Reflections on Personal Identity in Early America,* ed. Ronald Hoffman, Mechal Sobel, and Fredrika J. Teute, 206-237. Chapel Hill: University of North Carolina Press, 1997.

Jensen, Joan M. *Loosening the Bonds: Mid-Atlantic Farm Women, 1750-1850.* New Haven: Yale University Press, 1986.

Johnson, Walter. *Soul by Soul: Life Inside the Antebellum Slave Market.* Cambridge, MA : Harvard University Press, 1999.

Jones, Alice Hanson. "Wealth and Growth of the Thirteen Colonies: Some Implications." *Journal of Economic History* 44, no. 2 (June 1984): 239-254.

Jones, Douglas Lamar. *Village and Seaport Migration and Society in Eighteenth-Century Massachusetts.* Hanover, NH: University Press of New England, 1981.

Jordan, Constance. "Feminism and the Humanists: The Case of Sir Thomas Elyot's Defence of Good Women." In *Rewriting the Renaissance: The Discourses of Sexual Diference in Early Modern Europe,* ed. Margaret Ferguson, Maureen Quilligan, and Nancy J. Vickers, 242–258. Chicago: University of Chicago Press.

Kamensky, Jane. *Governing the Tongue: The Politics of Speech in Early New England.* New York: Oxford University Press, 1997.

Kansteiner, Wulf. "Finding Meaning in Memory: A Methodological Critique of Collective Memory Studies." *History and Theory* 41 (2002): 179-197.

Karlsen, Carol F. *The Devil in the Shape of a Woman: Witchcraft in Colonial New England*. New York: Norton, 1987.

Katz, Michael B. *In the Shadow of the Poorhouse: A Social History of Welfare in America*. New York: Basic Books, 1986.

Katz, Wendy. "Portraits and the Production for the Civil Self in Seventeenth-Century Boston." *Winterthur Portfolio* 39 (2005).

Kerber, Linda K. "The Paradox of Women's Citizenship in the Early Republic: The Case of *Martin vs. Massachusetts*, 1805." *American Historical Review* 97 (1992).

Kerrison, Catherine M. "By the Book: Advice and Female Behavior in the Eighteenth-Century South." Ph.D. diss., College of William and Mary, 1999.

Kerrison, Catherine M. *Claiming the Pen: Women and Intellectual Life in the Early American* South. Ithaca, NY: Cornell University Press, 2006.

Keyssar, Alexander. "Widowhood in Eighteenth-Century Massachusetts: A Problem in the History of the Family." *Perspectives in American History* 7 (1982): 83-119.

Kierner, Cynthia A. *Beyond the Household: Women's Place in the Early South, 1700-1835*. Ithaca, NY: Cornell University Press, 1998.

Koehler, Lyle. A Search for Power: The "Weaker Sex" in Seventeenth-Century New England. Urbana: University of Illinois Press, 1980.

Konig, David. *Law and Society in Puritan Massachusetts: Essex County, 1628-1692*. Chapel Hill: University of North Carolina Press, 1979.

Kulikoff, Allan. *Tobacco and Slaves: The Development of Southern Cultures in the Chesapeake, 1680-1800*. Chapel Hill: University of North Carolina Press, 1986.

Lane, Jr., G. Winston. "Economic Power Among Eighteenth-Century Women of the Carolina Lowcountry." In *Money Trade, and Power: The Evolution of Colonial South Carolina's Plantation Society*, ed. Jack P. Greene, Rosemary Brana-Shute, and Randy J. Sparks, 322-343. Columbia: University of South Carolina Press, 2001.

Lebsock, Suzanne. *The Free Women of Petersburg: Status and Culture in a Southern Town, 1784-1860*. New York: Norton, 1984.

Lee, Jean Butenhoff. "Land and Labor: Parental Bequest Practices in Charles County, Maryland, 1732-1783." In *Colonial Chesapeake Society*, ed. Lois Green Carr, Philip D. Morgan, and Jean B. Russo, 306-341. Chapel Hill: University of North Carolina Press, 1988.

Lemay, J. A. Leo. *Robert Bolling Woos Anne Miller: Love and Courtship in Colonial Virginia, 1760*. Charlottesville: University Press of Virginia, 1990.

Lloyd, Joanne. "Beneath the City on the Hill: 'Alley Society' and Interracial Community in Boston, 1700-1850." Ph.D. diss., Boston College, 2007.

Lockley, Tim. "Rural Poor Relief in Colonial South Carolina." *Historical Journal* (2005): 955-976.

Lopata, Helena Znaniecka. "Support Systems of American Urban Widowhood." *Journal of Social Issues* 44 (1988): 113-178.

Lopata, Helena Znaniecka. *Women as Widows: Support Systems*. New York: Elsevier North Holland, 1979.

Main, Gloria L. "The Distribution of Consumer Goods in Colonial New England: A Subregional Approach." In *Early American Probate Inventories*, ed. Peter Benes and Jane Benes, 153-168. Boston: Boston University Press, 1989.

Main, Gloria L. "Gender, Work and Wages in Colonial New England." *William and Mary Quarterly* 51 (1994): 39-66.

Main, Gloria L. *Peoples of a Spacious Land: Families and Cultures in Colonial New England*. Cambridge, MA: Harvard University Press, 2001.

Main, Gloria L. "Probate Records as a Source for Early American History." *William and Mary Quarterly*, 3rd series, 32 (1975).

Main, Gloria L. *Tobacco Colony: Life in Early Maryland, 1650-1720*. Princeton: Princeton University Press, 1982.

Main, Gloria L. "Widows in Rural Massachusetts on the Eve of the American Revolution." In *Women in the Age of the American Revolution*, ed. Ronald Hoffman and Peter J. Albert, 67-90. Charlottesville: University Press of Virginia, 1989.

Malmsheimer, Lonna M. "New England Funeral Sermons and Changing Attitudes Toward Woman, 1672-1792." Ph.D. diss., University of Minnesota, 1973.

Mancke, Elizabeth. "At the Counter of the General Store: Women and the Economy in Eighteenth-Century Horton, Nova Scotia." In *Intimate Relations: Family and Community in Planter Nova Scotia*, ed. Margaret Conrad, 167–181. Fredericton, NB: Acadiensis Press, 1995.

Matson, Cathy. *Merchants & Empire: Trading in Colonial New York*. Baltimore: Johns Hopkins University Press, 1998.

McCrae, Robert R., and Paul T. Costa Jr. "Psychological Resilience Among Widowed Men and Women: A 10-Year Follow-up of a National Sample." *Journal of Social Issues* 44, no. 3 (1988): 129-142.

McCusker, John J. *How Much Is That in Real Money? A Historical Price Index for Use as a Deflator of Money Values in the Economy of the United States*. Worcester: American Antiquarian Society, 1992.

McCusker, John J. *Money and Exchange in Europe and America, 1600-1775: A Handbook*. Chapel Hill: University of North Carolina Press, 1978.

McCusker, John J., and Russell R. Menard. *The Economy of British America*. Chapel Hill: University of North Carolina Press, 1985.

McKendrick, Neil, John Brewer, and J. H. Plumb. *The Birth of a Consumer Society: The Commercialization of Eighteenth-Century England*. Bloomington: Indiana University Press, 1982.

McLuskie, Kathleen. *Renaissance Dramatists*. Atlantic Highlands, NJ: Humanities Press International, 1989.

McNamara, Martha J. *From Tavern to Courthouse: Architecture & Ritual in American Law, 1658-1860*. Baltimore: Johns Hopkins University Press, 2004.

Martin, John Frederick. *Profits in the Wilderness: Entrepreneurship and the Founding of New England Towns in the Seventeenth Century*. Chapel Hill: University of North Carolina Press, 1991.

Menard, Russell. *Economy and Society in Early Colonial Maryland*. New York: Garland, 1985.

Miller, Marla R. *The Needle's Eye: Women and Work in the Age of Revolution*. Amherst: University of Massachusetts Press, 2006.

Miller, Marla R. "The Last Mantua Maker: Craft Tradition and Commercial Change in Boston, 1760-1845." *Early American Studies: An Interdisciplinary Journal* 4 (2006): 372-424.

Miller, Perry. *Errand Into the Wilderness*. Cambridge, MA: Belknap Press of Harvard University Press, 1981.

Monaghan, E. Jennifer. *Learning to Read and Write in Colonial America*. Amherst: University of Massachusetts Press, 2005.

Morgan, Edmund S. *American Slavery, American Freedom: The Ordeal of* Colonial Virginia. New York: Norton, 1975.

Morgan, Edmund S. *Inventing the People: The Rise of Popular Sovereignty in England and America*. New York: Norton, 1988.

Morgan, Edmund S. *The Puritan Family: Religion and Domestic Relations in Seventeenth-Century New England*. New York: Harper & Row, 1966.

Mulcahy, Matthew. "The 'Great Fire' of 1740 and the Politics of Disaster Relief in Colonial Charleston." *South Carolina Magazine* 99 (1998), 135–157.

Narrett, David E. "English Social Customs in a New World Setting: Patterns of Inheritance and Family Life in Colonial Suffolk County, New York." Unpublished paper presented at the Conference on British Studies, October, 31, 1981.

Narrett, David E. *Inheritance and Family Life in Colonial New York City*. Ithaca, NY: Cornell University Press, 1992.

Narrett, David E. "Patterns of Inheritance in Colonial New York City, 1664-1775: A Study in the History of the Family." Ph.D. diss., Cornell University, 1981.

Nash, Gary B. "Poverty and Poor Relief in Pre-Revolutionary Philadelphia." *William and Mary Quarterly* 33 (1976), 1–40.

Nash, Gary B. *The Urban Crucible: Social Change, Political Consciousness, and the Origins of the American Revolution*. Cambridge, MA: Harvard University Press, 1979.

Nash, Gary B. "Poverty and Politics in Early American History." In *Down and Out in Early America*, ed. Billy G. Smith. University Park: Pennsylvania State University Press, 2004.

Norton, Mary Beth. "The Evolution of White Women's Experience in Early America." *American Historical Review* 89 (1984): 593-619.

Norton, Mary Beth. *Founding Mothers and Fathers: Gendered Power and the Forming of American Society*. New York: Knopf, 1996.

Norton, Mary Beth. "Gender and Defamation in Seventeenth-Century Maryland." *William and Mary Quarterly*, 3rd series, 44 (1987): 3-39.

Norton, Mary Beth. "Getting to the Source: Hetty Shepard, Dorothy Dudley, and Other Fictional Colonial Women I Have Come to Know Altogether Too Well." *Journal of Women's History* 10, no. 3 (1998): 141-154.

Norton, Mary Beth. "Letter to the Editor." *William and Mary Quarterly*, 3rd series, 48 (1991): 639-648.

Norton, Mary Beth. *Liberty's Daughters: The Revolutionary Experience of American Women, 1750-1820*. New York: Little, Brown, 1980.

Norton, Mary Beth. "Reflections on Women in the Age of the American Revolution." In *Women in the Age of the American Revolution*, ed. Ronald Hoffman and Peter J. Albert, 479-493. Charlottesville: University Press of Virginia, 1989.

O'Donnell, Mary Ann. "Tory Wit and Unconventional Woman: Aphra Behn." In *Women Writers of the Seventeenth Century*, ed. Katherine M. Wilson and Frank J. Warnke, 341-374. Athens: University of Georgia Press, 1989.

Okin, Susan Muller. *Women in Western Political Thought*. Princeton: Princeton University Press, 1979.

Olivas, J. Richard. "'God Helps Them Who Help Themselves': Religious Explanations of Poverty in Colonial Massachusetts, 1630-1776." In *Down and Out in Early America*, ed. Billy G. Smith, 262–288. University Park: Pennsylvania State University Press, 2004.

Pagels, Elaine. *Adam, Eve, and the Serpent*. New York: Random House, 1988.

Panek, Jennifer. "'My Naked Weapon': Male Anxiety and the Violent Courtship of the Jacobean Stage Widow." *Comparative Drama* 34 (2000): 321-344.

Panek, Jennifer. *Widows and Suitors in Early Modern English Comedy*. Cambridge: Cambridge University Press, 2004.

Parrish, Susan Scott. *American Curiosity: Cultures of Natural History in the Colonial British Atlantic World*. Chapel Hill: University of North Carolina Press, 2006.

Pateman, Carole. *The Sexual Contract*. Palo Alto, CA: Stanford University Press, 1988.

Peck, Linda Levy. *Consuming Splendor*. Cambridge: Cambridge University Press, 2005.

Perlmann, Joel, and Dennis Shirley. "When Did New England Women Acquire Literacy?" *William and Mary Quarterly*, 3rd series, 48 (1991): 50-67.

Plane, Ann Marie. *Colonial Intimacies: Indian Marriage in Early New England*. Ithaca, NY: Cornell University Press, 2000.

Pointon, Marcia. "Women and Their Jewels." In *Women and Material Culture, 1660-1830*, ed. Jennie Batchelor and Cora Kaplan, 11–30. New York: Palgrave Macmillan, 2007.

Poovey, Mary. *Uneven Developments: The Ideological Work of Gender in Mid-Victorian England.* Chicago: University of Chicago Press, 1988.

Premo, Terri L. *Winter Friends: Women Growing Old in the New Republic, 1785-1835.* Urbana: University of Illinois Press, 1990.

Pruden, Elizabeth M. "Family, Community, Economy: Women's Activity in South Carolina, 1670-1770." Ph.D. diss., University of Minnesota, 1996.

Pruden, Elizabeth M. "Investing Widows: Autonomy in a Nascent Capitalist Society." In *Money Trade, and Power: The Evolution of Colonial South Carolina's Plantation Society*, ed. Jack P. Green, Rosemary Brana-Shute, and Randy J. Sparks. Columbia: University of South Carolina Press, 2001.

Rabuzzi, Daniel. "Eighteenth-Century Commercial Mentalities as Reflected and Projected in Business Handbooks." *Eighteenth-Century Studies* 29 (1995-1996): 169-189.

Roeber, A. G. *Faithful Magistrates and Republican Lawyers: Creators of Virginia Legal Culture, 1680-1810.* Chapel Hill: University of North Carolina Press, 1981.

Roeber, A. G. "Authority, Law, and Custom: The Rituals of Court Day in Tidewater Virginia, 1720-1750." In *Material Life in America, 1600-1860*, ed. Robert Blair St. George. Boston: Northeastern University Press, 1988.

Roelker, Nancy Lyman. "Introduction: Papers From the 1981 Berkshire Conference: Widowhood and Rational Domesticity: Modes of Independence for Women in Early Modern Europe." *Journal of Family History* 7 (Winter 1982): 376-378.

Rogers, Kim Lacy. "Relicts of the New World: Conditions of Widowhood in Seventeenth-Century New England." In *Woman's Being, Woman's Place: Female Identity and Vocation in American History*, ed. Mary Kelley, 36-47. Boston: G. K. Hall, 1979.

Rosen, Deborah. *Courts and Commerce: Gender, Law, and the Market Economy in Colonial New York.* Columbus: Ohio State University Press, 1997.

Rosenthal, Joel. "Aristocratic Widows in Fifteenth-Century England." In *Women and the Structure of Society: Selected Research from the Fifth Berkshire Conference on the History of Women*, ed. Barbara Harris and Jo Ann McNamara, 36-47. Durham: Duke University Press, 1984.

Rutman, Darrett B., and Anita H. Rutman. *A Place in Time: Explicatus.* New York: Norton, 1984.

Rutman, Darrett B. and Anita H. Rutman. "'Now-Wives and Sons-in-Law': Parental Death in a Seventeenth-Century Virginia County." In *The Chesapeake in the Seventeenth Century: Essays on Anglo-American Society*, ed. Thad W. Tate and David L. Ammerman, 153-182. Chapel Hill: University of North Carolina Press, 1979.

Rutz-Robbins, Kristi. "'Divers Debts': Women's Participation in the Local Economy, Albemarle, North Carolina, 1663-1729." *Early American Studies* 4 (2006): 425-441.

Ryan, Mary P. *Womanhood in America: From Colonial Times to the Present.* 3rd ed. New York: Franklin Watts, 1983.

Ryden, David B., and Russell R. Menard. "South Carolina's Colonial Land Market: An Analysis of Rural Property Sales, 1720–1775." *Social Science History* 29 (2005), 599–623.

St. George, Robert Blair. "Heated Speech and Literacy in Seventeenth-Century New England." In *Seventeenth-Century New England,* ed. David G. Allen and David D. Hall,272–322. Boston: University of Virginia Press for the Colonial Society of Massachusetts, 1985.

Salinger, Sharon V. *Taverns and Drinking in Early America.* Baltimore: Johns Hopkins University Press, 2002.

Salmon, Marylynn. "Equality or Submersion? Feme Covert Status in Early Pennsylvania." In *Women of America: A History*, ed. Carol Ruth Berkin and Mary Beth Norton, 92-111. Boston: Houghton Mifflin, 1979.

Salmon, Marylynn. *Women and the Law of Property in Early America.* Chapel Hill: University of North Carolina Press, 1986.

Salmon, Marylynn. "Women and Property in South Carolina: The Evidence From Marriage Settlements, 1730 to 1830." *William and Mary Quarterly*, 3rd series, 39, no. 4 (October 1982): 655-685.

Schultz, Martin, and Herman R. Lantz. "Occupational Pursuits of Free Women in Early America: An Examination of Eighteenth-Century Newspapers." *Sociological Forum* 3, no. 1 (1988): 89-109.

Selement, George. *Keepers of the Vineyard: The Puritan Ministry and Collective Culture in Colonial New England.* Lanham, MD: University Press of America, 1984.

Shammas, Carole. "Changes in English and Anglo-American Consumption from 1550 to 1899." In *Consumption and the World of Goods*, ed. John Brewer and Roy Porter, 177–205. London: Routledge

Shammas, Carole. "Early American Women and Control Over Capital." In *Women in the Age of the American Revolution*, ed. Ronald Hoffman and Peter J. Albert, 134-154. Charlottesville: University Press of Virginia, 1989.

Shammas, Carole. *The Preindustrial Consumer in England and America.* Oxford: Oxford University Press, 1990.

Shammas, Carole, Marylynn Salmon, and Michel Dahlin. *Inheritance in America From Colonial Times to the Present.* New Brunswick, NJ: Rutgers University Press, 1987.

Shields, David S. *Civil Tongues: Polite Letters in British America.* Chapel Hill: University of North Carolina Press, 1997.

Shoemaker, Robert B. *Gender in English Society, 1650-1850.* London: Addison Wesley Longman, 1998.

Sirmans, M. Eurene. *Colonial South Carolina: A Political History, 1663-1763.* Chapel Hill: University of North Carolina Press, 1966.

Sirmans, M. Eurene. "The Legal Status of the Slave in South Carolina, 1670-1740." *Journal of Southern History* 27, no. 4 (November 1962): 462-473.

Smith, Daniel Scott. "Inheritance and the Social History of Early American Women." In *Women in the Age of the American Revolution*, ed. Ronald Hoffman and Peter J. Albert, 45-66. Charlottesville: University Press of Virginia, 1989.

Smith, Daniel Scott. "Underregistration and Bias in Probate Records: An Analysis of Data From Eighteenth-Century Hingham, Massachusetts." *William and Mary Quarterly*, 3rd series, 32, no. 1 (January 1975): 100-110.

Smith, Joseph H. "The Foundations of Law in Maryland, 1634-1715." In *Law and Authority in Colonial America*, ed. George Billias, 92-115. Barre, MA: Barre, 1964.

Snyder, Terri. *Brabbling Women: Disorderly Speech and the Law in Early Virginia*. Ithaca, NY: Cornell University Press. 2003.

Somerville, James K. "The Salem (Mass.) Woman in the Home, 1660-1770." *Eighteenth-Century Life* 1 (1974): 11-14.

"Special Forum: Women's Economies in North America Before 1829." *Early American Studies* 4 (Fall 2006), 271–470.

Speth, Linda. "More Than Her 'Thirds': Wives and Widows in Colonial Virginia." *Women and History* 4 (1983): 5-41.

Spring, Eileen. *Law, Land, and Family: Aristocratic Inheritance in England, 1300-1800*. Chapel Hill: University of North Carolina Press, 1993.

Spruill, Julia Cherry. *Women's Life and Work in the Southern Colonies*. Originally published, 1938; reprint, New York: Norton, 1972.

Spufford, Margaret. *Contrasting Communities: English Villagers in the Sixteenth and Seventeenth Centuries*. New York: Cambridge University Press, 1974.

Starr, June, and Jane F. Collier, ed. *History and Power in the Study of Law: New Directions in Legal Anthropology*. Ithaca, NY: Cornell University Press, 1989.

Staves, Susan. *Married Women's Separate Property in England, 1660-1833*. Cambridge, MA: Harvard University Press, 1990.

Staves, Susan. "'Books without which I cannot write': How Did Eighteenth-Century Women Writers Get the Books They Read?" In *Women and Material Culture, 1660-1830*, ed. Jennie Batchelor and Cora Kaplan, 192–211. New York: Palgrave Macmillan, 2007.

Stout, Harry S. *The New England Soul: Preaching and Religious Culture in Colonial New England*. New York: Oxford University Press, 1986.

Stroebe, Margaret S., Wolfgang Stroebe, and Robert O. Hansson. "Bereavement Research: An Historical Introduction." *Journal of Social Issues* 44, no. 3 (1988): 1-18.

Sturtz, Linda. *Within Her Power: Propertied Women in Colonial Virginia*. New York: Routledge, 2002.

Todd, Barbara J. "Demographic Determinism and Female Agency: The

Remarrying Widow Reconsidered . . . Again." *Continuity and Change* 9, no. 3 (1994): 421-450.

Todd, Barbara J. "The Remarrying Widow: A Stereotype Reconsidered." In *Women in English Society, 1500-1800*, ed. Mary Prior, 54-92. London: Methuen Press, 1985.

Ulrich, Laurel Thatcher. "'Daughters of Liberty': Religious Women in Revolutionary New England." In *Women in the Age of the American Revolution*, ed. Ronald Hoffman and Peter J. Albert. Charlottesville: University Press of Virginia, 1989.

Ulrich, Laurel Thatcher. *Good Wives: Image and Reality in the Lives of Women in Northern New England, 1650-1750*. Oxford: Oxford University Press, 1980.

Ulrich, Laurel Thatcher. "Hannah Barnard's Cupboard: Female Property and Identity in Eighteenth-Century New England." In *Through a Glass Darkly: Reflections on Personal Identity in Early America*, ed. Ronald Hoffman, Mechal Sobel, and Fredrika J. Teute, 238-273. Chapel Hill: University of North Carolina Press, 1997.

Ulrich, Laurel Thatcher. "Housewife and Gadder: Themes of Self-sufficiency and Community in Eighteenth-Century New England." In *"To Toil the Livelong Day": America's Women at Work, 1780-1980*, ed. Carol Groneman and Mary Beth Norton, 21-34. Ithaca, NY: Cornell University Press, 1987.

Ulrich, Laurel Thatcher. "John Winthrop's City of Women." *Massachusetts Historical Review* 3 (2001).

Ulrich, Laurel Thatcher. "Sheep in Parlor, Wheels on the Common: Pastoralism and Poverty in Eighteenth-Century Boston." In *Inequality in Early America*, ed. Carla Gardina Pestana and Sharon V. Salinger, 182–200. Hanover, NH: Univesity Press of New England, 1999.

Ulrich, Laurel Thatcher. "Vertuous Women Found: New England Ministerial Literature, 1668-1735." *American Quarterly* 28 (1976).

Underdown, David. *Revel, Riot, and Rebellion: Popular Politics and Culture in England, 1603-1660*. Oxford: Clarendon Press, 1985.

Vachon, Mary L. S., and Stanley K. Stylianos. "The Role of Social Support in Bereavement." *Journal of Social Issues* 44 (1988): 175-190.

Vickery, Amanda. *The Gentleman's Daughter: Women's Lives in Georgian England*. New Haven: Yale University Press, 1998.

Waciega, Lisa Wilson. "A 'Man of Business': The Widow of Means in Southeastern Pennsylvania, 1750-1850." *William and Mary Quarterly*, 3rd series, 44 (January 1987): 40-64.

Waciega, Lisa W[ilson]. "Widowhood and Womanhood in Early America: The Experience of Women in Philadelphia and Chester Counties, 1750-1850." Ph.D. diss., Temple University, 1986.

Wall, Helena M. *Fierce Communion: Family and Community in Early America*. Cambridge, MA: Harvard University Press, 1990.

Wall, Richard. "Women Alone in English Society." *Annales de démographie historique* 16 (1981): 303-317.

Walsh, Claire. "Shops, Shopping, and the Art of Decision Making in Eighteenth-Century England." In *Gender, Taste, and Material Culture in Britain and North America, 1700-1830*, ed. John Styles and Amanda Vickery, 151–177. New Haven: Yale University Press, 2006. Walsh, Lorena S. "Community Networks in the Early Chesapeake." In *Colonial Chesapeake Society*, ed. Lois Green Carr, Philip D. Morgan, and Jean B. Russo, 200-241. Chapel Hill: University of North Carolina Press, 1988.

Walsh, Lorena S. "'Till Death Us Do Part': Marriage and Family in Seventeenth-Century Maryland." In *The Chesapeake in the Seventeenth Century: Essays on Anglo-American Society*, ed. Thad W. Tate and David L. Ammerman, 126-152. New York: Norton, 1979.

Walsh, Lorena Seebach. "Charles County, Maryland, 1658-1705: A Study of Chesapeake Social and Political Structure." Ph.D. diss., Michigan State University, 1977.

Waters, John J. "Patrimony, Succession, and Social Stability: Guilford, Connecticut in the Eighteenth Century." *Perspectives in American History* 10 (1976): 131-160.

Waters, John J. "The Traditional World of the New England Peasants: A View From Seventeenth-Century Barnstable." *New England Historical Genealogical Register* 130 (January 1976): 3-21.

Weir, Robert M. *Colonial South Carolina: A History*. Millwood, NY: KTO Press, 1983.

Wells, Robert V. *The Population of the British Colonies in America Before 1776*. Princeton: Princeton University Press, 1975.

Williamson, Marilyn L. *Raising Their Voices: British Women Writers, 1650-1750*. Detroit: Wayne State University Press, 1990.

Wilson, Lisa. *Ye Heart of a Man: The Domestic Life of Men in Colonial New England*. New Haven: Yale University Press, 1999.

Wilson, Lisa. *Life After Death: Widows in Pennsylvania, 1750-1850*. Philadelphia: Temple University Press, 1992.

Winslow, Ola Elizabeth. *Samuel Sewall of Boston*. New York: Macmillan, 1964.

Winthrop, R. C. *A Difference of Opinion Concerning the Reasons Why Katharine Winthrop Refused to Marry Chief Justice Sewell*. Boston: Privately printed, 1885.

Wood, Kirsten E. *Masterful Women: Slaveholding Widows From the American Revolution Through the Civil War*. Chapel Hill: University of North Carolina Press, 2004.

Wood, Kirsten E. "'The Strongest Ties That Bind Poor Mortals Together': Slaveholding Widows and the Construction of Family in the Southeast, 1790-1860." In *Negotiating Boundaries of Southern Womanhood: Dealing with the Powers that Be*, ed. Janet L. Coryell, Thomas H. Appleton Jr., Anastasia Sims, and Sandra Gioia Treadway. Columbia: University of Missouri Press, 2000.

Wood, Kirsten E. "See You at the Tavern: Women's Participation in Associational, Political, and Musical Gatherings at Early Republican Taverns." Paper presented annual meeting for the Society for Historians of the Early American Republic, Philadelphia, July 21-24, 2005.

Wood, Peter H. *Black Majority: Negroes in Colonial South Carolina from 1670 Through the Stono Rebellion*. New York: Knopf, 1974.

Woodbridge, Linda. *Women and the English Renaissance: Literature and the Nature of Womankind, 1540-1620*. Urbana: University of Illinois Press, 1986.

Wulf, Karin. *Not All Wives: Women of Colonial Philadelphia*. Ithaca, NY: Cornell University Press, 2000.

Young, Jeffrey Robert. *Domesticating Slavery: The Master Class in Georgia and South Carolina, 1670-1837*. Chapel Hill: University of North Carolina Press, 1999.

Zabin, Serena. "Women's Trading Networks and Dangerous Economies in Eighteenth-Century New York City." *Early American Studies: An Interdisciplinary Journal* 4 (2006): 291-321.

Zaeske, Susan. *Signatures of Citizenship: Petitioning, Antislavery, & Women's Political Identity*. Chapel Hill: University of North Carolina Press, 2003.

Zuckerman, Michael. "The Fabrication of Identity in Early America." *William and Mary Quarterly*, 3rd series, 34, no. 2 (April 1977): 183-214.

Index

About the Author

VIVIAN BRUCE CONGER is Associate Professor of History at Ithaca College.